CROSS ROADS

CHOOSE THE HARDER RIGHT

I0793967

RANDAL A. WRIGHT
WITH SCOTT O'NEIL

CROSS ROADS

CHOOSE THE HARDER RIGHT

CFI
An imprint of Cedar Fort, Inc.
Springville, Utah

Paperback ISBN 13: 978-1-4621-4703-8
eBook ISBN 13: 978-1-4621-4769-4

Published by CFI, an imprint of Cedar Fort, Inc.
2373 W. 700 S., Suite 100, Springville, UT 84663
Distributed by Cedar Fort, Inc., www.cedarfort.com

Library of Congress Cataloging Number: 2024931623

Cover design by Shawnda Craig

Edited and Typeset by Julie Irvine

Printed in the United States of America

10 9 8 7 6 5 4 3 2 1

Printed on acid-free paper

Contents

Foreword

Each year, Randal Wright's classes at BYU Campus Education Week are filled to capacity. Regular attendees know that to avoid the overflow, they need to arrive early. For years, Lisa O'Neil and her mother have been two such attendees. They don't miss any of Randal's classes, which is how Randal became friends with Lisa's husband, former Philadelphia 76ers CEO Scott O'Neil.

I first met Randal while working as an Especially for Youth counselor eight years ago, and because he is a person who truly practices what he preaches, he has remained a friend and influence in my life in the years since. Two years ago while I was working at Deseret News, Randal emailed me with a story idea: Lisa O'Neil, a member of The Church of Jesus Christ of Latter-day Saints, was married to her husband, Scott, for twenty years before he made the decision to be baptized into the Church himself.

As an avid basketball fan, I was intrigued by Scott's story, so with Randal's help, I met with Scott and Lisa to discuss his conversion. I have found over my two-year friendship with Scott that while their careers may be different and they might initially seem unlikely friends—given Randal's Texas drawl and Scott's northeastern demeanor—the two men are actually cut from the same cloth. They are men of their word, men who love their wives and children, men who want to do what is right, men who care about building relationships of trust, and men who strive daily to become better human beings.

During a recent crossroads in my life, I sought the advice of both Randal and Scott. Both could have easily sent me a quick email response of encouragement, but instead, both took hours of their time on separate occasions to sit with me in person. As I sat with Scott and Lisa in a hotel restaurant, and later with Randal, I thought of how many people would pay big money to receive guidance from these wise human beings. But they weren't just offering rote advice; they were showing me how much they cared about me. I tell you this so you will know that the things you read from them in this book are not just nice ideas. They are principles these authors actually believe in and, more importantly, principles they live.

This book is a gold mine of stories, quotes, and personal insights collected by two of the best men I know. As I read, I felt a desire to speak more positively, wake up earlier, and love more intently. I wanted to be a better daughter, sister, and friend. I wanted to set goals and persist until I achieved; I wanted to help others do the same. I wanted to record my experiences so they do not go wasted.

These crossroads moments in our lives can be overwhelming and scary, but as the Lord said in Doctrine and Covenants 38:30, "If ye are prepared ye shall not fear." This book will prepare anyone for moments of decisions, decisions that will—as President Thomas S. Monson said—determine our destiny. I hope that as you read, you will imagine yourself sitting with Randal and Scott, in a hotel restaurant or in a university library, talking with them one-on-one. That is what they would do if they knew you personally. After all, as Scott signs every email, "Anything, any time."

Morgan Jones Pearson

INTRODUCTION

A crossroads is defined as an intersection of two or more roads or a point at which a crucial decision with far-reaching consequences must be made.[1] It is interesting how many times we all come to crossroads in life. Often we make decisions between a road with easy tasks, which the majority usually take, and one with harder undertakings chosen by the minority. The natural man tendency is to avoid harder roads even though it takes effort to grow and make progress. No one gets physically strong sitting in a recliner watching television or driving to the gym to watch other people work out. The same applies to our spiritual, social, emotional, and cognitive development. It takes effort. And anything that requires effort seems to have a high dropout rate. President Henry B. Eyring gave this valuable insight in determining which path we should take when we reach a crossroads. He said, "If you are on the right path, it will always be uphill."[2]

Some crossroads occur once in a lifetime, some unfold over time, and some happen daily. Just this morning we all came to a crossroads and had to choose between the uphill less-traveled road of arising early or the well-traveled road of sleeping longer than needed. We also faced similar crossroads throughout the day concerning prayers, scripture study, proper nutrition, and exercise. Strength and progression seldom come without exertion and struggle, whether it be spiritual or physical. Following are examples of how the two authors came to a crossroads in life and chose the harder right rather than the easier wrong and the blessings that resulted.

Scott O'Neil

About the time my cousin Michael Esposito was accepted to the Harvard Business School, I was rejected by seven of the nine universities I applied to. I ended up selecting Villanova over Syracuse and was wait-listed at Georgetown and Notre Dame. After being a straight A student, president of the student body, and captain of three varsity sports teams, the rejection brought humility and more than a few tears. It convinced me that I was not as smart as my cousin. To counter these feelings, I decided to work so hard that I would prove them (and myself) wrong and someday attend Harvard.

I look back today and smile about how naive I was. I took it personally that I wasn't considered smart enough to attend a certain school. I carried a big chip on my shoulder for a long time and thought getting into the graduate school of my choice would be a panacea for my insecurities. But sometimes naivete, youth, and inexperience come together in just the right doses.

Villanova was an incredible academic and social experience. Perhaps the chip on my shoulder motivated me to take a couple of semesters of Japanese and calculus as electives just to show myself that I could do it. I rarely missed class, and I sat in the front row and studied a lot. I graduated with honors and found a true love and interest in learning.

After graduating, I went to work in the sports business at the New Jersey Nets as a marketing assistant. Then, after a promotion and job change, I moved to the Philadelphia Eagles and began to manage people, deal with budgets, write business plans, and do other things I didn't feel qualified for. In time, however, I came to a crossroads in life and with my career. I knew I needed to learn more to be effective and continue to grow. I also wanted to run a professional sports team someday and knew the current path I was on was not going to get me there.

After a lot of prayer, thought, and conversations with my wife, Lisa, I decided to apply to graduate school to acquire a stronger baseline in business. This time I only applied to Harvard, even though I only had an 11 percent chance of being accepted. I had heard a rumor that the three Ms had the best chance of getting in—Mormons, Military, and McKinsey. I wasn't a member of that religion, I did not attend a military academy, nor did I work for the prestigious worldwide management consulting firm.

I was an underdog again, and the vision of my undergraduate rejection letters burned in my memory. Why was I only applying to Harvard? Was it false bravado, the chip on my shoulder, overconfidence, raw ambition, or the amazing business program? Maybe I just wanted to prove people wrong. Looking back, it was likely a combination of all those things.

I was excited when I received the acceptance letter. I spent quite a bit of time speaking to friends, mentors, and colleagues, asking if I should leave a job I loved and the city that felt like home when my life was going so well. A longtime mentor, Bruce Schilling, said I would be crazy not to go, while my boss, Len Komoroski, offered the exact opposite counsel. The thing that may have tipped the scales was when team president Joe Banner and the owner, Jeff Lurie, wished me well and said if I ever wanted to return, there would be a spot for me with the Eagles. I chose the harder right and was off to Cambridge, Massachusetts.

When I first arrived on campus, some of the excitement of being accepted left, and I couldn't manage to do anything other than worry. It is hard to describe the raw humility I felt realizing the harder right road suddenly felt very much like the wrong road. I was surrounded by people who were smarter, had more relevant experience, and were more confident. The campus was comprised of smart, type A, talented, aggressive people, and it seemed everyone was great at something. Yet I also began to realize that everyone else felt vulnerable and uncomfortable in the beginning too. In time, I stopped seeing other students as competitive or insecure and started to get to know them individually. I rooted for them, and they rooted for me. The community was like a family, which brought me peace.

I tried to use my strength at building relationships to my advantage. I played a lot of basketball and was the daily ringleader. I was a writer and eventual humor editor for the school paper, the *Harbus*. I tended to stir things up a bit in class, take chances, and make people laugh. I found relationships. Trust and love overcame insecurity, fear, and panic. I had fun! I did fine in class, although I wasn't the best student and didn't aspire to be for the first time in my life. I let it come to me. I smiled more. I relaxed. I enjoyed the moment. I rarely said no to any challenge or invitation and was surprised to be selected by my fellow classmates to be the student speaker on graduation day.

The harder right road seems much more obvious in hindsight than it did at the time of the decision. Now it seems like a slam dunk, a no-brainer. Back then, it was not that easy and certainly not that simple, but it was the *right* path. Because of that decision, I learned to see the world like a CEO does and was able to build a network that I draw on today. Oftentimes, we underestimate and rarely appreciate the impact and blessings of one right decision. But my decision to follow my inner voice that whispered "Apply to Harvard" became *the* decision! The rewards of this one decision have had an exponential impact on my life and will continue to impact generations of O'Neils for eternity.

But why did attending Harvard impact our family for eternity? Let's back up, because there is more to the story. Shortly after Lisa and I were married, her grandmother Dorothy Holt summoned me over to her chair in the corner of the family room in Lisa's parents' home. She sat quietly taking in all the chaos that her grandchildren and great-grandchildren were stirring up. She pulled me close so she could say something in my ear. As I listened intently and curiously, she said, "Scott, when the time is right, you will bring thousands of people into this church. We need you." She gave me a hug and sent me on my way. I was perplexed by her comment since I was Catholic and my parents, grandparents, and ancestors on both sides for multiple generations were Catholic. Later Lisa asked me what her grandmother had said to me. I stammered a bit, eyes on the ground, and said she wanted to wish us a merry Christmas. I wasn't ready.

After more than twenty years of a happy, faithful, and fulfilling marriage to an incredible multigenerational member of The Church of Jesus Christ of Latter-day Saints, Lisa Reynolds O'Neil, and the growing testimonies of our three daughters, I finally decided to be baptized. I looked out at the friends and family who had traveled from ten states to our ward building in rural West Chester, Pennsylvania, and my only thought before being submerged in the baptismal font was to ask myself what took me so long to make this decision. Why do we sometimes avoid or procrastinate the harder right choices? I don't know.

My conversion is a story of a thousand steps rather than one lightning bolt moment. For years, I had a strong testimony of Jesus Christ as the Savior of the world and the Son of God. I even believed Joseph Smith to be a true prophet of God and wholeheartedly believed the Book of Mormon to be another testament of Jesus Christ. But life was good. We made it all work fine and were happy, so why change? After all, our family was close knit. We laughed a lot, read scriptures together, held home evenings, counted our blessings, and attended church on Sundays. Most of the members of the ward who didn't know us assumed I was a member of the Church. I was active and often had assignments from the bishop or stake president.

I don't imagine there is a typical conversion story. In fact, no two stories have ever sounded the same to me. I have always been fascinated by hearing what I call the "story of how I got here" from other converts. With that in mind I decided to share mine in hopes that it might light a spark, inspire hope and patience, or simply provide an opportunity to teach or learn just like thousands of stories have inspired and influenced me over the years.

There is an old proverb of unknown origin that says, "It takes a village to raise a child." In other words, it takes the people of an entire community to teach and interact with children for them to learn and grow in a safe environment. Often the same principle applies in gathering Israel. Following are a few of the more notable people and experiences that had a significant impact on my conversion over time.

Harvard Business School: The incredible members of The Church of Jesus Christ of Latter-day Saints I met at the Harvard Business School had a significant impact on my eventual decision to join the Church. Although Catholic, I attended Latter-day Saint church meetings with Lisa, along with the business school's dean, Kim Clark, and its most prominent professor, Clayton Christensen. Several members became my lifelong friends. Wilford Cardon, who I met at the business school, baptized me, after asking me every time I saw him whether I was ready to join. His wife, Nicole, continues to be a beacon of strength and love to our family. Greg and Demi Davis, Tagg and Jen Romney, Matt and Amy Eyring, and Drew and Joanna Johnson attended my baptism and sealing to my family for all eternity a year later in the Philadelphia Pennsylvania Temple. Jared Stone, who served as the president of the Tennessee Nashville Mission, and his wife, Jani, continue to be a guiding light in our lives. David Young, who was at the John F. Kennedy School of Government during my time in Cambridge, and his wife, Rebecca, were strong forces for good. David became our home teacher when we ended up in the same New Jersey ward years later.

Friends: Moving to New Canaan, Connecticut, after a sudden prompting from Lisa, doubled my commute (not so good), but added spiritual giants into our lives (really good) who offered much toward my conversion at this point in time. Scott and Melissa Cutler, Ben and Megan Sibbett, and Brian and Krista Blair were all with us when we went through the open house for the Manhattan New York Temple. These friends provided an incredible foundation for how I want to live, and their impact cannot be overstated.

The Temple: The experience of seeing a temple being built in Philadelphia, having my children participate in the youth cultural celebration, and being there for the dedication were all among the most spiritually moving moments in my life. However, attending the VIP open house tours, led by President Vai Sikahema and his wife, Keala, with my family and friends is still one of the most powerful moments in my life. Standing in the sealing room, President Sikahema leaned over and whispered in my ear that this is where I would be when Alexa (my oldest daughter) got married. We both hugged and cried because I knew then it was just a matter of time.

Home Teachers: I had some of the greatest home teachers in the world. Peter Pilling, David Young, Chester Elton, Bob Kinney, and Clark Maxwell, a counselor in our stake presidency. President Maxwell was the person I called when I was ready to be taught by the missionaries. He was the person who came to every meeting with those missionaries. He also confirmed me a member of The Church of Jesus Christ of Latter-day Saints and was a witness at my and my wife's sealing a year later. President Maxwell was and is as impactful a person in my spiritual journey as there is.

Missionaries: The two missionaries who made the biggest impact over the years were my nephews Josh and Jeremy Reynolds. I visited Josh on his mission in Dallas, Texas, and his light, his questions, and his challenge to me to read the Book of Mormon again while listening to the Spirit stayed with me. A couple years later, Jeremy was serving his mission in Sendai, Japan, when his mission president asked whether he had any relatives who were not members of the Church. "Those members of your family who are not yet members of the Church just became your biggest investigators," his mission president said. Jeremy later stated when he wrote home each week that I was the one he had in mind. I read his letters and felt the Spirit so strongly I was brought to tears.

Randal Wright: Lisa had heard Randal speak at BYU Campus Education Week several years in a row. Lisa, her mother, and her sisters planned their schedules around Randal's classes. She had all his books, quoted him as often as relevant, took pages of notes, and said he was the best speaker she'd ever heard. The legend of Randal Wright was long and strong in the O'Neil house. Lisa and our daughters were out west for a month or so, and she came back to find Randal's book *The Book of Mormon Miracle* on my nightstand. I had been reading, praying, and thinking about the power of an eternal family while they were gone.

Family: Lisa is a wonderful example in terms of how to live and has had the most influence on me, the life I live, and my conversion. Lisa had incredible examples in her home growing up, and her parents continue to show selfless service and undying faith. Our daughters, Alexa, Kira, and Eliza, are faithful members of the Church. They are diligent scripture readers, they find power and connectivity in the Church and in the gospel, and they set a great example for me to aspire to live. Our home evenings mattered. Our scripture reading before bedtime mattered. Our family prayers mattered. Our blessings on meals mattered. The spirit in our home mattered. It all mattered, and it still matters in keeping us on the covenant path.

After my final meeting with Elders McGlaughlin and Carter, I sent out a text to hundreds of members of the Church I had met over the years with a Bitmoji of me dressed as a missionary (tag and all) with my arms open wide, exclaiming, "I believe."

Back to August 13, 2016. As I emerged from beneath the surface of the water, without thinking I crossed my fingers (our sign for I love you in the O'Neil household) and searched for Lisa's eyes, which I found. The world seemed to stop. I was at peace. I was happy. I was home. And now, about bringing those people to the Church as Grandma said . . . I need to get to work!

Randal Wright

My grandmother Epsie was born in southeast Texas and later baptized in The Church of Jesus Christ of Latter-day Saints in 1900 when she was eighteen years old. She married my grandfather James, who was not a member of the Church, at age twenty-five. He was a lumberjack by trade and over time became a heavy drinker and was often abusive to his family. My dad, Cooper, was born in southwestern Louisiana in 1917, the eighth of eleven children. His family lived in temporary lumber camps during his formative years, and he and his siblings had little opportunity for formal education.

My mother, Mabel, was born in 1924 and grew up in southern Alabama, the oldest daughter of a sharecropper and a fourth-generation member of the Church. When my mother was thirteen, her mother died in childbirth, leaving her to care for her three younger siblings, who were eleven years old, nine years old, and twenty-two months old, while my grandfather worked long hours in the fields. Mom was forced to drop out of school to take on her mother's responsibilities in the home.

In 1942, my mom and dad met at a Church dance in Mobile, Alabama, and were married that same year. A few months after their marriage, my dad was drafted into the US Army. After his discharge and with little formal education and only a slight chance for well-paying jobs, my father and mother became entrepreneurs. They started several businesses over the years, which required working twelve or more hours a day, six days a week. They were never out of work but perhaps were out of money on several occasions. My father was a good man, but because of his work schedule, I don't remember him attending one activity I was involved in. He was also unaffectionate. I never once heard him say the words "I love you" to anyone, nor did he tell me I could make myself into something extraordinary.

So unlike Scott's parents, who both obtained PhD degrees, my parents never even made it to high school. However, both desired that their children obtain good educations. They didn't have the time nor the background to help in that area, although they worked hard to provide us with educational opportunities.

I did well in school until the beginning of fifth grade. Shortly after school started that fall, I was finishing the lyrics of a mushy love song I'd been working on all summer. Written about a girl I had a crush on, I was focused on the task while sitting at my desk in school. Unfortunately for me, my teacher Mr. Singer happened to walk past my desk and noticed I was working on something other than the assignment he had given. He grabbed the paper with the words to my almost finished song and started laughing as he walked to the front of the classroom. He then read the words aloud to the entire class. It was the most humiliating experience of my life. My classmates laughed hysterically, and many pointed their fingers at me. At the end of the previous school year, I had all As on my final report. By the end of my fifth-grade year, I had straight Cs. Mr. Singer's actions that day destroyed my confidence and desire to learn and perform well in school. I lacked the confidence and support system to pull myself back into my past achievement.

From that point on, I basically shut down in school and only put forth enough effort to pass my classes. I didn't like teachers and avoided speaking in class. To make matters worse I was the youngest and smallest boy in my grade and looked much younger than I was. I was not the student body president nor the captain of three sports teams. The only award I would have been qualified for was "most likely to repeat senior year." However, they didn't have that award, so I didn't get any. Graduating from high school, I had no idea what I was going to do with my life. But with my mother's encouragement, I applied to a small junior college and was accepted. At that point I discovered the easy road I had been taking for years did not lead to positive outcomes, even at a junior college.

Soon I found myself at a major crossroads. I realized that each time I followed the path of least resistance, I always came to the same dead end, discovering there was absolutely nothing there. One day while reading the local newspaper, I noticed an ad for the Dale Carnegie Public Speaking Course. An inner voice whispered to me, "You need to take this course." Because the course was expensive and I was terrified to speak in public, I refused to seriously consider even calling about the course. For days I tried to brush off the strong feeling that this was my answer, but the thought would not go away. I felt compelled to take the course and somehow found the money and the nerve to sign up.

Feeling uncomfortable walking into the first class, I thought I had wasted a lot of money and considered asking for a refund. I was by far the youngest person in class and easily the least experienced. Driven men and women already successful business executives, managers, and salespeople, along with the minister of a large local church, were part of the class. I wondered why I had committed to go down this path when it seemed too difficult for me. I was totally out of my comfort zone but decided to stay that night. It's hard to describe what happened to me during the next several weeks, but I began to change and became more confident. I never missed a class throughout the duration of the course.

I went from being terrified to speak in front of the group to looking forward to it—that is, until my final speech on the last night of the course. While I was struggling to come up with a topic, my inner voice whispered, "Talk about Joseph Smith and the Book of Mormon." At first I thought there was no way I'd choose to stand up in a room full of successful men and women from other faiths and speak on this topic. However, as much as I tried to produce another subject, I drew a total blank. I even brought copies of the Book of Mormon for everyone in the class, not knowing if I would follow through with the prompting. I was still debating whether I had the nerve to speak on this theme as I rose from my seat and faced the group. I went through with the speech I was prompted to give with confidence and passion.

The next speaker was Jerry Kirk, leading salesman for the largest beer and wine distributor in the area. I wondered whether he would blast me for my religious topic in that secular setting. I was shocked when he said, "I had a speech prepared, but I've decided not to give it. I want everyone to know that I am a member of The Church of Jesus Christ of Latter-day Saints, but I haven't been active. I've decided after the previous speech to go back to church this Sunday." Utter surprise overtook me later that night when I was chosen for the most outstanding speech.

I stood at a crossroads and made the difficult decision to act on the prompting to pay for the public speaking course. On the last night of the course, I followed through on the prompting to speak about Joseph Smith and the Book of Mormon and even followed through and gave everyone in the class a copy of that amazing book of scripture. The decision to participate in the class changed the course of my life. It motivated me in ways that are hard to describe. I began studying harder at Lamar University and ended up transferring to Brigham Young University. Jerry Kirk found himself at a crossroads and chose the harder right by quitting his job and going back to college. At one point, he and his wife, Patty, lived in the apartment next to ours when we were both seeking degrees at BYU. Later Jerry and I served in a bishopric together.

I went from harboring a strong distrust for teachers to teaching college-aged students and from being terrified to speak in my own ward to speaking to large groups in more than 250 cities in the United States and several foreign countries. Instead of taking the path of least resistance in school, I climbed higher and obtained a PhD. I don't say these things to boast but only to say that I have a strong testimony of the counsel given by President Thomas S. Monson when he said, "May we maintain the courage to defy the consensus. May we ever choose the harder right instead of the easier wrong."[3]

We All Face Difficult Choices

While few face the same crossroads in life, we all must constantly choose between the more frightening and difficult right path and the simpler and easier wrong one. So why should we intentionally choose the more challenging path? Because as Zig Ziglar said, "Difficult roads often lead to beautiful destinations."

For years Randal Wright and Scott O'Neil have been interested in discovering behaviors that lead to personal growth in individuals. During research for this book, over three hundred individuals were asked to respond to the prompt "Describe a pivotal experience, decision, or event in your life that changed you for the better." These stories came from individuals who approached the crossroads in life and decided to follow the road less traveled by the masses, one that led them to progress and become a better person. Reading their contributions was life changing in many ways for both of us. We realized, however, that it is impossible to include even a small percentage of the valuable input we received. To eliminate any bias, we had several readers choose experiences they thought fit well with the topic discussed in each chapter. Sixteen of these experiences are placed at the beginning of each chapter, and others are scattered throughout the book. Our intent is to encourage all to choose the harder right rather than the easier wrong.

CHAPTER 1

Change Yourself to Change Your World

Once any of us conclude—"That's just the way I am," we give up our ability to change. We might as well raise the white flag, put down our weapons, concede the battle, and just surrender—any prospect of winning is lost. While some of us may think that does not describe us, perhaps every one of us demonstrates by at least one or two bad habits, "That's just the way I am."[4]

Elder Donald L. Hallstrom

Merrilee Boyack

I was a freshman at Brigham Young University when my life profoundly changed in a matter of minutes. I was on campus a week early for a seminar. I was lonely and homesick. I'm talking about the terrible, ugly, physical, full-on, crying homesick. One day I wandered through the student center and saw a large group of people in the main auditorium. I sat in the corner out of curiosity. Up front a man was teaching the large group. At one point in his presentation, he called up two young men from the audience. He whispered something in the first young man's ear. That young man then walked across the stage and began waving. With a big smile, he pointed to people in the audience. Then the teacher whispered something to the second young man, who slowly shuffled across the stage hanging his head and looking away from the audience. The contrast between the two young men was glaring.

The teacher then asked those of us in the audience a compelling question that I have never forgotten. He asked, "Which of these young men would you want to meet and talk to?"

Everyone called out, "The first one," with someone shouting, "We wouldn't want to interrupt the pity party of the second guy!"

Another called out, "The first guy was super friendly!"

Then the teacher asked, "Which of these young men is acting with his true personality?"

We were stumped. How could we know the answer to that question? They were both total strangers.

The teacher then taught, "You had no clue who was truly friendly or truly shy. You were just reacting to how they acted. This is called the Act as If principle. If you act a certain way, people will interact with you as if that is who you really are. Eventually that will become your true personality."

That day I felt as if a light from heaven was shining down! My life was changed in that moment. I understood, finally, how to change. I walked out of that class smiling and waving to people across the campus—pretending as if I were an outgoing, confident young woman even though I was anything but that. A strange thing happened as I watched: everyone waved and smiled back at me. In three days, I kid you not, I had a marriage proposal. And no, I obviously didn't marry the guy, but that experience reinforced the power of the Act as If principle. That one simple lesson has profoundly impacted every single aspect of my life. I still use it forty years later. In minutes, I was taught a principle that changed everything for me.

Change Can Be Difficult

Merrilee had a life-changing experience by using a simple yet powerful technique first proposed by American philosopher, psychologist, and Harvard professor William James. He suggested, "If you want a quality, act as if you already had it."[5] In Merrilee's case, she was shy and homesick and needed to act as if she was outgoing and well adjusted. Continuing this principle of acting a certain way should in time make this character trait become part of you.

Merrilee fully embraced this concept and applied it to a weakness she was struggling with and was "changed in that moment." Her experience was something that perhaps many desire but few succeed in doing. Fortunately, Merrilee picked an area of life to change that resulted in instant rewards.

Obviously, not all change will come as quickly and as dramatically as Merrilee's did that day. For example, if people want to change their eating habits and lose excessive weight, it will take time and considerable effort. Change is seldom easy or instant, but the results are often well worth the effort. IT industrialist Narayana Murthy explained, "Growth is painful. Change is painful. But, nothing is as painful as staying stuck where you do not belong."[6]

Randal: A few years ago, I was skimming through old journal entries to see whether I was becoming a better person over time. Two entries caught my attention and taught me that change is not easy, and overcoming some weaknesses may be more difficult than overcoming other weaknesses. I have also learned that temporary change is far more common than permanent change. Both entries refer to a program designed to help people overcome self-defeating behaviors. The program was developed by psychology professor Jonathan Chamberlain. The two entries are almost exactly fifteen years apart.

> *Entry 1:* I just finished reading a book, *Eliminating Your Sdbs: Self-Defeating Behaviors*, by Jonathan Chamberlain. The idea is to choose a behavior to work on that you feel is holding you back in your progression. Dr. Chamberlain and other researchers have spent years developing techniques to help people change these behaviors. It is a powerful program. I chose procrastination as the self-defeating behavior that I would most like to eliminate in my life. . . . I feel good that I have accomplished a great deal since beginning the program this week.

> *Entry 2:* Lately I have been reading a book called *Eliminating Self-Defeating Behaviors* by Jonathan Chamberlain. It has been sitting in my bookcase untouched for years. I remember working on some self-defeating behaviors long ago, but I can't remember what they were. Something told me that I should go through the process again and try to eliminate a behavior that seems to be holding me back. The biggest problem I have right now in my life is that I'm a huge procrastinator. I put off everything you can think of. I was very aware today of my problem and how much it is holding me back.

I was a little shocked to realize the irony of making a great deal of progress eliminating procrastination from my life only to discover I was still struggling with it years later. I don't know what happened, but it appears I started off with a bang, procrastinated or let life get in the way, and then forgot I was even working to rid it from my life. At first I was down on myself, but I realized that some weaknesses are just part of our natural man tendencies and overcoming them will take intense effort and the Lord's help. President Dieter F. Uchtdorf pointed out, "God wants to help us to eventually turn all of our weaknesses into strengths, but He knows that this is a long-term goal. He wants us to become perfect, and if we stay on the path of discipleship, one day we will. It's OK that you're not quite there yet. Keep working on it, but stop punishing yourself."[7]

Many who want change are familiar with the remarkable promise made by Moroni. In the Book of Mormon we read, "And if men come unto me I will show unto them their weakness. I give unto men weakness that they may be humble; and my grace is sufficient for all men that humble themselves before me; for if they humble themselves before me, and have faith in me, then will I make weak things become strong unto them" (Ether 12:27).

Act as If

Benjamin Franklin was a brilliant polymath who became one of the United States' Founding Fathers. In 1726, at age twenty, he was inspired to embark on a personal improvement project to reach moral perfection. He said, "It was about this time I conceived the bold and arduous project of arriving at moral perfection."[8] His plan identified thirteen virtues he most desired and the things he needed to do to act as if he had that virtue.

Thirteen Virtues

1. Temperance: Eat not to dullness; drink not to elevation.
2. Silence: Speak not but what may benefit others or yourself; avoid trifling conversation.
3. Order: Let all your things have their places; let each part of your business have its time.
4. Resolution: Resolve to perform what you ought; perform without fail what you resolve.

5. Frugality: Make no expense but to do good to others or yourself, i.e., waste nothing.
6. Industry: Lose no time; be always employed in something useful; cut off all unnecessary actions.
7. Sincerity: Use no hurtful deceit; think innocently and justly, and, if you speak, speak accordingly.
8. Justice: Wrong none by doing injuries or omitting the benefits that are your duty.
9. Moderation: Avoid extremes; forbear resenting injuries so much as you think they deserve.
10. Cleanliness: Tolerate no uncleanliness in body, clothes, or habitation.
11. Tranquility: Be not disturbed at trifles, or at accidents common or unavoidable.
12. Chastity: Rarely use venery but for health or offspring, never to dullness, weakness, or the injury of your own or another's peace or reputation.
13. Humility: Imitate Jesus and Socrates.

He went on to say, "I determined to give a week's strict attention to each of the virtues successively. Thus, in the first week, my great guard was to avoid every the least offense against Temperance, leaving the other virtues to their ordinary chance, only marking every evening the faults of the day." Soon after beginning his project, Franklin realized that moral perfection was significantly more difficult than he had anticipated. He noted, "While my care was employ'd in guarding against one fault, I was often surprised by another."[9]

However, Franklin did not throw in the towel because of the difficulty of his quest to change and improve. He tracked his progress in a small book to make sure he was focused on his desired virtues. Every morning he asked, "What good shall I do this day?" He then made out a to-do list of things that came into his mind. At night, he examined himself by asking, "What good have I done today?" Although Franklin freely admitted that he did not always live up to the virtues he desired, his attempt made him a giant among men and one of the most admired and respected people in American history. He was a printer, philosopher, editor, author, diplomat, statesman, scientist, wealthy businessman, inventor (Franklin stove, bifocals, swim fins, lightning rod), musician (violin, harp, and guitar), and coauthor of the Declaration of Independence. Franklin was also the first president of what would become the University of Pennsylvania. His focus on changing himself for the better made him a role model for generations to come.

Scott: Several years ago, I was promoted to senior vice president of Team Marketing & Business Operations for the NBA. At thirty-four, I was inexperienced but full of confidence, commitment, and force of will. Shortly after my promotion, we had a board meeting scheduled. I had been going to the NBA board meetings for three years and thoroughly enjoyed them. This one proved to be a little bit different. David Stern, the NBA commissioner, summoned me to his office a few weeks before the meeting to inform me that I would be speaking in front of my bosses David Stern and Adam Silver, my peers at the NBA league office, thirty team owners, and several team CEOs. In so many words, he told me not to screw this one up. What could possibly go wrong?

I was nervous. So nervous that I hustled to the bathroom before I had to speak because I had a feeling I was going to lose my lunch. In the meeting, I was introduced but couldn't really hear anything as I walked up to the podium. I was sweating. I read for about twenty minutes, only looking up occasionally at the audience. I don't think they cared much about what I was lecturing on. I fielded a question or two and shuffled back to my seat. Shortly thereafter, we took a break, and people patted me on the back, said I did great, and wished me well.

The reality is that I was awful. I vowed never to put myself in that vulnerable position again. Tony Robbins said, "By changing nothing, nothing changes."[10] So I decided to change. From that point on, I began to act as if I were an engaging public speaker. I worked, prepared, practiced, and forced feedback from interested parties just like a professional speaker would do. I vowed to never shake, sweat, or read a speech again, because that is not what professional speakers do.

I recently gave a keynote address at a large conference held in Chicago. There was no sweating, nor reading, but there was a lot of storytelling and emotion. This was not born into me, but once I began to act the part of a public speaker, I began to see improvement. I believe this principle will help change not only behavior but attitude also.

But you must desire a change in your life, or there will be no improvement. Andy Warhol declared, “When people are ready to, they change. They never do it before then, and sometimes they die before they get around to it. You can’t make them change if they don’t want to, just like when they do want to, you can’t stop them.”[11]

You Can Change

Years ago, I attended a sales training meeting for my occupation. One of the presenters talked about human nature and said something that has always stuck with me. He suggested, “A person twenty-one years old or older will continue to do in the future as they have done in the past unless they have a spiritual experience or brain surgery.” Even though he said it tongue in cheek, with a big smile, I’m not so sure his conjecture is far off. Change can be difficult, and so often when a person does change, it is short lived.

Natural man tendencies seem to be a source of struggle and frustration for most of us. The Apostle Paul explained, “And lest I should be exalted above measure through the abundance of the revelations, there was given to me a thorn in the flesh, the messenger of Satan to buffet me, lest I should be exalted above measure” (2 Corinthians 12:7). Apparently, mortality is meant to be difficult. As Paul discovered, at least one issue may be a constant thorn to deal with.

I once talked to a friend I’ll call Sarah about her endless struggle with weight. She was depressed and down on herself because of so many failures. Only a few years earlier, she concentrated on eating only healthy food and exercising regularly, and she lost a considerable amount of weight. During that time, she experienced more happiness and confidence than ever before. Many can relate to what happened next. Once she reached her ideal weight, she began to allow herself a few “free days” to eat whatever she wanted. Within a short time, she completely backslid and ended up gaining the weight back, plus even more. As we talked, she mentioned how disappointed she was in herself and that she was truly miserable. I asked, “If eating healthy and exercising led to weight loss and brought you so much happiness and confidence, why did you quit?” She tried to answer but ended up crying.

President Monson said, "The battle for self-discipline may leave you a bit bruised and battered but always a better person. Self-discipline is a rigorous process at best; too many of us want it to be effortless and painless. Should temporary setbacks afflict us, a very significant part of our struggle for self-discipline is the determination and the courage to try again."[12]

It seems as if something holds everyone back. Stephen West was an attorney and former senior vice president and general counsel for Marriott International Inc. In a meeting I attended, he spoke about the importance of learning from our experiences and continually improving. To illustrate, he said he and other executives in his company met to consider candidates to fill an important leadership position. Someone suggested that a long-time employee be offered the job since he had twenty-six years of experience with the company. Another executive spoke up, "Actually, he only has one year of experience." Other committee members were puzzled; they all knew how long this man had been with the company. The executive then explained, "He has one year of experience repeated twenty-five times." Because the man had not improved himself over the years, he was passed over for a major promotion.

Change and improvement over time brings opportunity while the lack of it closes doors. Even making consistent small changes can add up to huge results. However, to be successful in making permanent change, your desire to improve must be greater than your desire to remain the same. And if by chance you occasionally fail at your goal to change, get back up and try again. President Monson taught, "One of God's greatest gifts to us is the joy of trying again, for no failure ever need be final."[13]

Be Open to Advice

Randal: Recently I read a magazine article about Aaron Franklin, owner of Franklin Barbecue, which is recognized as one of the best barbecue restaurants in America. His customers often endure a three- to four-hour average wait time to be served. In the article the writer stated, "Aaron Franklin's favorite barbecue (other than his own, presumably) is Valentina's Tex Mex BBQ."[14] I made a note of this recommendation and stopped by Valentina's, waited fifteen minutes, and got one of the best sliced beef sandwiches I've ever eaten. Later, I took my wife, Wendy, there and encouraged her to order the sliced beef sandwich, recalling how good it was. Instead, going against my expert advice, she ordered a pulled pork sandwich. I assured her she'd made a major mistake.

Several months later, she and I again stopped by Valentina's on our way to a movie theater. This time I strongly urged her to try the beef, but she again went against my advice and ordered the pulled pork sandwich. The thought occurred to me that one reason people don't change is that they refuse to listen to the good advice of those who know more than they do. We got our sandwiches to go. Since she was driving, I ate mine on the way to the movie. I expressed that the beef sandwich was even better than the last time and probably the best barbecue sandwich I had ever eaten. That's saying a lot because I've eaten barbecue in cities all across the nation. I reiterated how she really needed to be more open to suggestions and how she'd missed out by not getting the beef.

We arrived at the theater just in time for the movie to start, so she put her sandwich in her purse to eat in the nearly empty theater. After finding our seats, she pulled out her sandwich just as I left to buy popcorn. When I returned, she was visibly irritated with me and whispered, "You ate my sandwich! This is the beef sandwich you ordered!" There was no way out of it. I had mistakenly eaten her pulled pork sandwich, which turned out to be the best barbecue sandwich ever. I learned that night that we often fail to improve because we refuse to listen to advice from others, thinking we have it all figured out ourselves. If we never try others' suggestions, we have no idea whether this advice will benefit us or not. My friend Chris said, "Everyone should eat vanilla ice cream occasionally so they can appreciate rocky road!"

Live Life in Crescendo

I once observed a group of middle school-aged boys acting silly. At one point a girl their age sitting in front of them turned around and exclaimed, "You boys are so premature!" One of the boys stated, "It's *immature*, Julie, not *premature*." She replied, "Whatever the name—you are it." The word she used to describe the boys that night seemed quite accurate—premature!

Most individuals probably fit in the premature category in at least some aspects of life, and that is not a bad thing. It just means our greatest works lie in the future after we obtain a little more maturity and experience. Every year we should notice personal improvement and change for the better. In music, this concept is called a crescendo, meaning a gradual increase in loudness or intensity.

An unfortunate occurrence among people retired from full-time employment is using their newfound leisure time for unproductive activities. Retirees generally spend over four hours a day watching television, an hour a day reading, and forty-two minutes a day thinking and relaxing.[15] At a time when individuals have the most experience, wisdom, and potential to grow and help make the world a better place, many stagnate. While relaxation and recreation are necessary for a well-balanced life, surely they should not be the major focus of life. Imagine what our country could be if everyone had the philosophy that Stephen R. Covey made a part of his life. Here is what he said about the retirement years:

> I am now 76 years old and could easily retire. But I'm not retired and I don't plan to retire. I don't believe in retirement. Why people ask me? Simply, I have a life motto. It is: Live life in crescendo!
>
> Living life in crescendo to me means that my most important work is always ahead of me, never behind me. I believe that "where much is given, much is required." I have a sacred stewardship to contribute and not to retire to leisure. . . .
>
> Start living your life in crescendo—and remember your most important work is ahead of you, not behind you! There is so much more to do, to learn and contribute.[16]

Do Your Very Best

Randal: While serving in a volunteer leadership position, I had several opportunities to talk to Kasi, a high school student. At one point, I asked how she was doing in school. She said that everything was going well overall, but she was struggling in her Spanish class. We discussed what options she had to improve her Spanish grades. Her first suggestion was that she could quit watching so much television and spend more time studying. She then said that her friend Julie was good at Spanish and had volunteered to tutor her. Before we finished our conversation, she committed to try her hardest to earn an A on a test that was coming up in a couple of weeks. I was excited to see if she would put in the required work, knowing she could not only make excellent grades but also feel better about herself. President Monson explained, "Our responsibility is to rise from mediocrity to competence, from failure to achievement. Our task is to become our best selves."[17]

I saw Kasi twice before she took the test and asked her if she was doing what she had agreed to do as far as using her television time to study and having Julie tutor her. She assured me that she was doing what she had committed to. The weekend after the test, I was eager to hear about the test results and ask what lessons she had learned from her hard work. I asked her how she did on the test as soon as I saw her. I was shocked when she said, "I made a forty-five out of one hundred." Her answer was so unexpected I didn't even know what to say. I couldn't believe she had studied so hard and still failed the test.

I thought long and hard about lessons I could learn from her experience. After several weeks, a powerful message came to me. I learned that in some areas of life we can change and improve quickly just as Merrilee did by acting as if she were outgoing. In other areas, change can be difficult, but with determination and hard work those weaknesses can be turned into strengths. Then there are some things that are nearly impossible to acquire or change no matter how much a person wants it or how hard he or she tries. If you are born to be short in stature, it does no good to spend time trying to be tall. While I'm still confident Kasi could learn Spanish with enough sacrifice and hard work, surely it is possible and okay that learning languages is not one of her gifts. Over time she found that she had a knack for science and is now a registered nurse. Others perhaps have an easier time learning languages but find science nearly impossible to understand. In the scriptures we learn, "For all have not every gift given unto them; for there are many gifts, and to every man is given a gift by the Spirit of God" (Doctrine and Covenants 46:11).

Of course, there are plenty of examples where people have demonstrated that with determination and hard work they can acquire skills thought to be beyond their reach. On the other hand, isn't it okay if some people who have not been blessed with a gift in one area spend time improving in other areas within their reach? A quote often attributed to Albert Einstein says, "Everybody is a genius. But if you judge a fish by its ability to climb a tree, it will live its whole life believing that it is stupid."

The key is doing the best you can with what you have been given, while not getting down on yourself because you don't have the same gifts and talents that others have. In Matthew 25 we read about the parable of the talents. Most people are familiar with the details of the parable, where a man gives one of his servants five talents, another two, and another only one. The servant with five talents worked hard and obtained five more. The one given two went out, did the best he could, and gained two more. However, the servant who only received one talent buried his talent in the earth. To the first two servants the Lord offered his highest honor by saying, "Well done, thou good and faithful servant: thou hast been faithful over a few things, I will make thee ruler over many things: enter thou into the joy of thy lord" (Matthew 25:21). But to the one who buried the one talent he had been given, the Lord reserved a serious rebuke: "And cast ye the unprofitable servant into outer darkness: there shall be weeping and gnashing of teeth" (Matthew 25:30).

It is interesting that the servant who only gained two extra talents received the exact reward as the one who gained an extra five. Perhaps the Lord is saying if you will do the best you can with what you have been given, you will receive an eternal reward for your effort to change, improve, live life in crescendo, and, in scriptural terms, endure to the end.

Invitation to Act

1. Determine a weakness you most want to change to a strength and write it down.
2. Ask yourself why you have this weakness, and keep a journal of related thoughts, feelings, and actions.
3. Make a list of the long- and short-range prices you pay for holding onto this weakness.
4. List the positive things you miss out on because this weakness is holding you back.
5. Ask yourself every morning what good you should accomplish that day and write your thoughts. At night go over the list and ask if you accomplished your goal.

CHAPTER 2

Decisions Determine Destiny

Satan is an accomplished master at making devastating choices appear attractive, even reasonable. So be careful . . . The decisions you will make will profoundly affect life now and for eternity. Make them wisely and prayerfully.[18]
Elder Richard G. Scott

Melanie Nelson Wright

I was a people pleaser and wanted to be great at whatever I was part of. Immature in my thinking as a teenager, I completed Personal Progress at church, but I also found a lot of satisfaction in being part of the in crowd at school. I was a popular cheerleader and spent my weekends at parties and places where the Spirit didn't reside. I had two recognizable spiritual experiences by the time I had graduated high school, but neither was enough on its own for me to have a true testimony of the gospel. I remember talking to my bishop about my desire to be great at church but also with my school friends. Inspired, he read me a powerful poem about the folly of trying to go down two different paths at the same time.

My bishop's message left a big impression on me. A year later, I was finishing up my first year of college. That year my parents divorced, and four of my five siblings and my mom had stopped going to church. I had attended the Young Single Adult ward and institute classes enough that people knew who I was, but I missed enough that I would get fellowship visits from the missionaries. I continued to be very social in the party scene as well. At my brother's wedding at the end of my freshman year, I was visiting with a lifelong friend from the ward I grew up in. He was a returned missionary, but we were both drinking a beer and at the same time talking about wanting to get married in the temple. The irony of that conversation and our behavior was some sort of turning point for me. I felt like I was trying to straddle the fork in the road and going nowhere. I decided that night that it was time for me to experiment on the things I had been taught and to see for myself if they were true. I knew I had to figure this out. It would have been easier to just stop going to church. I would have been more accepted, certainly among my friends and even in my own family, had I stopped going to church and chosen the other path. But I wasn't ready to not believe without giving it a fair chance. So I told a nonmember friend of mine, "I'm just experimenting. I'm going to do what the Church teaches for a year and see what happens."

By the time my year experiment ended, I had changed. I was a different being with different desires, different habits, and different goals. There was no need to analyze the results and decide which way I wanted to go, because I was changed. Instead of looking for the light, I decided to *be* the light and ultimately found the light through my experiment. I thought I was confident as a cheerleader who could get in front of huge crowds and perform with no problem. But having a knowledge that I was a child of God gave purpose to my talents and gave me a completely different and more powerful confidence. I no longer needed to make decisions to try to please others, but rather, I was easily able to make decisions based on what kept me close to my Heavenly Father. True confidence is being who you really are, no matter who you are around, and feeling good about being that person. I believe we can achieve this only by being at one with our Father in Heaven's will and purpose. The change I went through during my experiment has shaped my entire life. I'm grateful my young mind was willing to take a chance and see what happened.

Decide Today

Melanie decided to follow the path of Christ suggested by the Book of Mormon prophet Alma when he said, "But behold, if ye will awake and arouse your faculties, even to an experiment upon my words, and exercise a particle of faith, yea, even if ye can no more than desire to believe, let this desire work in you, even until ye believe in a manner that ye can give place for a portion of my words" (Alma 32:27). The decision to try the straight and narrow path changed Melanie's life forever. She found the path that led to real confidence, a temple marriage, an eternal family, and true happiness. She is proof of what President Gordon B. Hinckley said: "You can determine the kind of life you will have in your thirties and forties by what you do in your teens."[19] It is also true that the decisions you make in your twenties, thirties, and forties will determine the kind of life you will have in your fifties, sixties, and seventies. The bottom line is that our decisions determine our destiny.

Randal: A few years ago, I had the opportunity to speak to a large group of twelve- and thirteen-year-old boys in Anchorage, Alaska, about making good decisions. During the talk, I shared an experience that my cousin Brian, who was visiting from out of state, and I had when I was their age. One day we went exploring and found a snapping turtle. Although these turtles were common where I lived, Brian apparently had never been around one. I asked the young men in Alaska if they knew how to play with a snapping turtle. Most had no idea, so I explained that you get a stick and poke around the turtle's open mouth until it clamps onto the stick.

Brian was having a lot of fun as the turtle repeatedly snapped onto the end of the stick with its powerful jaws. But Brian and I both learned a few things about snapping turtles that day. We first learned their necks are much longer than you think, allowing them to strike almost like a snake. We also learned their legs are powerful, and they can lunge forward quickly. We then learned that impulsive decisions can often come with unintended negative consequences. Those lessons came when Brian got too close to the turtle, and its jaws snapped onto one of his fingers like a vice.

Brian cried out in extreme pain as I stood by with no idea how to help. I asked the young men in Alaska what they thought I should have done. One boy said I should have gotten a stick and poked the turtle. I reminded him that was what had gotten Brian in this predicament to begin with. Another boy suggested I should have reached down and pried the turtle's mouth open. I told him there was no way I was going to put my fingers near the turtle's mouth. The next suggestion was that I take a knife and cut the turtle's head off. That was followed by cutting Brian's finger off. Their suggestions demonstrated the point I wanted to make. When we make a bad decision, there are seldom good solutions to get us out of the predicament.

When several boys asked what finally happened, I told them that Brian panicked and lifted the turtle off the ground with his finger. The turtle seemed to clamp down even harder, and Brian became terrified. At that point he did what he had to do to rid himself of the pain—a round-the-head helicopter move, which sent the turtle flying off his finger, along with some of his own flesh. This left him in even worse pain with his finger bleeding—and later a permanent scar. I suggested to my wide-eyed audience when they are faced with decisions in the future, they should study things out in their minds and then ask Heavenly Father if it is right (see Doctrine and Covenants 9:8).

I then asked the boys if any of them had physical scars. Almost every hand went up. I invited a few to share the stories behind their scars. The first shared how he was riding down the side of a mountain on a piece of tin and crashed, leaving a large gash. The second said he stood up under a trampoline while his brother was jumping on it and hit his head when he fell. I told the boys if they had studied their decisions out and asked if they were right, the boys could have avoided their scars. I then challenged them to use that formula to make decisions in the future. The last boy, with a visible facial scar, said, "I was sitting on the kitchen counter picking my nose with a knife and fell off the counter, landing on the knife." I emphasized that bad decisions can not only lead to physical scars but also emotional, mental, and spiritual ones.

Years ago, I was in the audience when a college student named Carla gave a speech on the importance of making good decisions. One thing she said has stayed with me and has resurfaced in my thoughts several times. She taught, "The decisions we make will either bring amazing rewards, horrible consequences, or something in between." The evidence of the statement she made is all around us.

Life is a never-ending process of deciding what we are going to do next. In the end, we become the sum of those decisions. We should constantly ask if the path we are taking is likely to lead to amazing rewards, horrible consequences, or something in between. Life is far too short to be making bad, thoughtless decisions. Kahlil Gibran made an excellent point when he said, "We choose our joys and sorrows long before we experience them."[20]

We live in a world bombarded with the message that the large and spacious building is where all fun and happiness occurs. Those in the building mock and point their fingers at those who decide to take a different path. They promote alcohol, immorality, drugs, tobacco, pornography, vaping, and more, as if these are just harmless fun. These vices can latch onto a person much like the snapping turtle on my cousin's finger—but with far more devastating consequences. Often these vices leave scars on our physical, emotional, mental, or spiritual well-being. Elder Neal A. Maxwell explained, "If we entertain temptations, soon they begin entertaining us!"[21]

Unfortunately, many in society have bought into the lies that the only way to have fun is to participate in some of these evils. That philosophy has gained a huge foothold on college campuses among even the nation's brightest students. Now those who choose not to drink alcohol or have premarital intimacy are often looked down upon and viewed as weird, boring, and out of touch with reality. However, with just a little "studying it out," anyone can easily see the decision to participate in these activities often leads to severe consequences for individuals, families, and society.

Winning Is Not an Accident

Many fail to consider the impact daily decisions have on long-term success and happiness. The tendency to follow the crowd down the path of least resistance and merely drift along with no overall vision or destination is all too common. The result is often somewhere in between the amazing rewards and horrible consequences that Carla mentioned in her speech. Perhaps this condition is what the Lord was referring to in Revelation 3:15–16: "I know thy works, that thou art neither cold nor hot: I would thou wert cold or hot. So then because thou art lukewarm, and neither cold nor hot, I will spue thee out of my mouth."

What is it that you would like to accomplish in life? Are you on the path that will lead to your desired finish line? You cannot expect to be on the road leading to Las Vegas and end up at Disney World. Neither can you expect to be on the road leading to Seattle part of the time and the road leading to New York City part of the time and expect to end up in either place. We simply must make decisions that will lead us to our desired destination. Not everyone has the talent, competitive fire, opportunity, or luck to be on the world stage. However, all have a chance to make a difference in the world in their own way with the talents they have been given.

You Are Free to Make Decisions

While in college, I took an organizational behavior class from a nationally recognized professor. One day before class, I heard a classmate say, "I won't be in class on Thursday because I have a tennis tournament." The student seemed a little surprised with the response he received. "No, you don't have to go to the tennis tournament. You choose to go rather than come to my class."

The student countered, "You don't understand! I'm on the university tennis team, and I have to go to the tournament."

Our wise professor then said, "I understand perfectly. You are a member of the tennis team and choose to go to the tennis tournament rather than come to my class."

Seemingly exasperated, the student responded, "Okay, I choose to compete in the tournament rather than coming to your class."

Our professor then said, "If I were on the tennis team, I would take part in the tennis tournament rather than come to class too. But I just want you to understand that you are free to choose what you do in life. Don't blame others or circumstances for your choices."

What a wonderful thing to realize that we can choose the path we take in life. However, we must remember that no one else is to blame for the choices we make.

Decide to Decide and Act

Some have a difficult time making any decisions. That can cause major problems along life's path. Those who fall into this category seldom accomplish what they are capable of. Former professional baseball player and five-time All-Star Bobby Murcer summed it up: "You decide you'll wait for your pitch. Then as the ball starts toward the plate, you think about your stance. And then you think about your swing. And then you realize that the ball went past you."[22] In other words, if we are to achieve amazing things in life, we must make decisions and act.

We all find ourselves standing at the crossroads of life with choices before us. Margaret Thatcher, British stateswoman and former prime minister of the United Kingdom, said, "Standing in the middle of the road is very dangerous; you get knocked down by the traffic from both sides."[23]

If we are to do anything amazing in life, we must decide what we want to accomplish then go quickly down the path that leads to that end.

We Make Decisions Daily

Our lives involve continuous tasks to determine what to do next. Think of decisions you have already made today. We make some decisions as if we are on autopilot. Some may seem insignificant today but if repeated over time could become significant. For example, if we consistently choose to eat an unhealthy high-sugar diet without exercising, we dramatically increase our chances of diabetes, obesity, heart disease, and early death. On the other hand, if we choose to eat nutritious meals and exercise consistently, we will likely increase our chances of living a long, healthy life.

While daily decisions made over time can dramatically affect our destiny, so can one-time impulsive decisions. For years, I drove past one of the largest businesses in the area where we lived. The CEO of that institution was an admired leader in both the business world and in community affairs. He was highly motivated, and his decisions led to great accolades. He had a JD from a top-rated law school, served on the boards of several other businesses, and held prestigious positions in cultural arts and service organizations. He was highly respected in the large Christian church he, his wife, and their children attended. His children were also popular at a local private school.

However, while attending a convention in a distant city, he made one thoughtless decision that would forever change his life. He decided to go against the advice of Karl Kraus, who said, "In case of doubt, decide in favor of what is correct."[24] He was arrested for soliciting an undercover police officer. The next day his picture and the story of his arrest made the front page of the local newspaper and shocked the city. That one impulsive decision immediately negated most of the things he had spent his entire life working for. Within a short time, he lost his good reputation and was fired from his prestigious job. He later went bankrupt. In his case, one hasty decision led to horrible consequences and changed the course of multiple lives.

Almost daily we read of those whose decisions have led to great success and amazing rewards or to lost friendships, physical injury, death, loss of respect, disgrace, divorce, financial ruin, addiction, regret, guilt, and more.

No wonder President Ezra Taft Benson taught, "Making decisions is probably the most important thing people ever do."[25]

Suggestions for Making Good Decisions

Learn from Past Decisions and from Others

Since our decisions can have such far-reaching consequences, it is imperative that they be well thought out. It is helpful to learn from the results other people have had from making similar decisions. For example, how many times have individuals in important positions been brought down by making unwise decisions? Even though these stories made headlines nationwide, others ignore the lessons right in front of them and repeat the same mistake with the same horrible results. No one needs to repeat the same mistakes that brought misery to those who chose that path.

Decisions are a part of life. Most likely, we've all made good decisions and some that are bad. We also can observe decisions made by others around us and read about others. It is always good to closely examine our own past decisions and others' decisions and ask, "And how did that work out?" Perhaps this is the reason Irish philosopher Edmund Burke is reported to have said, "Those who don't know history are doomed to repeat it."

Determine What You Value

Successful companies identify their core values. Most often, they incorporate these values into a mission statement, which then serves as a guide for almost every major decision. Amazon was launched in 1995 and has become the largest internet-based retailer in the world. Its first mission statement was short and simple, yet it drove almost everything Amazon does: "be Earth's most customer-centric company, where customers can find and discover anything they might want to buy online." How well is Amazon fulfilling its original stated mission? "Amazon sells more than 12 million products, not including books, media, wine and services. When Amazon Marketplace sellers are factored in, the total product count balloons to more than 353 million."[26] Even the company logo with an arrow going from A to Z was influenced by their mission statement.

One of the most important things an individual can do in life is to determine what he or she values. Roy Disney believed, "It's not hard to make decisions when you know what your values are."[27]

If, for instance, you value a healthy body and good quality of life, certain decisions become almost automatic. People who value their health will exercise, eat nutritious food, and avoid ingesting harmful substances. Smoking cigarettes would be out of the question since smoking is known to cause cancer, heart disease, stroke, lung disease, diabetes, and chronic obstructive pulmonary disease, which includes emphysema and chronic bronchitis. Cigarette smoking is also responsible for more than four hundred eighty thousand deaths per year in the United States.[28]

Have you ever written down the things you deeply value? Do you have a concise written mission statement that reflects those values? If so, it will be a tremendous help in making decisions, just as it is for companies like Amazon. Someone has said the best time to look for an emergency exit is before the emergency. It is also the best time to make decisions, when possible. President Spencer W. Kimball suggested, "Make certain decisions only once."[29]

Life Basically Involves Two Choices

Randal: For many years, I had a difficult time understanding 1 Nephi 14:10: "And he said unto me: Behold there are save two churches only; the one is the church of the Lamb of God, and the other is the church of the devil; wherefore, whoso belongeth not to the church of the Lamb of God belongeth to that great church, which is the mother of abominations; and she is the whore of all the earth."

One day I found myself in Gettysburg, Pennsylvania, standing on the field where the largest battle of the Civil War occurred. Fought between July 1 and 3, 1863, this battle involved approximately seventy-five thousand soldiers from the Confederate Army and eighty-two thousand for the Union Army. This awful battle resulted in over fifty thousand casualties, counting dead, wounded, and missing. While contemplating the battle, the scripture verse that had confused me for so long came to mind. I realized the soldiers involved in the Battle of Gettysburg made a choice to either fight for the North or the South. There were only two choices. At that point, the scripture made total sense to me. In the battle between good and evil, we are either in the Lord's church or the church of the devil. There are only two choices. However, even if we choose the right side, it does not necessarily mean we are good soldiers!

In a class, the instructor talked about how hard it is to constantly stay positive. He said, "I have a hard time staying happy all the time, unlike John here, who is always happy." He looked over at John, a man in his eighties who is the happiest, most positive guy you will ever meet. John responded with four words and then didn't say anything else. He simply said, "You have two choices." In other words, you can choose to be happy or not.

While life involves thousands of choices overall, we basically face only two choices at any given time. For example, every morning we can choose to get up early or not. To read our scriptures or not. Wear a certain outfit or not. Arrive at work on time or not. Someone may say this logic does not apply, for example, to buying a new car since there are 237 existing models with new models appearing each year. That of course does not include the hundreds of used cars available. However, doesn't it still come down to two choices? Do you want a Honda Accord or something else? Something else! Do you want a Toyota Camry or something else? Something else! How about a Chevrolet Malibu or something else? Yes, that is the car I want. But even when you've decided on a make and model, you still face multiple choices. Doesn't it still go back to two choices to make at any given time? Do you want a hybrid or not? Leather seats or not? The standard stereo or not, and so forth. Ultimately, we only face two choices at any given time, so we need to remember to choose the best one.

While making wise decisions is not always easy, the effort is worth the price required. It helps to keep the big picture in mind when making daily decisions. President Monson declared, "You are of a noble birthright. Eternal life in the kingdom of our Father is your goal. Such a goal is not achieved in one glorious attempt but rather is the result of a lifetime of righteousness, an accumulation of wise choices, even a constancy of purpose. Like the coveted A grade on the report card of a difficult and required college course, the reward of eternal life requires effort."[30]

Invitation to Act

1. Determine all the things that you deeply value in life and write them down.
2. Write a mission statement that reflects those values to guide your future decisions.

3. When making decisions in life, use this scripture: "But, behold, I say unto you, that you must study it out in your mind; then you must ask me if it be right, and if it is right I will cause that your bosom shall burn within you; therefore, you shall feel that it is right" (Doctrine and Covenants 9:8).

CHAPTER 3

Create a Vision with the End in Mind

How different our lives are when we really know what is deeply important to us, and keeping that picture in mind, we manage ourselves each day to be and to do what really matters most. If the ladder is not leaning against the right wall, every step we take just gets us to the wrong place faster. We may be very busy, we may be very efficient, *but we will also be truly* effective *only when we begin with the end in mind.*[31]

Stephen R. Covey

Damian Fink

Each year while I was a member of a Boy Scout troop, we participated in selling candy bars to raise money for troop activities. This was not something I liked to do because I lived outside of town and didn't enjoy the long walks between houses. It took a lot of time and effort, and I decided that it wasn't worth it. I asked my mom if she had any ideas. She suggested I try my grandpa, a well-known residential real estate agent in the area. I gave him a call, and he agreed to help. A few days later, he picked me up at my house, and we drove to pick up the candy.

Upon our arrival, the person handling the effort asked how many bars we wanted. The previous year I had sold fifteen or twenty bars but didn't know if I could do that again. I wasn't sure what my grandpa had in mind, so I started to ask about the open box that had about ten or fifteen bars left, thinking that it wouldn't be too hard to sell that many. As I reached down to get the bars, Grandpa asked the person in charge how many candy bars were left to be sold.

"Well, this is all we have left," he answered.

There were ten cases of candy bars on the wooden pallet, but one was open. "That will be fine," Grandpa said. "We'll take all of them."

He popped the trunk open and started loading cases. At first, I stood there shocked and a bit confused. We filled the trunk and the back seat with the boxes. He was trying to teach me to see the big picture. He then said, "Let's go." We traveled in relative silence as I tried to work through how many doors we'd need to knock on to sell all the candy. My brain couldn't process what was going on.

Our first stop was the office building of a title company. Grandpa opened the trunk, and I reached into the open box, asking him how many I should bring. He was about to teach me a lesson that would forever change me. He smiled and said, "We don't sell by the bar, we sell by the box." In other words, if you want to be successful in life, you are going to have to start by thinking big. He reached down, grabbed a box of candy bars, closed the trunk, and headed to the office.

What played out at that first stop repeated over the next few hours. We walked into an office, and Grandpa dropped a box on the reception desk. The owner or manager of the office we happened to be in came out, and Grandpa introduced me. I then explained what I was doing.

True to his word, we did not sell by the bar, even though at several stops many people tried to negotiate for a bar instead of a box. The close rate that day was 100 percent! At every office, we sold either a half box or a full one. I won a bike for being a top seller in the state of California with 962 candy bars sold in one afternoon. That experience certainly raised the bar for me.

From that point on, no matter what I was involved in, I tried to envision the result at the end as something big. Later, when choosing a career, I decided on real estate. However, residential real estate did not appeal to me. Selling one home at a time was like selling one candy bar at a time. When I encountered commercial real estate, it reminded me of selling cases of candy as a boy. I thought, "I was born for this." Once you begin to envision accomplishing big things with the end in mind, life gets exciting.

Envisioning Your End Goal

The word *visualize* means to form a mental image. What Damian's grandfather did was give him a mental image of accomplishing big things in life. That day forever changed how he viewed the world. Can you imagine how much time and effort it would have taken to sell 962 candy bars one or two at a time? Having a vision of the end goal being something big can have incredible implications for many facets of life.

Many are stuck on the ground thinking small thoughts not fully realizing their potential to soar. Believing in yourself and seeing the big picture is exciting and has the potential to not only change you but also to change the world around you. Elder Merlin R. Lybbert told the following story: "An enterprising turkey gathered the flock together and, following instructions and demonstrations, taught them how to fly. All afternoon they enjoyed soaring and flying and the thrill of seeing new vistas. After the meeting, all of the turkeys walked home."[32]

The lesson of this tale is obvious. If you want to enjoy the thrill of having a new outlook, you must stop thinking like a normal turkey and believe you can fly. You have to allow those beliefs to change how you act. Otherwise, you stay on the ground. Isn't it time to see new vistas?

Believing in Yourself

Publisher and author William Walker Atkinson offered this insight to those contemplating what they want to accomplish. "Visualization is simply the creation of a strong mental image of the thing desired, the perfecting it each day until it becomes almost as clear as an existing material thing."[33]

Once you can visualize yourself achieving something grand, you begin to believe you can do it. That belief then moves you toward your end goal. Darren Johnson discovered this important truth in an unusual way while home for Christmas break one year. Think about this experience and the potential implications of his accidental discovery.

> In the 1990s, I returned home from college to spend the Christmas holidays with my family. My older brothers, KC and Kevin, were also home. KC introduced us to a single-player computer video game called *Minesweeper*. The objective was to clear a rectangular board containing hidden mines without detonating any in the shortest amount of time

possible. We decided to compete on the intermediate level to see who would end up with the fastest time for the week.

We took turns sitting at the computer console trying to figure out how to one-up the current record holder. I took an early lead in the competition with a solve time of 160 seconds, but that score did not last long. If I left the computer for any length of time, I returned to find another brother's name on top. It took a few days before we managed to get our times below 100 seconds. I had thought that score was impossible at first, but once we broke that barrier, the times continued to fall even lower. I completed the puzzle in 80 seconds, only to come back an hour later to find that Kevin had it solved in 72 seconds. I sat down and dropped my score to 64 seconds, only to come back later to find that KC had completed it in what seemed to be an impossible 48 seconds. By the end of the week, the low score stood at 26 seconds, six times faster than my original low score. I gave up way too much family time and tried every way possible to beat that score, but it was impossible to beat. The best I could do was 27 seconds. As our holiday week ended, much to my chagrin, I had to concede the competition to my brother who had beaten me by one second.

It was then that my brothers let me in on a little secret. Neither of them had managed to complete the puzzle in less than 100 seconds. KC, a software developer, knew how to hack the system code and change the name and time for the high score. Every time I beat the score, he went back into the system files and made it appear as if they had topped me again.

I now wonder if I had not seen scores faster than mine whether I would have believed such scores were possible or achieved the times that I did. In my naivete, it never occurred to me that the scores I saw were unachievable. Instead, my belief fueled the innovation I needed to reclaim the top scorer spot each time.

The trick Darren's brothers played on him teaches that truly believing what you envision increases the likelihood it will happen. Author Roy T. Bennett wrote, "Don't let others tell you what you can't do. Don't let the limitations of others limit your vision. If you can remove your self-doubt and believe in yourself, you can achieve what you never thought possible."[34]

Begin with the End in Mind

Randal: A few years ago, my friend Kent and I entered a wood carving shop and saw a beautiful carving of a Native American chief. The detail was incredible. My friend asked the wood-carver, "How did you do this?"

I thought he would mention his training or years of experience, but he simply said with a smile, "I just carved away everything that wasn't a chief, and this is what I had left." In other words, he envisioned exactly where he was going with the piece of wood before he started. If he wanted to end up with a cowboy or pirate, I'm confident the old carver could have produced them also. What would the wood-carver have created if he began carving without a clear vision of the end results? Most likely just a pile of wood shavings! I'm sure Michelangelo envisioned his sculpture David and all his other creations before he started the actual work.

In life, we are both the wood-carver and the piece of wood. Are you creating something beautiful, producing a pile of wood shavings, or just looking at the piece of wood in the mirror every day? You must be able to perceive the end before you know where to even start. Jesus Christ knows exactly what His end goal is. We read in Moses 1:39, "For behold, this is my work and my glory—to bring to pass the immortality and eternal life of man." Every program in His church fits under that one-sentence vision. Do you have a mental picture of your end goal fixed firmly in your mind?

The Founding Fathers

Our country began when inspired patriots envisioned the results of their actions. Fortunately, their vision for this country was written in inspired documents preserved for the entire world to see. If only all people would give as much thought to their purpose in life. Even for those who have thought about their end objective, few have mission or vision statements to serve as a road map and constant reminder of what they visualize for the outcome.

The *Founding Fathers* is a term used to describe the individuals living in the Thirteen Colonies who led the American Revolution against the British Crown. Perhaps the most influential of these visionaries were Thomas Jefferson, Benjamin Franklin, John Adams, Alexander Hamilton, John Jay, James Madison, and George Washington. They envisioned their end goal, which eventually led to the adoption of the Declaration of Independence on July 4, 1776, and the signing of the remarkable US Constitution on September 17, 1787. As you carefully read the words the Founding Fathers penned, consider how these documents have blessed the lives of millions worldwide.

- The Declaration of Independence: "We hold these truths to be self-evident, that all men are created equal, that they are endowed by their Creator with certain unalienable Rights, that among these are Life, Liberty and the pursuit of Happiness."
- Preamble to the US Constitution: "We the People of the United States, in Order to form a more perfect Union, establish Justice, insure domestic Tranquility, provide for the common defense, promote the general Welfare, and secure the Blessings of Liberty to ourselves and our Posterity, do ordain and establish this Constitution for the United States of America."

According to the *Oxford English Dictionary* a constitution is "the system or body of fundamental principles according to which a nation, state, or body politic is constituted and governed."[35] President Dallin H. Oaks pointed out, "The United States Constitution was the first written constitution in the world. It has served Americans well, enhancing freedom and prosperity during the changed conditions of more than two hundred years. Frequently copied, it has become the United States' most important export. After two centuries, every nation in the world except six have adopted written constitutions."[36]

What the Founding Fathers envisioned for their new country was unparalleled in human history. America is now over 240 years old and the world's oldest continuous republic. The prosperity and opportunities for growth and success coming from these early inspired documents are unmatched. Irish playwright George Bernard Shaw said, "You see things; and you say, 'Why?' But I dream things that never were; and I say 'Why not?'"[37]

The Founding Fathers dreamed of having a country like no other in history and said, "Why not?" Thinking big led to envisioning big, which led to belief and then action.

Other Inspiring Men and Women

Let's look at a few individuals from various walks of life who saw a big picture, believed, and helped make their visions reality.

Joseph Smith

In 1834 Joseph Smith called for a meeting to be held in Kirtland, Ohio. President Wilford Woodruff recorded, "The Prophet called on all who held the Priesthood to gather into the little log school house they had there. It was a small house, perhaps fourteen feet square. But it held the whole of the Priesthood of the Church of Jesus Christ of Latter-day Saints who were then in the town of Kirtland. . . . The Prophet said, 'Brethren, I have been very much edified and instructed in your testimonies here tonight, but I want to say to you before the Lord, that you know no more concerning the destinies of this Church and kingdom than a babe upon its mother's lap. You don't comprehend it. . . . This Church will fill North and South America—it will fill the world.'"[38]

Randal: I had an experience while working for the Church Educational System that taught me the importance of creating a vision. My supervisor, Kelly Shepherd, invited me to accompany him to a worldwide area directors meeting held in Utah. It was an amazing experience to be with area directors from Chile, Brazil, Mexico, Japan, Korea, England, Canada, Africa, Russia, the Philippines, and many more. During one of the closing meetings, a short film about Joseph Smith and his legacy was shown. Included was a scene of a large modern printing press running off copies of the Book of Mormon, and then the famous quote by Joseph Smith flashed on the screen. It is obvious the Prophet could see where the restored gospel would end up. He wrote, "The Standard of Truth has been erected; no unhallowed hand can stop the work from progressing; persecutions may rage, mobs may combine, armies may assemble, calumny may defame, but the truth of God will go forth boldly, nobly, and independent, till it has penetrated every continent, visited every clime, swept every country, and sounded in every ear, till the purposes of God shall be accomplished, and the Great Jehovah shall say the work is done."[39]

Sitting on the side at the front of the room, I had a clear view of those in attendance. At the end of the film, I noticed many wiping tears from their eyes. I, too, was overcome with emotion, realizing that I was with those from across the world carrying out the end of the vision Joseph Smith began with. Those area directors had responsibility for the seminaries and institutes throughout the entire world.

Karl G. Maeser

On October 14, 1855, talented teacher Karl G. Maeser was baptized in his native Germany by Franklin D. Richards. After being forced to leave his home by the Dresden police, he and his family immigrated to America. Maeser taught in several Utah schools until Brigham Young asked him to move his family to Provo and establish an academy in the name of the Church. The last instruction he received from President Young before the move was this: “You ought not to teach even the alphabet or the multiplication tables without the Spirit of God.”[40]

By the beginning of 1884, nine years after Maeser first accepted the assignment, the Brigham Young Academy had nearly four hundred students and appeared to be financially stable. However, on the night of January 27, 1884, a fire destroyed the building the academy occupied. During the next eight years, the fledgling school held classes in temporary buildings and drifted toward financial collapse. The faculty often went without pay and became increasingly discouraged. During this difficult time Maeser wrote this to the First Presidency of the Church: “I am worn out and sick in spirit, . . . and with all my love for this Academy, I feel that I owe it to my very life, which is needlessly wearing itself out here in an apparently hopeless task, to accept any change that will promise me opportunities for permanent usefulness.”[41]

At that point Maeser told his wife and daughter to get ready to move back to Salt Lake City. Unable to make a living at the academy, he had decided to accept a position at the University of Deseret. Several days after packing up their possessions, his daughter asked her father when they were leaving for Salt Lake.

He responded, “I have changed my mind. I have had a dream—I have seen Temple Hill filled with buildings—great temples of learning, and I have decided to remain and do my part in contributing to the fulfillment of that dream.”[42] The buildings he saw, of course, make up the Brigham Young University of today.

Helen Keller

Helen Keller was born in Tuscumbia, Alabama, on June 27, 1880. At nineteen months old, she contracted an unknown illness leaving her both deaf and blind. Despite severe challenges, Keller was extremely bright and by age seven learned more than sixty signs to communicate with her family. About that time, Keller's mother, Kate, read an account in Charles Dickens's *American Notes* about a deaf and blind woman named Laura Bridgman who was successfully educated. This gave Keller's parents hope, and they sought help. Keller's father, Arthur, took her to a noted physician in Baltimore. He, in turn, referred Keller's father to Alexander Graham Bell, who was working with deaf children. Bell suggested they contact the Perkins Institution for the Blind in Boston, where Laura Bridgman had been educated. It was here that a twenty-year-old former student, also visually impaired, was assigned to be Helen's teacher. Her name was Anne Sullivan.

Anne moved to the Keller home in Alabama in 1887 and immediately began to communicate with Keller by spelling words in her hand. Within a short time, Keller understood that every object had a word to identify it. The next year Keller began her formal education at the Perkins Institution and later at the Wright-Humason School for the Deaf in New York. During each step of her educational journey, Anne Sullivan was by her side.

Keller's physical limitations did not prevent her from conceptualizing a vision of who she was and what she could become in the end. In 1900, she was accepted to Radcliffe College, a prestigious women's liberal arts college in Cambridge, Massachusetts. She became the first deafblind person to ever earn a bachelor of arts degree, and she did it with honors. In time, Keller learned to speak to and understand other people by using her fingers to read their lips. She became the author of twelve published books and was a world-famous speaker. Between 1946 and 1957, she visited thirty-five countries on five continents.[43]

Here is a summary of one speech given in Menomonie, Wisconsin: "According to those who attended, Helen Keller spoke of the joy that life gave her. She was thankful for the faculties and abilities that she did possess and stated that the most productive pleasures she had were curiosity and imagination. . . . Keller also spoke of the joy of service and the happiness that came from doing things for others. . . . Keller imparted that "helping your fellow men were one's only excuse for being in this world and in the doing of things to help one's fellows lay the secret of lasting happiness." She also told of the joys of loving work and accomplishment and the happiness of achievement. Although the entire lecture lasted only a little over an hour, the lecture had a profound impact on the audience."

Helen was once asked by a reporter, "What can be worse than being blind?" She replied, "Having eyes to see but no vision."[44] In 1999, *Time* magazine named Helen Keller one of the one hundred most influential people of the twentieth century.[45] While she could not see with her physical eyes, her mental vision was twenty-twenty.

Walt Disney

Walt Disney was also a visionary icon. He developed an interest in drawing at an early age and got a job as a commercial illustrator at age eighteen. In his early twenties, he moved to California and started Disney Brothers Cartoon Studio with his brother Roy. At age twenty-seven, Walt and Ub Iwerks developed the character Mickey Mouse. At that point, his studio prospered, and Disney produced several full-length cartoon films like *Snow White and the Seven Dwarfs*, *Pinocchio*, *Fantasia*, and many more.[46]

For years, Disney envisioned building a theme park where both children and parents could have fun together. The dream became reality when Disneyland opened in July 1955. The opening ceremony was broadcast to seventy million viewers on the ABC television network and had over three million guests in the first year. In October 1971, another theme park opened called Walt Disney World near Orlando, Florida. The property covers twenty-five thousand acres and currently employs over sixty thousand people. It is the most visited vacation resort in the world with over fifty-two million visitors annually. Disney now has twelve theme parks and fifty-two resorts worldwide.[47]

Walt Disney left a legacy that has touched the lives of hundreds of millions. He had an incredible ability to turn his vision into reality. Surely almost every individual in America has either bought, watched, listened to, or visited something Walt Disney first saw in his mind. Disney is one of the best-loved media and entertainment companies in the world. The company currently owns ABC, ESPN, Lucasfilm, Marvel, Pixar, Disney

Cruise Line, Disney on Ice, and Disney Parks, Experiences and Products. Walt Disney once said, "If you can dream it, you can do it."[48]

When you begin by envisioning the end, it is as if a map comes into your mind showing the roads leading to your destination. However, like a wood-carver, if you can't see at the start where you are going, you may end up with wood shavings in life. Walt Disney passed away five years before the grand opening of Walt Disney World. Shortly after it opened, "someone said to Mike Vance, the director of Disney Studios, 'Isn't it too bad that Walt Disney didn't live to see this? Vance replied, 'He did see it—that's why it's here.'"[49]

What Is Your Gift?

In 1967, President Kimball gave a speech to the students at Brigham Young University called "Education for Eternity." In it, he shared a vision he had for church members so bold that it surprised those who heard his message. He shared the names of some of the most visionary and creative men and women in recorded history. Most of the names are so well known that first names are not needed: Da Vinci, Curie, Michelangelo, Goethe, Rembrandt, Raphael, Pasteur, Einstein, Shakespeare, and others. His message was for Church members to step up and be their equals or even superiors.

At one point he said, "Then we ask, 'Can there never be another Michelangelo?' Ah! Yes! His *David* in Florence and his *Moses* in Rome inspire adulation. Did all such talent run out in that early century? Could not we find an embodied talent like this but with a soul that was free from immorality and sensuality and intolerance?"

He continued, "The story of Mormonism has never yet been written nor painted nor sculptured nor spoken. It remains for inspired hearts and talented fingers yet to reveal themselves. They must be faithful, inspired, active Church members to give life and feeling and true perspective to a subject so worthy. Such masterpieces should run for months in every movie center and cover every part of the globe in the tongue of the people, written by great artists and purified by the best critics."[50]

Are you one of those he was talking about who need to step out of the shadows and accomplish a remarkable mission in life? If so, you must first see the end from the beginning and turn your vision into reality.

Invitation to Act

1. What lessons can you learn from Darren going from 160 seconds to 27 seconds in the game *Minesweeper*? How could his discovery apply to you?
2. Find a quiet place to pray and write down answers to the following questions:
3. Who am I? Why am I here? Where am I going?
4. Write a short vision statement of your end goal in life. Write a detailed plan of how you are going to reach your objective.

CHAPTER 4

Set and Achieve Life Goals

An unwillingness to set standards or goals for ourselves, of course, can result in a Mormon malaise, going nowhere but very anxiously.[51]
Elder Neal A. Maxwell

Harry Simmons

When I was about sixteen, I attended a presentation about setting goals and was challenged to write down one hundred goals for my life. I did it. At the time, I was in high school and involved in many things, including being on the wrestling, football, and track teams. I had spent most of my life on a small farm. After graduation I went to Brigham Young University and majored in horticulture. Life was good! After my mission, I missed being part of a team, so I tried out for and made the university rugby team. One of our first games was against the Colorado School of Mines. I was asked to play hooker, which is like a center in football. I had no idea what I was doing because I had only played the game for a short time and had never played that position.

During the game, I ended up on the ground with several players piled on top of me. My face was pinned to the ground. I felt my body twist and a sharp pain in my neck. I heard three loud pops and then felt a chill travel from my neck to my toes. Most of my face was still in the turf even though I was lying on my back. The trainer ran out and asked me if I could feel this or that, but I didn't know what she was talking about. An ambulance was called, and I was placed on a flat board with my head taped down. Later at the hospital, I saw my rugby coach crying. That was unusual, and I wondered what was wrong. As soon as an MRI was taken, I was immediately placed in halo-gravity traction to keep my head and neck still. Once my broken neck was back in place, I had surgery to fuse the vertebra. I spent the next six months in the hospital and rehab.

I returned home to Louisiana and later was allowed to return to college to finish my degree. Before graduating, one of my professors commented that it would be difficult to do horticulture confined to a wheelchair for life. He suggested I think about something less physical, like law school. Following his advice, I applied to ten law schools and was accepted into nine. I decided on the University of Texas at Austin. Back at home before starting law school, I used the $10,000 I had received from insurance to buy two duplexes in my hometown and rent them out. I focused on property law, graduating in 1998. For five years, I built a real estate portfolio.

In 2003, I happened to look at the one hundred life goals I had written down as a teenager. Here is a sample of those goals:

- Learn five languages
- Visit one hundred countries
- Visit all seven continents
- Retire at age thirty-five
- Get married
- Own a farm
- Get a bachelor of science degree
- Get a master's degree
- Get a doctorate degree

At that point, I had received my BS and JD. I was thirty-five years old, and my real estate investments were paying off well. With the freedom to do so, I applied to a college in Thailand to earn an MS in tropical horticulture. With that degree, my three educational goals were complete, and I was also able to learn the Thai language. I was already proficient in English, Spanish, Portuguese, and Chinese, totaling five languages. While in Thailand, the dollar was strong and flights were cheap, so I traveled almost every other weekend, visiting forty-seven countries and six of the seven continents. I also met and married my wife.

Even though I officially retired at age thirty-five, my wife and I now own Simmons Family Farms. We have two properties, which total 358 acres. In addition to year-round vegetable crops, we have numerous fruit trees, blackberry plants, laying hens, and beef. We also grow sixty species of small ornamental noninvasive clumping bamboos.

Recently Randal Wright visited our farm. I reminded him that he was the speaker who gave the talk on setting one hundred life goals during my teen years. I was glad I could share how those written goals had guided my life and kept me going through the hard times after my accident.

Leave Something Behind

Randal: Visiting Harry and seeing his accomplishments and the positive way he looked at life was an emotional and motivating experience for me. I was shocked when he told me that I had given the talk that led to him setting his life goals. I witnessed firsthand the impact of setting life goals. What Harry continued to accomplish made me think of a billboard I often noticed on my way to the airport. The message was only three words long, but its positive meaning has stayed with me. It simply stated, "Leave something behind!" Under the message was the name John D. Rockefeller. I have asked myself many times what thing of value I was leaving behind. Harry helped me realize that I can do so much more.

What did John D. Rockefeller leave behind? He is considered one of the greatest businessmen and respected philanthropists in US history. His donations helped make the University of Chicago a world-class research institution. He funded the Rockefeller Institute for Medical Research (now called the Rockefeller University) in New York, which has brought forth dramatic medical breakthroughs and helped produce twenty-six Nobel Prize winners in chemistry and medicine. He also founded the Rockefeller Foundation, which helped establish the Johns Hopkins Bloomberg School of Public Health and the Harvard T.H. Chan School of Public Health. The foundation contributed to the development of the yellow fever vaccine. It also supported education and other causes in the United States for over one hundred years. Rockefeller left behind an incredible legacy that has blessed the lives of millions. So what will you and I leave behind?

Before we set out to accomplish anything, we need to clearly understand what a goal is. The word goal is a modern word meaning an end or objective. Worthy goals give purpose and meaning to life. The lack of goals creates turmoil and indecision, often leading to bad decisions. President Kimball explained, "Failure to plan brings barrenness and sterility. Fate brushes man with its wings, but we make our own fate largely."[52]

Short and Lifelong Goals

Randal: While working on my undergraduate degree, I was fortunate to be mentored by two motivating and inspirational professors in one semester. Each impacted me deeply in different ways. Both placed an emphasis on self-improvement. One (Reed Bradford) presented the fact that each of us has an inner desire to make a difference in the world. He further pointed out that it was up to us to decide to live a life of greatness or mediocrity. His teachings and encouragement made a profound impact on my life. The other professor (Stephen R. Covey) asked us what we would be doing in ten years and encouraged us to write down our ten-year goals. I did.

That semester I spent a great deal of time thinking about my goals and what I wanted to do with my life. Would it be a life of mediocrity or greatness? I ended up writing down a ten-year plan on a 5″ x 7″ index card and filed it away somewhere. Years later, my mother was cleaning a closet and found a shoebox filled with several items from my college days. After she dropped it by my work, I opened the box and saw on top the card titled "My 10-Year Goals." It is hard to describe the excitement I felt when I realized it had been almost exactly ten years since I first wrote them. I realized going down the list I had either achieved or was currently working on all the written goals. However, after a few weeks the excitement wore off, and I found myself dissatisfied with my life and job. I had written a ten-year plan but set no goals for the rest of my life.

During this time, I read an article about a man named John Goddard, who, at age fifteen, decided to write down his goals for life. He ultimately listed 127 things he planned to accomplish during his lifetime. His goals included things like explore the Nile, Amazon, and Congo Rivers; study primitive cultures in the Congo, New Guinea, Borneo, and Ethiopia; climb Mounts Ararat, Kenya, Fuji, and Kilimanjaro; and visit the Great Wall of China, Taj Mahal, and Easter Island. Other goals were to land on and take off from an aircraft carrier, learn to play the violin, make a parachute jump, run a five-minute mile, learn French, Spanish, and Arabic, and of course, many more.[53]

The *Los Angeles Times* once called Goddard "the real life Indiana Jones."[54] John's occupation included filming his adventures around the world and sharing his message with thousands. At the time of his death in 2013, he had achieved 109 of his life goals. He stated, "Most people go about their lives dreaming, wanting to do things, and hoping to do things, but they have no real plan. And nothing is built from a parking lot to a cathedral, unless you have some sort of a blue print."[55]

Even though I had no desire to be a world-renowned adventurer and explorer, reading what he accomplished had a dramatic impact on my life at a critical time. His story caused me to ask myself what I really wanted and needed to do with the rest of my life.

During this period, I followed Paul's example when he asked, "Lord, what wilt thou have me to do?" (Acts 9:6). At that point, I began writing down the goals I felt I needed to accomplish in life. These goals were specific so I could easily measure my progress and know when the goal was completed. I kept adding to my list until I reached one hundred specific goals to achieve in my lifetime. Some of them seemed unrealistic at the time, but I wrote them anyway: obtain master's and PhD degrees, teach at a major university, lecture throughout the United States, write twelve books, visit Israel, and many more. Since that time, I noticed my life drifting toward these goals, and I have accomplished many of them. These goals have greatly influenced who I am today.

When we write our goals and review them often, we become alert to the opportunities that help us reach them. French writer Antoine de Saint-Exupéry wisely said, "A goal without a plan is just a wish." While there is nothing magical about setting one hundred life goals, it does force you to think deeply about what you were sent to Earth to achieve. It also allows you to set goals in various areas of your life like your career, family, health, finances, education, talents, and spirituality. With one hundred goals to accomplish, you are almost guaranteed to stay excited and busy for life. Hall of Fame football coach Lou Holtz said, "If you are bored with life, if you don't get up every morning with a burning desire to do things—you don't have enough goals."[56]

Having Goals Is Motivating

Randal: One of my students from the past was a remarkable girl from Bozeman, Montana, named Carlee Clark. She came to the University of Texas at Austin on a track scholarship after being state champion in multiple events all through high school. She and one of my daughters became good friends, so she was in our home often. One night I talked to her about the power of goals and challenged her to pray for help then write down one hundred goals for her life. The next year she transferred to BYU, where she continued her track career. Several years later she came to a presentation I gave at BYU Campus Education Week on setting life goals. During the presentation, I invited Carlee to the front of the room to explain to the crowd how she was doing with her life goals. She had completed many of the goals she had written down and was working on several others. I then asked her if she would share with the audience a couple of the goals she'd set for herself and a few experiences relating to them.

We learned that before starting her senior year at BYU, Carlee got married and her priorities began to change. She debated whether to even continue with track. What was once an essential part of her life was suddenly not as important. During this time of confusion, she came down with mononucleosis. The virus's incubation period of four to six weeks with necessary rest helped Carlee decide it was time to quit her track career and move on with life. But after coming to this conclusion, she felt turmoil knowing she was giving up on two of her life goals. One was to make All-American status, and the other was to be invited to the Olympic trials.

She became motivated to compete during her senior year and at least try to complete her last two competition goals. Carlee competed in several meets around the nation but so far had fallen short of reaching her goals, even though she was invited to compete at the NCAA Division I championship meet in Des Moines, Iowa. That week a tragic car accident claimed the life of one of her teammates, with the funeral held the same day as the track meet. Carlee chose to run the last race of her career in honor of her teammate. The *Deseret News* reported what happened that day: "In Saturday's final day of the 2008 NCAA National Track and Field Championship, BYU senior Carlee Clark-Platt competed in her final collegiate race, finishing in seventh place in the 800-meter final and earning All-American honors. . . . With her collegiate career over, Clark-Platt will now turn her attention to the Olympic trials later this month in Eugene, Ore."[57]

Suggestions for Setting Goals

You may already have some good strategies for setting goals, or you may wonder, "Where do I start?" The following suggestions will help make the goals you set more meaningful, significant, and integral to your life.

Know Where You're Going

Carlee knew exactly what goals she wanted to accomplish during her track career. It is remarkable that she qualified as an All-American in the last race of her college career, which led to an automatic invite to the Olympic trials. Knowing where you are going in life will be a huge help in setting specific goals to get there.

Years ago Iraq invaded the oil-rich country of Kuwait to pay off its debts after a bitter war with Iran. The United States began a massive military buildup in Saudi Arabia in preparation for liberating Kuwait. Among the preparations were ships being loaded with military equipment to be sent to the Middle East. Imagine for a moment hearing a seaman on one of those ships asking his captain where they were going. What are the chances of the captain saying, "I have no idea where we are going! I think we will just drift and see where we end up." Unfortunately, many go through life like our imaginary ship captain, drifting and seeing where life will take them. However, once the ship captain knew that the destination was the Jeddah Islamic Port, he made detailed plans and delivered the equipment. Yogi Berra said, "If you don't know where you are going, you'll end up someplace else."[58]

When individuals discover what they were sent to Earth to accomplish, goal setting becomes much easier. President Russell M. Nelson gave this counsel: "Learn *for yourselves* who you really are. Ask your Heavenly Father, in the name of Jesus Christ, how He feels about you and your mission here on earth. If you ask with real intent, over time the Spirit will whisper the life-changing truth to you. Record those impressions and review them often, and follow through with exactness."[59]

Once you realize who you are and why you are here on Earth, you can write a short statement of what your mission is. With a mission statement in place, your life goals will be much clearer. While there are no set rules for what your mission statement will look like, most agree it should be concise, well defined, challenging, and inspiring.

Set Realistic Goals

Over the years many have acted on the concept that anything is possible if you are willing to work hard enough. For example, Abraham Lincoln taught, "You can have anything you want if you want it badly enough."[60] While these kinds of statements may sound good in a motivational speech, the philosophy causes some to spend their lives pursuing things they will never accomplish. Leadership consultants Tom Rath and Barry Conchie said, "If you spend your life trying to be good at everything, you will never be great at anything. While our society encourages us to be well-rounded, this approach inadvertently breeds mediocrity."[61] Unfortunately, many let their real gifts and talents lie unused, underdeveloped, or even unrealized by envying and chasing the gifts and talents they have not been blessed with.

Some goals can be developed and achieved with enough desire and hard work while others cannot. How many young boys would love to be an NBA player? Currently three in ten thousand high school basketball players will make it to the NBA. The key to making a difference in the world is to discover your gifts, talents, passions, and most importantly, your overall mission in life. Once you discover your purpose in life, you can accomplish amazing things. Sister Elaine S. Dalton explained the importance of matching your gifts and talents with the divine missions we've all been given. She said, "Your gifts and talents, and your preparation now, will help you to accomplish your divine mission—and each of us has one. . . . So today, I say to each of you . . . *dare great things!*"[62]

It is our responsibility to discover our gifts and talents and to set goals to accomplish the mission the Lord has for each of us.

Some individuals learn what their designated purpose is early on, and it unfolds over time. Do what you can now to discover your mission, and your life goals will naturally fall into place. Some of the goals you set may seem a little unrealistic at present, but you'll know deep down that you can achieve them with the Lord's help. Ellen Johnson Sirleaf, the first female head of state in Africa, believed, "The size of your dreams must always exceed your current capacity to achieve them. If your dreams do not scare you, they are not big enough."[63]

Have a Plan

Those who visit Chicago see many impressive skyscrapers. There is one, however, that stands out above all others. It is a huge black building called the Willis (Sears) Tower. At 1,451 feet tall, it towers high above everything else in the city. At one time, it was the world's tallest building. Can you imagine the amount of planning that went in to making that building a reality? How many pages of blueprints would be required? Every minute detail of the tower had to be strategized long before the construction started. Once all the detailed plans were in place and construction began, it took approximately two thousand workers three years to complete the project.

During the Savior's mortal ministry, he gave instructions to those who plan to build a tower. Those involved in planning the Willis Tower surely followed these instructions closely. Christ said, "For which of you, intending to build a tower, sitteth not down first, and counteth the cost, whether he have sufficient to finish it?" (Luke 14:28). In other words, we should think through the feasibility of any goal we have and what is required to complete it. Once we set the goal and determine it to be realistic, we need specific plans or a blueprint. When Christ gave His counsel on building towers, He obviously wasn't talking about just earthly towers. A similar process was used in the premortal existence in planning for this earth and our mortal experience. Bryant S. Hinckley clarified, "Before the earth was framed or man appeared upon its surface, a plan was worked out in the councils of heaven by infinite minds for his progress and development. If man will reach his destiny he too must have a plan."[64]

Just as it would be ludicrous to attempt building the Willis Tower without an organized design, it is foolish to believe we can reach our life goals without a plan. If we are to achieve the mission we were sent to Earth to accomplish, surely we will need to set goals to do so. Those responsible for the Willis Tower set a goal, counted the cost, drew up detailed plans, and began the difficult task of construction. If we are to achieve any worthy goal, we need a plan. Sterling W. Sill observed, "Any good builder can erect a magnificent building if the architects can conceive it and know how to follow a blueprint."[65]

Find an Accountability Partner

Most of us would never think of planning an activity with good friends and then not showing up. To stand them up repeatedly would be out of the question. It is safe to say that most of us keep the commitments we make to our friends. Why then do so many of us think nothing of breaking the promises we make to ourselves? How many times, for instance, have you or I agreed to read the scriptures every day, lose weight, exercise regularly, or eat healthier? How did that turn out?

A study by Statistic Brain Research Institute found that only 9.2 percent of 1,273 respondents felt they had been successful in achieving their New Year's resolutions for the previous year.[66] Often a resolve to lose weight is broken a few days later when the vow comes face-to-face with ice cream or candy. Of course, everything will be okay because we'll for sure start again tomorrow, next Monday or at the first of next year . . .

If you are one who keeps commitments to a friend but has trouble keeping those made to yourself, there is an obvious solution. Share your goals with a friend and ask him or her to help you progress and be held accountable. It also helps to have a specific day and time for reporting to your friend. Having an accountability partner can dramatically increase the likelihood of accomplishing a goal.

President Monson taught, "When performance is measured, performance improves. When performance is measured and reported, the rate of improvement accelerates."[67] Dr. Gail Matthews, psychology professor at Dominican University of California, conducted a study concerning the factors that influence goal achievement. She found that "more than 70 percent of the participants who sent weekly updates to a friend reported successful goal achievement, compared to 35 percent of those who kept their goals to themselves, without writing them down."[68]

Once you are focused on a goal with a detailed plan as well as committed and ready to carry it out, you should also set a deadline. Have you ever been to a post office on April 15? By setting a deadline, the IRS motivates people to action every year. Your overall plan for achieving a goal should include setting deadlines along the way and sharing them with an accountability partner. There is something motivating about having an anticipated deadline for completion.

Rewards or Consequences

One of the time-honored ways to encourage good behavior is the carrot-and-stick approach. The name is derived from a cart driver who dangled a carrot in front of a mule while holding a stick behind it. We often see this method used by parents who are teaching children. The carrot is "If you clean your room, I'll take you to get an ice cream cone." The stick is "But if you don't clean your room, you're going to be grounded." Adults are usually good at applying this type of discipline on children but seldom use it for *self*-discipline. When is the last time you withheld privileges or sent yourself to time-out for not doing what you said you would do? On the other hand, do you reward yourself if you accomplish something significant?

Many have found this approach works well for accomplishing goals. As adults, we seldom have anyone to apply consequences when we fail to follow through. What is the answer? We need *self*-discipline of course! Perhaps a self-applied reward or consequence would help us reach more goals. Theodore Roosevelt once said, "With self-discipline most anything is possible."[69]

Continuous Improvement

Scott: The purpose of life goals is to help us continuously improve and to help others along the way do the same. Goals are no longer a bucket list to be checked off as we focus on what *we* want. Yes, as a young man, I thought I wanted to have a fancy sports car. I now drive a Dodge Ram pickup truck to my daughters' basketball games. Back then I craved VIP invitations to the Grammys and Super Bowl. Now I leverage that access to provide experiences that help boost others. I would rather stay home with my family for pizza and movies. I once aspired to sit courtside for an NBA team, but now one of my greatest joys is to bring fans down to the court for a picture after the game and create a priceless memory for them. If I craved having a big house in the "right" zip code, it certainly isn't where we ended up. While I do love our beautiful home, it is one that my wife chose because of its proximity to our church and our daughters' schools. It isn't that one way is necessarily better than another; as you gain perspective, often the things you thought you wanted most in the past matter least given some time.

Today I create goals that support my family and marriage, challenge me professionally and spiritually, and push me physically. I live with the Kaizen principle, which is a Japanese business philosophy of continuous improvement. Embrace change. Improve yourself. Learn something new each day. Learn from someone new.

However, be self-aware enough to realize that if you charge ahead toward your goals with blinders on, you may miss the opportunity to build something incredible along the way. Allow your goals to live and breathe. Be flexible and open to adjusting or improving them or admitting when they may have been misguided.

We are trying to be winners in the game of life. Fortunately, we don't have to compete against anyone else to win. It is all about being the best we can possibly be. I like how basketball great Larry Bird put it: "A winner is someone who recognizes his God-given talents, works his tail off to develop them into skills, and uses these skills to accomplish his goals."[70]

Invitation to Act

1. Ask the Lord what He would have you do in life the same way Paul did: "And he trembling and astonished said, Lord, what wilt thou have me to do?" (Acts 9:6).
2. Read your patriarchal blessing closely to help gain inspiration to determine your life mission; that will help you set life goals.
3. Use your patriarchal blessing as a guide to help you write out a mission statement.
4. Once you have an idea of what your life mission is, pray and ask for help writing out one hundred life goals.
5. When you begin to focus on a specific goal, come up with the detailed plan (blueprint) to accomplish it.
6. Get to work!

CHAPTER 5

The Power of Self-Discipline

Be strong—be strong in the discipline of self. How many otherwise good men squander their strength and dissipate their will and literally destroy their lives because they have not the power of self-discipline.[71]
President Gordon B. Hinckley

Brent Jones

When I was in eighth grade and living in upstate New York, I played in an interfaith youth basketball league hosted at my church building. We played games every Saturday during the season. It was great to interact with players and fans from several different local churches. At the end of the season, I was awarded the most valuable player award for the league. I felt like I was on top of the world! Separately, my team held another award ceremony and gave me the team MVP award. Two MVP awards—I was ecstatic!

After accepting that team MVP award, I turned to go back to my seat, but the presenter grabbed my arm and exclaimed, "Not so fast! We have another award for you." He then pulled out a bag of Atomic Fireballs candy and informed the audience that I had won the Hothead award, referring to my tendency to get a little hot and angry in the heat of the competition! It was given to me in good fun and everyone had a good laugh, including me. That was, of course, until something suddenly made me stop laughing. I thought about my sweet, kind, and righteous mother. Then, I thought about what that Hothead award indicated about my character and the poor way I had conducted myself during many of those basketball games. I thought about how disappointed she must be in my lack of self-discipline and how I acted. She had shown me a better path and expected more of me.

Suddenly, those two MVP awards meant nothing to me as they became overshadowed by the darkness of what the Hothead award represented. My mother never said anything to me about how I acted during those basketball games, but she didn't need to. All I had to do was think about her example. I immediately wanted to change and be more disciplined. My mother was the real MVP!

From this experience, I learned that a person's good example has more power than nearly anything else to motivate and inspire us to be better in our lives, as my mother's example did for me. The reverse is also true. A bad example has a greater impact than anything good we might say. People are watching our behavior more than we realize. The Hothead award woke me up to this fact and motivated me to have more self-discipline and correct my anger issues.

I went on to play on my school's junior varsity team as a freshman and then on the varsity basketball team my sophomore, junior, and senior years. I remained aware of my behavior. The best feedback I received that showed I had overcome my hotheadedness was that my varsity basketball teammates, knowing I was a religious person, asked me to say a prayer before each game during our pregame huddle. I will forever be grateful for my mother, who is a saint, and the Hothead award, which served as a catalyst for positive change in my life.

Becoming Self-Disciplined

Discipline of self is not an easy task. If it were easy, far more people would have it. We all have weaknesses, and self-disciple is required to overcome them. For Brent, it was anger on the basketball court. For others, it may be procrastination, impatience, judgment, tardiness, selfishness, a negative attitude, or other weaknesses. Whatever your flaws, overcoming them will most likely not be easy. Brigham Young asked, "Now, brethren, can we fight against and subdue *ourselves*? That is the greatest difficulty we ever encountered, and the most arduous warfare we ever engaged in."[72]

Those who rise to the top in any field are highly disciplined. They are willing to do things that most avoid because of the difficulty involved. They may not like to do hard things any more than the average person, but they realize the rewards justify the effort required. Many realize that there is a certain power that comes to those who are in control of themselves. President Hinckley counseled, "Cultivate within yourselves the mighty power of self-discipline."[73]

When Benjamin Franklin was involved in his grand project to reach mortal perfection, he wanted to give up many times because the battle was so difficult and his failures so frustrating. I'm sure most of us can relate to this entry from his autobiography:

> This article, therefore, cost me so much painful attention, and my faults in it vexed me so much, and I made so little progress in amendment, and had such frequent relapses, that I was almost ready to give up the attempt, and content myself with a faulty character in that respect, like the man who, in buying an ax of a smith, my neighbour, desired to have the whole of its surface as bright as the edge.
>
> The smith consented to grind it bright for him if he would turn the wheel; he turn'd, while the smith press'd the broad face of the ax hard and heavily on the stone, which made the turning of it very fatiguing. The man came every now and then from the wheel to see how the work went on, and at length would take his ax as it was, without farther grinding. "No," said the smith, "turn on, turn on; we shall have it bright by-and-by; as yet, it is only speckled." "Yes," said the man, "but I think I like a speckled ax best." And I believe this may have been the case with many, who, having, for want of some such means as I employ'd, found the difficulty of obtaining good and breaking bad habits in other points of vice and virtue, have given up the struggle, and concluded that "a speckled ax was best."[74]

Because of the difficulty of mastering ourselves, far too many become satisfied with a speckled axe instead of the shiny one they could have. President Hinckley was referring to this tendency when he said, "One of the great tragedies we witness almost daily is the tragedy of men of high aim and low achievement. Their motives are noble. Their proclaimed ambition is praiseworthy. Their capacity is great. But their discipline is weak. They succumb to indolence. Appetite robs them of will."[75]

By the end of Benjamin Franklin's life most would say he became a brightly polished axe in many areas of his life. He chose thirteen virtues to acquire and in time mastered many of them. In one of President Monson's last sermons, he counseled everyone to do the same when he said, "May we maintain the courage to defy the consensus. May we ever choose the harder right instead of the easier wrong."[76]

From the moment we wake up until the time we go to sleep, a war rages between our spiritual side and the natural man tendencies we are all born with. This inclination is the temporal part of us that allows physical desires to override our inborn spiritual yearnings. Winning the war will obviously take self-discipline. The path to developing the control needed does not happen haphazardly. It takes real effort but becomes less onerous when we follow certain practices.

Suggestions

The following suggestions may help you develop the willpower and self-discipline needed to accomplish what you desire in life.

Stand Up

There is a well-quoted saying that simply states, "Misery loves company." In the Book of Mormon, the prophet Lehi gives credence to this statement and divulges the source of misery. He said, "For [the devil] seeketh that all men might be miserable like unto himself" (2 Nephi 2:27). It seems that anyone who is miserable tries to get others to join in. The tendency to bring others down is often associated with mocking, social pressure, and manipulation in our society. These actions are seldom used to encourage behaviors that bring happiness. How often do our youth, for example, hear, "You big wimp, why don't you read your scriptures and go to the temple more often?" No, social pressure is highly associated with trying to invite and entice others to try things that lead to misery like alcohol, pornography, vaping, immorality, dishonesty, and much more. Abraham Lincoln, taught, "When I do good I feel good, when I do bad I feel bad."[77] He could have easily added, "And when I feel bad, I want others to join me."

In a message to his future readers, Moroni shares this: "Wherefore, all things which are good cometh of God; and that which is evil cometh of the devil; for the devil is an enemy unto God, and fighteth against him continually, and inviteth and enticeth to sin, and to do that which is evil continually" (Moroni 7:12). In this verse, we learn that all good comes from God, and evil comes from the devil. The dictionary defines *good* as that which is praiseworthy in character[78] and *evil* as morally reprehensible.[79]

What if we asked whether what we are doing right now is right or wrong—more specifically, whether we are following God or the devil? How frightening to think we could be deceived into following someone who is openly opposed and hostile toward God.

Some may ask how the devil gains so many followers? Does he say, "Hey, guys, who wants to be miserable like me?" No, of course not. A former First Presidency of the Church said this of Satan: "He is working under such perfect disguise that many do not recognize either him or his methods."[80]

As Moroni points out, Satan invites and entices all to do evil. *Invite* means to make a friendly, polite request to go somewhere or to do something. *Entice* means to attract or tempt by offering pleasure or advantage. He knows human nature and every trick in the book on how to make sin appear pleasurable.

It is hard to name anything the Lord invites us to do that does not take self-discipline. Whether it is attending church, studying scriptures, ministering, researching family history, writing in our journals, attending the temple, exercising, going to bed early, getting up early, forgiving, eating healthy, cleaning church buildings, giving a talk, teaching a lesson, serving in a calling, or anything else—it all takes discipline. Unfortunately, anything that requires discipline often has a high dropout rate.

Imagine someone comes up to you and offers you a drink. When you ask what it is, they say it is alcohol. When you ask why you should drink it, they reply that everyone is doing it. When you ask if there are any possible negative consequences of drinking it, they say, "Addiction, shrinking brain, heart and liver damage, pancreatitis, infertility, diarrhea, sexual dysfunction, malnutrition, hallucinations, cancer, slurred speech, lung infections, fatigue, thinning bones, aggression, birth defects, muscle cramps, headaches, sleep disruption, vomiting, absenteeism, depression, accidents, loss of productivity, reduced quality of life, mood disorders, financial problems, job loss, poor decisions, domestic violence, conflict, divorce, fights, violent crime, neglect of others, injuries, and death (motor vehicle crashes, drowning, falls, fires, and gunshots)." When you ask how much they will pay you to drink it, they laugh and declare that you will pay a lot to drink it. In fact, a four-ounce shot of alcohol mixed with other juices usually costs about the same as an entrée in most restaurants.

No one could possibly be enticed to drink alcohol knowing the incredible risks involved. Right? Look around. Almost every restaurant, club, convenience store, stadium, arena, and supermarket in America sells alcohol, taking in over $71 billion a year. Unfortunately, it is not profitable for society since "the cost of excessive alcohol use in the United States reached $249 billion in 2010."[81] Somehow alcohol is associated with everything fun, including New Year's, Fourth of July, Christmas parties, Super Bowl parties, sporting events, boating, dances, picnics, weddings, graduations, recreational events, watching television, and even more. How does the devil pull it off? Remember to entice is to offer pleasure or advantage. If you drink, you can feel pleasure. Drinking is to your advantage, because if you don't drink you will be a social outcast.

For those willing to stand up to the adversary on things like alcohol, he will simply invite and entice you to do other things to block your progress. Fortunately, Moroni informs us that there is another voice trying to invite and entice us. He taught, "But behold, that which is of God inviteth and enticeth to do good continually; wherefore, every thing which inviteth and enticeth to do good, and to love God, and to serve him, is inspired of God" (Moroni 7:13).

The following imaginary morning is far too real for many of us. If I'm not mistaken, the first voice that often starts the day off inviting and enticing belongs to the adversary.

Alarm Goes Off: Game on.

Me: Okay. I promised myself I would get up early, exercise, and read the scriptures, so I'm just going to push the snooze button one time.

Adversary: I know you said you were going to do wonderful things early this morning, but you went to bed later than you planned. You really need to sleep longer so you are not tired throughout the day. You don't need to feel bad about this. You are a good person and can start tomorrow. Just turn the alarm off.

Me: No, I said I would get up early today, exercise, and read my scriptures, so I'm going to do it.

Adversary: I really admire your desire to do good, but just get the rest you badly need this morning. Then you can go to bed early tonight and be rested today. You can start tomorrow.

Me: But I promised myself that I was going to do it today.

Adversary: You didn't say "I promise." You merely set a goal, not realizing you were going to have to stay up late last night. If you get up now, you will be grouchy and will probably offend someone. Do you want to be a bad example? Is that what you want? You need your rest.
Me: I have been saying I was going to do this for a long time and have not been doing it.
Adversary: How many good people do you know get up at this ridiculous hour? Why aren't they up? Because they are night people. Did you ever consider that you were not born to be a morning person?
Me: I guess you have made some good points. I did stay up too late last night. Maybe the reason I stay up so late is that I really am a night person, because I'm tired every time I go to bed late and get up early. Besides, I know plenty of people who read their scriptures and exercise at night.
Alarm Turned Off: Game over.

The voice of the adversary sounds so rational and his message so easy to agree with that it is hard to recognize. This of course explains his success. No one would listen if the voice were harsh or demanding. His tactic is to lull us away without raising the alarm. Also, if we do try to engage in a conversation or debate with him, the odds are stacked against us. He is a champion debater and seldom loses to those willing to spar with him. Many find that when the alarm goes off and they immediately get out of bed, the adversary has no chance to begin his tempting argument. Push the snooze button even once, and the chance of getting up, exercising, and reading scriptures will drop dramatically.

It also seems as if the voice that invites and entices us to do good is quiet until we act. When we immediately act on what we have committed to do, something amazing happens. The voice that was quiet before we acted suddenly offers support and becomes our cheerleader. In the New Testament, James teaches that the adversary will back down if we stand up. He says that we should "submit [ourselves] therefore to God. Resist the devil, and he will flee from you" (James 4:7).

Do What You Say

Imagine for a moment that you get a call on Sunday from a good friend you haven't seen in years. You're excited to hear of his plans to be in town all week. During the conversation, your friend asks if you are available to meet at Ruth's Chris Steak House the next night (Monday) at seven o'clock with the offer to buy your dinner and talk about old times. Would you go? Of course! You arrive at a quarter to seven excited to see this friend. However, by seven thirty you're still waiting. You try to call but there is no answer. At nine o'clock you receive a call from your friend, asking if you can meet for dinner at the same restaurant the next night. When you ask why he didn't show up that night, he says, "Oh, I decided to go to the movies instead!"

Would you go on again on Tuesday night? Let's say you do go, and he fails to show again. At nine o'clock, the call you get is your friend asking you to dinner on Wednesday night. When asked why he stood you up again, he says he decided to go out with another friend instead.

Recalling your past friendship, you drive to the restaurant on Wednesday but are stood up the third time. Later that night, you receive the familiar call inviting you to dinner on Thursday night. When asked what the reason was for not showing, you're told that he stayed in the hotel room and watched television. On Thursday night, after the fourth no-show, you're informed that he needs to attend to some errands. The friend expresses regret for not being able to get together but says he would love to take you out for dinner and conversation the next time he is in town. What would you think about this friend? Would you trust him to do what he says in the future?

In the last chapter we asked if you would you ever tell a good friend to meet you at a specific time and place and not show up. Of course not! But again, what if the friend happens to be *you*? Have you ever planned on a Sunday night to start a diet Monday morning and not done it? Have you said on a Monday night you'd begin an exercise program on Tuesday and then are a no-show? What about saying you will get up early, read your scriptures daily, work on family history, write in your journal, and not doing it? Is saying you are going to do something and not following through a problem for you? If so, why is it that you would never do it to a friend but do it to yourself repeatedly?

Henry Kravis said, "If you don't have integrity, you have nothing. You can't buy it. You can have all the money in the world, but if you are not a moral and ethical person, you really have nothing."[82] Part of having integrity means doing what you say you will do. Some people have failed to act on what they have said they would do so often that they don't believe a word they say. Honoring your word and your commitment demonstrates integrity. Spencer Johnson said, "Integrity is telling myself the truth. And honesty is telling the truth to other people."[83]

What a sad thing if we can't trust ourselves to do what we commit to. When you reach a point where you can totally rely on promises you make to yourself and to others, you have acquired an important element of developing the self-discipline needed for success.

Have a Daily Routine

Picture in your mind living in a society where businesses (gas stations, supermarkets, pharmacies, and others) have no specific opening or closing times. One day they may open at six o'clock in the morning and close at nine o'clock at night and the next open at ten o'clock in the morning and close at five o'clock in the evening. Or perhaps business owners would not open their businesses at all if they stayed up too late the night before. Fortunately, we live in a day when businesses operate on a set schedule. Barring natural disasters or unforeseen events, businesses open and close when they say they will. There is something beneficial about having a set schedule.

Do you have trouble reading your scriptures daily? If so, perhaps the answer to your challenge is obvious. Usually, the reason people have trouble reading scriptures, writing in their journals, exercising, or completing other goals is because they don't set a specific time to do so. If someone asked you what time you read scriptures every day, how would you reply? Many who commit to good daily practices fail to set a specific time to accomplish them. Having no set time makes it difficult to ever develop a habit, because other things come up that take precedence. However, even setting a specific time like seven o'clock in the evening can be problematic. How many things in our society start at that time? Most successful scripture readers, exercisers, and other achievers select a specific time early in the morning when conflicts are few. President Nelson shares what his daily morning routine involves: "I get up before anybody else, and that gives me time for personal scripture reading."[84]

Having a daily routine eliminates the need to rely on motivation and sheer willpower to accomplish your goals. What you do repeatedly will eventually become a habit, eliminating the need to even think about it. It is as if you are doing good things on autopilot. Let's say for example that you resolve to get up at five thirty every morning to read scriptures, pray, plan your day, exercise, and write in your journal. Would that schedule take motivation and self-discipline for you to accomplish at this point in your life? If you did it repeatedly, over time it would become a normal part of your day like brushing your teeth, getting dressed, and eating breakfast. Having daily morning rituals will greatly increase your efficiency and spirituality and will help you start your day feeling good about yourself.

Having a daily routine is a powerful way to achieve success in any endeavor in life. Most people who care about leaving behind a legacy do what others refuse to do. John C. Maxwell said, "You will never change your life until you change something you do daily. The secret of your success is found in your daily routine."[85]

One of the most exciting things about a daily routine is how much doing a little each day adds up to be a lot over time. A Tanzanian proverb says, "Little by little, a little becomes a lot." By taking small steps every day, you eventually arrive at a wonderful destination. For example, practicing the piano 30 minutes every day adds up to 182.5 hours a year and eventually proficient playing. If you read the Book of Mormon 30 minutes a day, the average reader can complete the entire book over 10 times a year. Running 10 miles a week adds up to 520 miles a year, which is the equivalent of almost 20 marathons. If you write out just one experience from your life every day, you will accumulate 365 a year. Imagine leaving behind basically everything important you ever learned in life for your posterity. Over time, you will become skilled and even expert in those things you do repeatedly.

Plan Your Day

As president of the Bethlehem Steel Corporation, the largest shipbuilder and the second-largest steel producer in America, Charles M. Schwab was one of the richest men in the world in the early 1900s. In a quest to increase his own and his management team's efficiency, Schwab reached out to Ivy Lee, a respected productivity consultant and pioneer in the field of public relations. Lee told Schwab he could increase his management team's efficiency and company sales if Lee could spend fifteen minutes with each member of Schwab's team. Schwab asked how much his services would cost. Lee told him that it would not cost him anything unless Lee's advice worked. After three months, Lee told Schwab to send him a check for whatever Schwab thought Lee's services were worth to the company. The deal was made. Lee met with each executive and asked him for a commitment to do something for ninety days before he left work each day. Now termed the Ivy Lee Method, this way of accomplishing tasks is still used in the business world today. Here is what the Bethlehem executives agreed to do:

1. Write down the six most important tasks that need to be completed tomorrow.
2. Review each task, ranking them in order of importance.
3. The next day, start with the first task. Don't move on to any other tasks until it is completed.
4. Place any unfinished tasks at the top of the next day's list.

During the next three months, productivity at Bethlehem Steel increased dramatically. Schwab paid Lee $25,000 dollars, a huge sum of money in the 1920s. This method is not limited to business but can be used by anyone wanting to get more accomplished each day. The efficiency advice is free other than the small amount of self-discipline needed.[86]

Would you benefit from writing down a list of the six most important tasks you needed to complete tomorrow? This pondering takes little effort, but the results are well worth your time.

Get Uncomfortable

Our friend Camille Ballou shared an experience of a time when she struggled to gain the self-discipline needed to improve her life.

> During a time in my life when I was running a lot, I set many personal goals to improve my performance and new personal records for each half marathon I ran. I hired a personal trainer, who became a valued friend. He helped me lose weight and improve my running time by thirty minutes from one race to the next. I was ecstatic. And then I plateaued. The weight loss stalled out, and my finishing times stayed about the same. I wasn't getting any faster or stronger no matter how hard I worked or rather, how hard I *believed* I had worked.
>
> One day as I was doing lunges around the track, my trainer walked beside me as we discussed my progress. The weight loss and the thirty-

minute time improvement was easy. It was low hanging fruit that was easily plucked from the tree. What remained was the hard stuff. The uncomfortable stuff. And I was not comfortable being uncomfortable. My trainer observed that even in that moment as I was lunging one-fourth of a mile around the track, I was not pushing myself. I was only dropping my knee far enough for it to be considered a lunge without causing discomfort. After finishing the distance set, my trainer told me I had to do it all over again, this time with my knee touching the ground with each step. It took me forty-five minutes to lunge the track a second time, but when I was done, I felt invincible. I learned my lesson: if I want to progress, I must be comfortable being uncomfortable.

A comfort zone is "the level at which one functions with ease and familiarity."[87] While the definition sounds somewhat like describing heaven, staying in our comfort zone leads to a life with little growth or stress—and ultimately mediocrity and stagnation. It is like going to the gym every day and sitting in an easy chair feeling safe, at ease, and without stress while watching others choose to be uncomfortable while working out. How ironic is it that putting stress on the body through exercise relieves stress.

Self-improvement is not for the unmotivated or the quitter. It comes from an internal fire to better yourself. It requires choice, commitment, and self-discipline that moves you out of your comfort zone. Self-improvement comes when you pay the price to conquer and surpass yourself. It requires that you compel yourself do things you know are good for you whether you feel like doing them or not. President M. Russell Ballard instructed, "You control to a large degree your own destiny. You control your own life. . . . When we apply the ingredient of self-discipline, there is not much that any one of us . . . could not accomplish."[88]

Self-Discipline Is Required

Everything of real value in life has a price connected to it. In the case of personal improvement, the price required is self-discipline. And yet many seem to almost feel sorry for those who are the most disciplined and give up the most to improve themselves.

No matter what innate talents one possesses, those unable to motivate themselves to act seem destined for mediocrity. One must be willing to delay gratification in the short term to receive the reward of success in the long term. Insurance executive Benjamin N. Woodson taught, "The quality which sets one man apart from another—the factor which lifts one man to every achievement to which he reasonably aspires while the other is caught in a slough of mediocrity for all the years of his life—is not talent, nor formal education, nor luck, nor intellectual brilliance, but is rather the successful man's greater capacity for self-discipline."[89]

Invitation to Act

1. Beginning today, stop doing one thing you know you shouldn't do. Start one thing you know you should be doing!
2. Starting tomorrow, get up at five thirty and go to bed no later than ten thirty Record the daily results of this habit for fourteen days.
3. Get up immediately upon hearing your alarm go off, without pushing the snooze button.
4. Implement a specific schedule to know exactly what time certain things will take place, such as scripture reading, planning your day, writing in your journal, exercising, as well as other important activities.
5. Do one thing every day that gets you out of your comfort zone.
6. Every evening write down six specific things you need to get done the next day.

CHAPTER 6
Persistence Pays Off

I believe that perseverance is vital to success in any endeavor, whether spiritual or temporal, large or small, public or personal. . . . All significant achievement results largely from perseverance.[90]
Elder Joseph B. Wirthlin

John W. Wright

I grew up in a log house on blocks in Houston, Texas, in a lower middle-class family. My father was a machinist, and my mother stayed at home with the kids. During my childhood, my parents bought an encyclopedia, one volume at a time, with their purchases at a local grocery store. I was fascinated when looking through the pages of those encyclopedias and dreamed of being a scientist one day. During this time, my family took a trip to Idaho, and I found that the mountains also fascinated me. I couldn't decide between being a scientist or a mountain man.

Upon entering eighth grade, I was excited to try out for football. I was usually the kid who could whip anyone my age, so I was confident I would be a star. However, I was out of shape, and when I saw I was not the best on the team, I quit. Nevertheless, the next summer I asked my mom to drop me off at the gym at nine o'clock in the morning and pick me up at three o'clock every day. I filled the day with weights and running to get into top shape. That fall I played on the ninth-grade football team, but we didn't win one game and only scored one touchdown all year. I continued playing football into tenth grade. Although I didn't like it much, I played to be accepted by my peers. My interest continued in science. I was making As and Bs in my classes.

During my junior year, my school became integrated, and I began to love football. We won the city championship but lost in the quarter finals of the state playoffs. During my junior and senior years, I quit trying at school and made almost all Cs. I had also lost some of my passion for science. I did win two awards from peers, however. I was voted laziest and least likely to succeed. In my mind, I would get a major college football offer but was crushed when my coach told me I wasn't big enough or fast enough to play college ball.

After graduation, I took a job driving a cement truck but didn't like it at all. Then the husband of one of my mom's friends helped me get a job with the railroad as a fireman trainee. It was my dream job. It was great fun riding locomotives with my head out the window. I thought I could do that job forever. At two o'clock one morning, I could not see the lantern signals. I derailed a locomotive and was fired. Not knowing what to do next, I applied to Texas A&M University. Although my high school GPA wasn't good, my score on the SAT was, so I was accepted. I started taking premed classes but soon realized that was not for me. I went to see a university counselor who suggested that becoming a welder appeared to be a good option for me. I did that for a year but found it wasn't what I really wanted.

At that point, I met some guys going to the Texas A&M Maritime Academy in Galveston. I was looking for adventure, so I applied and went there. During this time, I got married, even though I didn't know her very well. She told me she did not want to be married to a sea captain who was gone all the time, so I went back to the same college counselor at Texas A&M. Looking at my credits after three and a half years in school, the counselor said I would lose the fewest number of credits by pursuing a mechanical engineering degree. At that point, I got serious and put my energy into trying to pass the difficult engineering classes. I took a math course called differential equations but could not grasp it and had to withdraw. I took it again and withdrew again. Out of options, I persisted and took it a third time. It was then that I began to understand math. In fact, it made total sense to me, and I loved it. That was a great lesson in persistence for me. Albert Einstein once said, "It's not that I'm so smart, it's just that I stay with problems longer."[91]

I graduated with a BS degree in engineering in 1978 and worked for a year at Eastman Chemical Company. At that point, I wanted to earn more money and have more adventure in life. I learned engineers were needed to work offshore in the Gulf of Mexico. I applied and got a job working ten days on and five days off with very high pay. The job was grueling and often required that we stay up for days at a time. I was often seasick and traveled back and forth between rigs in helicopters at night. That was adventurous! I learned about the oil and gas business firsthand, and it became a passion.

Over time, I began to specialize in capping oil rig blowouts underground and in 1989 formed the John W. Wright company. Our business was to provide engineering services for relief wells and underground blowouts for the oil and gas industry. Over the years, I had managed forty relief well projects and was successful in capping all of them. In the spring of 2010, the Deepwater Horizon drilling rig, owned by British Petroleum, exploded in the Gulf of Mexico, killed eleven people, and caused the largest marine oil spill in history. Experts tried to cap it for months without success.

The only long-term solution was a relief well—my specialty. My assignment was to drill down with a bit about the size of a fist and try to hit a target the size of a dinner plate eighteen thousand feet below the water's surface. On September 18, 2010, newspapers around the world announced that the relief well was successfully capped and the largest environmental disaster in US history was finally over. News organizations around the world carried this line: "The relief well was the 41st successful drilling attempt by John Wright, a contractor who led the team drilling the relief well aboard the Development Driller III vessel. Wright . . . has never missed his target."[92]

I think back on my experience taking the differential equations math class three times. I could have easily given up after the first failure and was tempted to do so but instead persisted and took it again. When you fail something the second time, you begin to doubt your abilities and might be tempted to throw in the towel. British social reformer Thomas Fowell Buxton said, "With ordinary talent and extraordinary perseverance, all things are attainable."[93] Following that line of reasoning, I took the class the third time, and finally it clicked. Because I understood math, I could lead the team that finally capped the Deepwater Horizon oil spill.

Persistence Equals Effort

For many, life is a constant battle between starting to accomplish something significant and quitting before its completion. In the beginning, John's story is a typical one of repeatedly starting and quitting. However, he found his passion in a demanding job that stirred something within him. Persistence led him to become the world's leading expert in his field. Calvin Coolidge once said, "Nothing in the world can take the place of persistence. Talent will not; nothing is more common than unsuccessful men with talent. Genius will not; unrewarded genius is almost a proverb. Education will not; the world is full of educated derelicts. Persistence and determination are omnipotent."[94]

It is unusual to find anyone willing to spend the amount of time and effort required to achieve elite status in any field. Many quit various endeavors before they even become run of the mill. I once asked an experienced piano teacher to estimate how many of her students quit playing before they reached proficiency. She thought for a moment and said, "I would say about 90 percent." While that estimate may or may not reflect all piano students, it is likely safe to say the dropout rate is quite high with beginners.

Could the same be said of those who start playing the flute, clarinet, trumpet, French horn, oboe, and trombone? At some point, many will close the cases on their instruments and never play again. What about those who begin karate, soccer, gymnastics, or dance lessons? Quitting various endeavors does not stop once a person reaches adulthood. How many start a diet or exercise program in January only to quit before February rolls around? Is it safe to say that anything requiring intense effort over time will have few who persevere? Legendary football coach Vince Lombardi seemed to have it right when he said, "Once you learn to quit, it becomes a habit."[95]

Most worthy goals in life require effort to complete. How can we reach a goal if we quit moving forward toward the objective? When we give up easily, we never really learn who we are or what we are capable of. Self-esteem increases and a feeling of immeasurable satisfaction comes when we stay with a difficult task or goal from start to finish. *Perseverance* means "continued effort to do or achieve something despite difficulties, failure, or opposition."[96]

Examples of Not Quitting

Gene Schrecengost came to see me right after finishing his first semester of a prestigious MBA program. He was seeking advice from friends and family members about whether he should drop out of the program. I asked why he had applied to the program to begin with if he was going to drop out before completing his degree. He divulged the reason he applied was to provide a good living for his family and have a job he enjoyed. We talked about the financial advantages he would reap if he stayed with the program. When he left that day, I didn't get the idea that the financial aspect motivated him enough to continue. I was surprised to hear later he had decided to stick with the program. I wondered what had changed his mind. Here is his story:

I was in my first semester at the University of Texas at Austin pursuing my master's in business administration and feeling overwhelmed and discouraged. I had just graduated the previous semester with a liberal arts degree and felt totally unprepared to be enrolled in a top-twenty business school. To add to the stress, I was married, and we had a small child at the time. It didn't take long to discover that my classmates were extremely intelligent, engaged, and dedicated. There were no slackers here! In fact, the majority had quit good jobs to pursue additional education. I was sitting next to former Wall Street brokers and consultants from one of the Big Three consulting firms. I did not have a business background, experience in the workplace, or related undergraduate classes.

These feelings of inadequacy deepened, and before the first semester ended, I began to wonder if I had made a huge mistake in choosing this path. The workload was very heavy compared to my undergraduate experience, and the bar seemed so much higher. I was at the top of my class in my undergraduate program, but I was not confident that I would survive the rigors of this program. In fact, I was miserable due to the potential of failure. I had never failed at anything significant in my life, but now this seemed a high probability. I shared these feelings with my wife and friends and sought their counsel. After much reflection and discussion, I decided that I should quit the program and get a job, so I researched my job options. My wife and friends all supported that decision.

I felt like there was one person remaining I needed to check in with—my father-in-law. I respected him tremendously and knew that I couldn't make this type of decision without his counsel. I remember our conversation as if it were yesterday even though it was nearly three decades ago. I explained the situation and my plan to quit the program and get a job. His six-word response has changed the course of my life. He stated simply, "I always finish what I start." As soon as I heard those words, I knew that I would finish my MBA. It was like a lightning bolt had struck me. We all have moments of self-doubt, and we also all need someone to inspire us to continue!

There would be no quitting for me. Embedded in his words was not just a message that I should not quit but an even more important message of his confidence in me. I could not let him down. I stayed in the program. It was not easy, especially in the beginning. But it got easier, and I graduated with a 3.5 GPA—not outstanding but nothing to be ashamed of either. This simple counsel of finishing what I start has been a critical factor in my career.

Gene prayed to know what to do after receiving his bachelor's degree. His answer was to take the GMAT and apply to an MBA program. Surely when the letter of acceptance arrived, Gene was extremely excited. So what happened to the enthusiasm and excitement he felt? He came face-to-face with accounting and statistics and decided to run. Six simple words from his inspired father-in-law led to a commitment that changed his life. His perseverance brought countless blessings for himself, his family, and others.

Randal: As a child, I had little self-confidence and would often quit things that were difficult. Much later, I set a goal to do something that would require tremendous effort and expense over an extended period. I knew this decision would be a huge benefit to me for the rest of my life. I was excited about it and shared my plans with my father. He reacted differently than I expected. He was not excited at all about my decision and even seemed irritated with me. At one point while we were discussing my plan, he said six words that made a dramatic impact on my life. Since then, I, too, have faced my own "accounting and statistics" fears many times and wanted to run from them. However, because of my dad's words I did not quit. What did he say to me? He said, "You are nothing but a quitter." Those words hurt me deeply at first. The thing that bothered me the most was that I knew what he said was true.

My dad has been gone for many years, but one day I hope to thank him for calling me a quitter. His words have replayed in my head hundreds of times and have helped me persist when I wanted to quit. For example, like Gene, I was overwhelmed in graduate school. Several of my classmates dropped out because of the pressure, but I decided to stay with it. I thought I might be kicked out of the program for poor performance, but I wouldn't quit no matter how badly I wanted to. Abraham Lincoln said, "You cannot fail unless you quit."[97] It is hard to describe my feelings when my doctoral committee chair announced, "Congratulations! You're finished!" I mentally thanked my dad for changing my life by calling me a quitter.

The quest to achieve a difficult goal can be discouraging at times. Thoughts of quitting are always close to the surface. However, the thrill of finishing a demanding but worthwhile goal will be a positive memory for the rest of your life. On the flip side, the pain of quitting something you felt inspired to do will linger a long time. Occasionally, I run across those in my program who walked away before finishing their degrees. I can hear the regret in their voices as they talk about not finishing what they at one point felt strongly about. American philosopher and psychologist William James explained, "Most people never run far enough on their first wind to find out they've got a second."[98]

While babies learn to walk, they are unsteady and fall repeatedly. The natural tendency for those watching is to try to prevent them from falling. However, babies need to learn to fall before they can learn how to walk. It is exciting to watch the persistence these little ones use to master this important task. Even though most fall constantly, they keep getting back up until they succeed and become "elite" walkers. Why is it that so many adults give up trying after a few falls? Can you imagine what the world would be like if every adult had the same persistence as infants? A quote from Ralph Waldo Emerson that President Heber J. Grant loved to reference says, "That which we persist in doing becomes easier for us to do—not that the nature of the thing is changed, but that our power to do is increased."[99]

President Grant was one who possessed a childlike determination to improve himself. I love reading about his persistence in his quest to discover and develop his talents. He believed that anyone could improve and develop a greater capacity to accomplish things over time. As a youth, he learned that persistent hard work allowed him to accomplish things that seemed almost impossible. Although not born with a natural singing voice, he wanted to learn to sing. He said this about his quest:

> From the time I was a child of nine, I tried to sing. I tried time and time again without any apparent success. When I was about forty-three years of age, I had a private secretary with a beautiful baritone voice. I told him I would give anything in the world if I could only carry a tune. He laughed and said, "Anybody who has a voice and perseverance can sing." I immediately appointed him as my singing teacher.
>
> My singing lessons started that night. At the end of two hours' practice I still couldn't sing one line from the song we had been practicing. After practicing that one song for more than five thousand times, I made a mess of it when I tried to sing it in public. I practiced it for another six months. Now I can learn a song in a few hours.[100]

I can't imagine practicing one song more than five thousand times. Heber J. Grant is an icon for persistence. He shared his formula for success with these words, "I know of no easy formula to success. Persist, persist, PERSIST; work, work, WORK—is what counts in the battle of life."[101]

What Is Your Objective?

People who know what they want to accomplish and are passionate and persistent often get what they set out to obtain. Do you know what you want to accomplish? Do you know where you want to end up?

Cha Sa-soon, a grandmother from South Korea wanted to obtain her driver's license so she could do something special with her grandchildren. In April 2005, at age sixty-four, Cha took the forty-question written portion of the test, which took fifty minutes to complete. She failed the test and could not take the driving portion until she achieved a certain grade. Being persistent, she took the test a second time but failed again.

She was disappointed but knew what she wanted and used her grandchildren as motivation to take the test a third time. Unfortunately, she failed again. Apparently, Cha was a believer in the philosophy Albert Einstein set forth when he said, "You never fail until you stop trying."[102] She kept trying and took it a fourth, fifth, and sixth time with the same results. But like an infant learning to walk, she refused to quit. Over the next three years, Cha continued to study and took the driving test once a day, five days a week. After three years on that schedule, she cut back and took it two times a week for two more years.

In 2010, Cha Sa-soon, then sixty-nine years old, became a national celebrity in South Korea. News outlets ran a story about her accomplishment and Hyundai-Kia, Korea's largest carmaker, gave her a brand-new Kia Soul and featured her in some of their ads. Why all the attention? Cha finally passed the written portion of her driver's test on her 960th try. She then passed the driving portion. In an article by Malcolm Moore, she explained her motivation to persist toward her goal. She said, "I wanted to get a driver's license so I could take my grandchildren to the zoo."[103]

Discover Your Talents

It is comforting to know that God gave each of us a mission to perform on Earth and at least one gift or talent to help us achieve that mission. I'm sure we would feel uncomfortable returning to His presence with our talents undiscovered, undeveloped, or underutilized and our mission aborted. One of the most bitter rebukes Jesus gave during his mortal ministry was to the servant who buried the talent he was given (see Matthew 25: 28–30). President Grant said, "I believe that we can accomplish any object that we make up our minds to . . . God has given to some people ten talents; to others, he has given one; but they who improve the one talent will live to see the day when they will far outshine those who have ten talents but fail to improve them."[104]

Yearly Gift to Christ

I met Phillip several years ago at a retreat held for employees and spouses of the organization we both worked for. During the event, we enjoyed a talent show put on by anyone willing to share. Phillip's wife volunteered him to play a song on the piano. He consented and played an extremely difficult classical piece with no music in front of him. It was amazing! When he finished, some asked for an encore. He said, "I would love to, but I don't know how to play the piano." Many of us laughed at his obvious joke until he told us that he was serious and really didn't know how to play. He then explained how he had always loved that song and wanted to learn to play even though he had never taken piano lessons. It took him an entire year learning a few notes at a time until he mastered it. He did say that he planned to learn to play the piano in the future.

His wife spoke up and told us that at the start of each new year Phillip would pick a new talent he wanted to develop and work on it all year. I learned in my association with him during the next few years just how talented he had become using that simple idea. From becoming an accomplished tennis player to learning Greek, he showed what could be accomplished in a year's time using persistence. Phillip's yearly tradition motivated me to follow his example. However, I decided I would give a yearly gift to Christ to celebrate His birth and express my gratitude. My goal is to spend all year either developing a new talent, turning an unwanted weakness into a strength, or working on a major project. My goal is always to be finished by Christmas Day. This tradition has brought me much joy and happiness and has allowed me to practice being persistent because of the obstacles that always come up when I try to do something meaningful.

Endure to the End

The dictionary definition of the word *endure* is "to remain firm under suffering or misfortune without yielding."[105] That word does not exactly bring up pleasant thoughts, yet a loving God tells us that it is required for eternal life. That phrase is not just used once in the standard works but sixteen times. Nephi had this to say about endurance: "And now, my beloved brethren, I know by this that unless a man shall endure to the end, in following the example of the Son of the living God, he cannot be saved" (2 Nephi 31:16).

In 1892, a young boxer named James Corbett faced the legendary heavyweight champion John L. Sullivan, whose record was forty wins, zero losses. The fight went twenty-one rounds and included one hour of actual fighting time, which required incredible endurance. In the fight, Corbett, the definite underdog, knocked out the great Hall of Fame champion. Boxing, a brutal sport, is not unlike our fight with the adversary during our earth life. Later, James Corbett shared his secret to his stunning victory. His advice should have meaning to us in our battles to overcome Satan and achieve the missions we were sent to Earth to accomplish. Corbett explained, "Fight one more round. When your feet are so tired that you have to shuffle back to the center of the ring, fight one more round. When your arms are so tired that you can hardly lift your hands to come on guard, fight one more round.

When your nose is bleeding and your eyes are black and you are so tired you wish your opponent would crack you one on the jaw and put you to sleep, fight one more round—remembering that the man who always fights one more round is never whipped."[106]

Facing the constant battle required in life can make enduring to the end seem daunting. President Monson helps put the Lord's requirement in perspective with these inspired words: "Seek heavenly guidance one day at a time. Life by the yard is hard; by the inch it's a cinch. Each of us can be true for just one day—and then one more and then one more after that—until we've lived a lifetime guided by the Spirit, a lifetime close to the Lord, a lifetime of good deeds and righteousness."[107]

To have the needed persistence to endure to the end, we need to envision our end goal, which is to be saved in the celestial kingdom. At times enduring to the end may seem almost impossible. But it becomes possible when we choose to be true for just one day as President Monson suggested. It is a matter of asking God for help every day, listening to the Spirit, following the promptings we receive, then repeating the process tomorrow. Soon our persistence in following the voice of the Spirit each day turns into a week, a month, and a year, until one day it becomes the last day of our mortality and we have endured to the end. Looking at the Lord's requirement in one-day-at-a-time increments helps put things into proper perspective. Surely any of us can be persistent in following the Savior for one day.

Invitation to Act

1. To practice persistence, pick one thing you will do daily to be closer to the Lord and one thing you will not do.
2. Pick a talent or hobby that you have always been interested in and work diligently on it for the year as a gift to Christ.
3. Try to envision the potential benefits that will come into your life when you develop your talents and use them to do good.
4. Devise a specific plan to reach your objective with milestones along the way to celebrate when completed. Don't focus on how far you must go but on how far you have come.
5. Devote a set amount of time each day to work on your talents.
6. Place a reminder of what you are trying to accomplish in a prominent place.

CHAPTER 7

The Price of Success Is Hard Work

Without hard work, nothing grows but weeds. There must be labor, incessant and constant, if there is to be a harvest.[108]
President Gordon B. Hinckley

Derick Lucas

While I was in college, I secured an internship for two summers in the field of my studies—engineering. The opportunity took me out of the state I grew up in and submerged me in a new environment. As the internship was wrapping up, my wife and I started to wonder and worry about what our next step would be since I didn't have full-time employment the following year. The small company I was interning for didn't have any full-time employment to offer either.

During this time my uncle, who lived in the area, invited me to help him move one of his neighbors into their new home. Several others had come to help get the family settled. As we finished moving furniture and boxes, we gathered in the crowded kitchen to get a drink of water. An older man and I began to talk about the city and his history there. When employment came up, he asked what brought me to town. I explained my current internship situation and my concern for what the future would hold. It turned out that he had worked in the same industry since he had finished high school. He asked if he could get a copy of my resume and stated that he would take it to a few engineers where he worked. I didn't get too excited because there were not many companies hiring at the time.

Nevertheless, I interviewed with the company he worked for and received a job offer before starting my last year of school. That turned out to be a great blessing since it allowed me to focus entirely on my studies.

After starting my employment, I talked with the man who had helped me get the job. He said that he had watched me the afternoon we moved the family in and was impressed by the way I worked. He knew I didn't know the family personally and was just there to offer help to someone in need without expecting anything in return. The only reason he asked for my resume and hand delivered it to the engineers at his place of employment was because of what he observed on that moving day. He appreciated seeing the hard work and effort I put in to helping a stranger.

Having him tell me that was a humbling and defining experience for me. It reiterated the importance of always working hard and giving it my all, whether in a professional or personal setting, without expecting compensation, acknowledgment, or reward. It also made me grateful for parents who taught me the meaning of hard work and the concept of giving and receiving. When I showed up to help that day, I had no idea that a life-changing moment would occur for me and my family. I still work for the same company and have continued to advance in my profession. I have a close friendship with the man who helped me secure the job. I truly believe we should always work hard, even when there is no known potential of a worldly reward.

Hard Workers Get Noticed

At one time, we owned a forty-acre weekend ranch and raised a small herd of cattle. We often needed to purchase hay for the cattle during drought periods. We always called Gabe, a kind, uneducated father of six. He worked six days a week but took off Sundays to attend an evangelical church with his family. I can still see Gabe pulling multiple fifty- to seventy-five- pound square bales of hay from his trailer, one in each hand, stacking them as fast as he could go. As he was leaving one hot, humid day after unloading our hay, I asked what was next that day. He said he was spending the rest of the day loading new bales from a large field and stacking them in a barn. As Gabe drove off in his well-used truck, I realized how much I admired him. He was a good man trying to worship with his big family and working hard at difficult manual labor. In my mind, I could hear the Lord saying to Gabe at the judgment bar, "Well done, good and faithful servant" (Matthew 25:23).

On the way home that day I asked my wife how she wanted to be remembered. She first stated, "a good wife and mother" but then added, " a hard worker." There is no doubt she was thinking of Gabe's example as she expressed her feelings. Hard workers are unusual and stand out from others. They also tend to rise to the top of whatever they are involved in and are usually highly respected. On the other hand, those who are lazy also stand out and get noticed. Most individuals, however, seem to fit in between being a hard worker and being lazy.

Derrick stood out and got noticed when he worked hard helping someone he didn't know. What an honor it would be to be viewed by others as a hard worker. How incredibly sad to be remembered as being lazy. President J. Reuben Clark Jr. once said, "There is no curse equal to the curse of idleness. It destroys the man, the group, the people, or the nation, who suffer under it."[109]

We live in a time with more time-saving technology available than any time in history. Think for example about the number of food options available compared to those in the past. Many ask why they need to grow a garden when supermarkets are right down the street. Why even cook, for that matter, when restaurants can be found on every corner? Or why even leave the house when you can have prepared food delivered to your door? Think about all the options available for communicating. Who remembers when you used to get letters in the mailbox? We have come a long way since the pony express days or even the telegraph. What about your travel options now versus the wagon or handcart days of the not-so-distant past? Remember buying maps or stopping at gas stations to ask for directions? In this environment, it is tempting to take the easy way out. Why mow your own yard when you can pay to have a lawn service do it for you? Why clean your own home if you can afford a cleaning service? What are we doing with all the extra time we are saving?

In our affluent culture, it is also tempting for parents to provide everything for their children and require little in return. Recently a young single adult shared her concern about her friend Anthony. She said he was never required to work during his teen years, yet he always wore expensive name-brand clothes, had all the latest electronic devices, traveled frequently, and was given an expensive car for his sixteenth birthday. The result? During his first year of driving, he got so many tickets he had his driver's license suspended, although his parents paid the expensive fines he incurred. After graduation Anthony took his entitled attitude to a Church college with all expenses paid by his parents. He was told to "concentrate on school" and not be distracted by a job. While at college he kept a running tab on a credit card for his parents to pay. Anthony ended up getting kicked out of school during his second semester for drug use. If not for drugs, he would have been dismissed at the end of the semester anyway because of failing grades. Is Anthony all that unusual? Pope Paul VI said, "Those who have everything given to them become lazy, selfish, and insensitive to the real values of life. The very striving and hard work that we so constantly try to avoid is the major building block in the person we are today."[110]

Hearing Anthony's story reminded me of some parents I know on the opposite end of the spectrum. Steve and Kris Bloomfield didn't believe in giving their children an allowance. They felt it sent the wrong message to reward kids for no effort. Not surprisingly, their children thought of ways to earn money. As a young teenager, their oldest son, Kyle, started a lawn business and was later joined by younger brothers Travis and Mason. Their father, Steve, was an executive with a high-tech company and oversaw 300 to 350 employees at any given time in the US and Asia. While Steve did not believe in giving his sons money or buying them cars, he was willing to give them his time. He often went with his boys to their lawn appointments and worked alongside them. I asked Steve why he spent his time doing manual labor with his boys. He mentioned three purposes:

1. I want to teach my boys how to work hard.
2. I want to spend quality time with my boys.
3. I want to check their work to make sure they're doing a good job.

The result? Recently I received an email from Kris and Steve's second son, Travis. Their family had moved away from our area several years ago. He sent the email to make me aware of an organization called Rising Star Outreach, whose mission is to help the leper colonies in India become thriving, self-sufficient communities through medical, educational, and economic rehabilitation. Travis said the following:

Since my early years in high school, I have always been heavily involved in service events and volunteer organizations. I am currently an executive director of a Big Brothers Big Sisters mentoring organization at BYU. It is something I just love. We are all God's children. If there is an opportunity to help someone change for the better, I know that person will go on to help others as well. Service always leaves a bigger impact than we anticipate, and that is why I love it. With work this summer I am hoping to make enough money for the upcoming semesters, as well as aid in funding this volunteer trip. I want to do the most I can in making an impact for the people affected by leprosy and help them enjoy life in a comfortable situation where they don't have to sacrifice as much every day.

This young man grew up in a family with the means to provide him with all his financial needs. Instead, he and his siblings were taught to work hard and to feel the joy and satisfaction that comes with it. Imagine what the world would be like if everyone worked hard. The great Leonardo da Vinci said, "Thou O God, dost sell us all good things at the price of labour."[111]

Work is an eternal principle and required of all who want to make progress. God the Father and His Son, Jesus Christ, show by example the importance of work. This world and worlds without number were not created by chance. Jesus Christ said, "My Father worketh hitherto, and I work" (John 5:17). What work was Jesus Christ sent to do? "For behold, this is my work and my glory—to bring to pass the immortality and eternal life of man" (Moses 1:39). Mortal men and women are also sent to Earth to do a special work. To Moses, God declared, "I have a work for thee" (Moses 1:6). What work does the Lord have for you?

Being Busy or Working

Some see themselves as hard workers because they are always busy. However, being busy may not be even closely related to hard work. The dictionary defines *busy* as "engaged in action."[112] However, work is not just about being active. *Work* is "sustained physical or mental effort to overcome obstacles and achieve an objective or result."[113]

Ask yourself multiple times a day if what you are doing at any given time is only to be active or to exert effort to achieve a purpose or result. President Monson once said, "We become so caught up in the busyness of our lives. Were we to step back, however, and take a good look at what we're doing, we may find that we have immersed ourselves in the 'thick of thin things.' In other words, too often we spend most of our time taking care of the things which do not really matter much at all in the grand scheme of things, neglecting those more important causes."[114]

An old story goes like this: a preacher asked a young boy in his congregation about his favorite New Testament story. The little boy thought for a moment and said, "I really like the story about the guy that loafs and fishes." Unfortunately, it seems to be the favorite story of far too many. Anne Frank showed wisdom beyond her years when she wrote, "You must work and do good, not be lazy and gamble, if you wish to earn happiness. Laziness may appear attractive, but work gives satisfaction."[115]

Many spend a large amount of discretionary time looking at the internet on a small screen. Ironically much of this screen time is spent looking and listening to hard working news anchors, politicians, singers, musicians, athletes, comedians, actors, and speakers. This type of loafing has grown exponentially over the years. "A new Nielsen Company audience report reveals that adults in the United States devoted about 10 hours and 39 minutes each day to consuming media during the first quarter of this year."[116] Imagine the results if even a portion of that time was used for self-improvement or working hard on something meaningful.

Staying busy with media is also making those involved more impatient, which, in turn, affects their ability to do hard work. New research shows students in this generation to be easily distracted, with short attention spans. This phenomenon is affecting adults as well. University of Massachusetts Amherst professor Ramesh Sitaraman found that internet users begin to become impatient waiting for a video to load after two seconds. After five seconds, 25 percent have given up, and at ten seconds, half have abandoned the process.[117] The expectation for instant results is showing up in all aspects of life, including work. A new occurrence with possible dangerous results to the rising generation has surfaced in the past few years. Young people are now watching peers become instant celebrities when their YouTube or other social media videos go viral. They forget that most things of value take time and hard work. Ray Kroc, who built McDonald's into the largest fast-food corporation in the world, said this about his seemingly quick success: "I was an overnight success all right, but thirty years is a long, long night!"[118]

Find Your Purpose

Austrian neurologist, psychiatrist, and Holocaust survivor Viktor Frankl believed, "Everyone has his own specific vocation or mission in life to must carry out a concrete assignment which demands fulfillment."[119] Those who discover their passion and mission often find the motivation needed to work hard to carry out their purpose. Michelangelo, Thomas Edison, and Thomas Jefferson are examples of those who discovered their life missions, resulting in huge impacts on their work ethics. These three and countless others have had a lasting influence on history. They learned who they were and why they were here and were willing to work extremely hard to accomplish what they felt they needed to do. American writer Frederick Buechner wrote, "To find your mission in life is to discover the intersection between your heart's deep gladness and the world's deep hunger."[120]

Michelangelo

While visiting Rome I saw some of the works of the great painter and sculptor Michelangelo. I was amazed by his incredible talent. I soon understood why he is considered one of the greatest artists of all time. His sculptures, paintings, and architecture are among the most famous ever produced. Michelangelo painted the ceiling of the Sistine Chapel between 1508 and 1512. Featured on the ceiling are nine scenes from the Book of Genesis, with the best known being *The Creation of Adam*. At the time of his commission, Michelangelo was thirty-three years old and considered himself a sculptor rather than a painter, having completed two of his most famous sculptures, *La Madonna della Pietà* and *David*, before he was thirty. It is said that he worked day after day in the chapel with his head bent back as far as he could on scaffolding over sixty feet in the air. Michelangelo worked for four years on the ceiling.

Twenty-five years after completing the ceiling, Michelangelo created the giant fresco called *The Last Judgment*, which took over four years to complete. Michelangelo also became a renowned architect later in his life and designed the Laurentian Library and the dome of St. Peter's Basilica.[121]

The Sistine Chapel and Michelangelo's other works attract about five million tourists each year.[122] I would think that most people who view his works are stunned by his incredible talent. Yet he declared, "If people knew how hard I have had to work to gain my mastery, it wouldn't seem wonderful at all."[123]

Thomas Edison

Thomas Edison was labeled the Wizard of Menlo Park and often described as America's greatest inventor. By the end of his career, he held 2,332 patents worldwide. He believed in developing his talents and encouraged others to do the same. He said, "If we all did the things we are really capable of doing, we would literally astound ourselves."[124] If we are capable of doing astounding things, what are we missing?

The impact of Edison's inventions is felt around the world to this day. He obtained patents for the incandescent light bulb, phonograph, motion picture camera, stock ticker, sextuplex telegraph, electric vote recorder, carbon microphone, commercial fluoroscope for X-ray examinations, alkaline storage battery, and the first commercial electric light and power system. He was an inventor but also a successful manufacturer and businessman who created the world's first industrial research laboratory. While still in his thirties, Edison became one of the most famous men in the world because of the influence of the devices he created and major new industries he developed.[125]

What Thomas Edison left behind to make the world a better place is incredible. His inventions did not just happen, however. He obviously had the same views as Michelangelo about where his success came from. He said, "Genius is one percent inspiration, ninety-nine percent perspiration."[126]

Thomas Jefferson

On April 29, 1962, at a White House dinner honoring Nobel Prize winners, John F. Kennedy said, "I think this is the most extraordinary collection of talent, of human knowledge, that has ever been gathered together at the White House, with the possible exception of when Thomas Jefferson dined alone."[127] Why would President Kennedy be so impressed about this great statesman?

Jefferson was one of America's foremost polymaths. He was one of the nation's Founding Fathers and the principal author of the Declaration of Independence. He served as the first secretary of state, was elected second vice president, and became the third president of the United States. During his presidency, Jefferson doubled the size of the young republic through the $15 million dollar Louisiana Purchase. Jefferson was a surveyor, architect, author, gardener, and prolific letter writer. He played the violin and cello and spoke English, French, Italian, and Latin. He signed legislation establishing the United States Military Academy at West Point, was the president of the American Philosophical Society, and founded the University of Virginia. He designed the Rotunda on that campus. He also designed his beloved eleven-thousand-square-foot Monticello, which became his private residence.[128]

While it is obvious Jefferson was a genius, that fact alone does not explain what he accomplished. Many brilliant people accomplish nothing of significance in life. What was his secret? He explained, "Determine never to be idle. No person will have occasion to complain of the want of time who never loses any. It is wonderful how much may be done if we are always doing."[129]

Twenty-Four Hours a Day

Angela, a young woman in our stake, shared an experience worth considering. She was sitting behind a girl she considered a super achiever in her high school class. The girl played several musical instruments and was a dancer, was ranked number two in her class, and had just received a scholarship to a prestigious university. Angela said one day the girl turned around and stated, "Isn't it interesting that everyone in the world has the same exact amount of time in a day!" That is all she said before she turned back around. We all have the same time in a day as Michelangelo, Thomas Edison, and Thomas Jefferson. We also have the same amount of time in a day as Joseph Smith and President Nelson. What are we doing with that time? President Hinckley asserted, "The work of the world is not done by intellectual geniuses. It is done by men of ordinary capacity who use their abilities in an extraordinary manner."[130]

Using our time to work hard often leads to accomplishment and success. Work is the thing that can transform talent and desire into a potential masterpiece. Dr. Alan Stockdale taught, "God left a world unfinished for man to work his skill upon. He left the electricity still in the cloud, the oil still in the earth. He left the rivers unbridged and the forests unfelled and the cities unbuilt. God gave to man the challenge of raw materials, not the ease of finished things. He left the problems unsolved and the pictures unpainted and the music unsung that man might know the joys and glories of creation. God created the quarries, but he carves the statues only by the hand of man."[131]

Always Something to Do

Scott: I learned there was always something to do while working at my first real job with the New Jersey Nets. That lesson had a profound impact on me and how I see the world. I was hired out of college to be an assistant to "Arnie" Prives, chief marketing officer, but most people thought I was an intern. During the first month, I was the first one to arrive at the office every day and sat in the lobby until someone came to the arena and entered the door code. I realized the opportunity I had been given, and it motivated me.

Arnie was a wonderful boss, but I was not cut out to be an assistant in the traditional sense. I was eager, hardworking, passionate, and proactive, but I'm administratively weak. Once I sent letters from Arnie to each of the other twenty-nine teams in the league. They all said, "Dear Jack." I had changed the address, but every team executive who received a letter from my boss was named Jack. These things happened from time to time.

I found there was always something to do when I looked. I created, picked up, offered, and contributed in just about every proactive way imaginable around the office. One night I stayed to fill and stuff envelopes for a season ticket mailing. It gave me an opportunity to work with the box office staff and get to know each of them. They seemed to appreciate an extra set of hands.

I was always around, always asking questions, and always proactive. Routinely, I would stay late to assemble proposals for the sponsorship group. It was tedious work. The group was short on resources, so an extra set of hands helped, plus it built relationships. If I had downtime, I was out asking if I could be of help. Need lunch? Want me to grab your dry cleaning while I am out? You need me to meet the bus? Where? "Anything, any time" was a principle I started my career with and still carry forward today. There were always plenty of projects to take on just by looking for them. I never found myself sitting with nothing to do. A side benefit is that I discovered I am happiest and most comfortable when I am up and doing.

Now as a CEO, the individuals who realize there is always something to do and take the initiative to get it done are those who impress me. Many fit into that category within our organization. Look around for tasks to be accomplished and take the opportunity to act.

I think industrialist Andrew Carnegie was indirectly talking about this formula when he said there are "two types of people who never achieve very much in their lifetime. One is the person who won't do what he or she is told to do, and the other is the person who does no more than he or she is told to do."[132] Leaders tend to love those with extraordinary desires to help their organizations or teams succeed and who don't constantly ask, "What do I do now?" All involved need to understand the mission of the task being asked and catch the vision of how to get it done. Bishop H. David Burton taught, "After the Fall, Adam was told, 'In the sweat of thy face shalt thou eat bread' (Genesis 3:19). As with any other commandment, there is joy in its keeping. To work—honestly and productively—brings contentment and a sense of self-worth."[133]

Benefits of Hard Work

Leads to Better Health

The world we live in tends to encourage a sedentary lifestyle, one associated with more than forty medically recognized chronic diseases such as high blood pressure, coronary heart disease, type 2 diabetes, obesity, stroke, mental illness, dementia, and some cancers. It also leads to a reduced quality of life and, perhaps most importantly, unhappiness.

Overall, our prophets and apostles are the epitome of health and quality of life. On average, they live extremely long and productive lives. The Lord has always used ordinary mortals with weaknesses to do His work on Earth. However, I can't imagine any of them being lazy. Members of the Quorum of the Twelve Apostles are usually not called until the age when others in society are retiring. They have all demonstrated a tremendous work ethic their entire life before being called. Their hard work does not diminish as they begin their ministry but seems to intensify.

President Hinckley summed up the "live life in crescendo" philosophy I'm confident all of them share:

> I'm given to meditation and prayer. I would enjoy sitting in a rocker, swallowing prescriptions, listening to soft music, and contemplating the things of the universe. But such activity offers no challenge and makes no contribution.
>
> I wish to be up and doing. I wish to face each day with resolution and purpose. I wish to use every waking hour to give encouragement, to bless those whose burdens are heavy, to build faith and strength of testimony.[134]

Think for a moment what President Hinckley accomplished in his lifetime. Among his many notable achievements were the construction of the Conference Center, the publication of The Family: A Proclamation to the World, and a tremendous increase in the number of temples being built. He became the greatest temple builder in history up to that time. Now consider the fact that his greatest accomplishments came after he was eighty-five years old

Now stop for a moment and make a mental list of everything that has happened in The Church of Jesus Christ of Latter-day Saints during the presidency of Russell M. Nelson. When did all these things occur? After he was ninety-four years old.

President Uchtdorf had this to say about hard work: "When our time in mortality is complete, what experiences will we be able to share about our own contribution to this significant period of our lives and to the furthering of the Lord's work? Will we be able to say that we rolled up our sleeves and labored with all our heart, might, mind, and strength? Or will we have to admit that our role was mostly that of an observer?"[135]

Blesses Other People

One of the reasons we were sent to Earth was to work on perfecting ourselves. In 3 Nephi 12:48 we read, "Therefore I would that ye should be perfect even as I, or your Father who is in heaven is perfect." The work required to make progress toward the goal of perfection is time consuming and strenuous. However, we are not only required to perfect ourselves but also to love our neighbors and to help them succeed. Horace Mann, a great American educational reformer, worked tirelessly to promote public education. He had this advice for others: "Be ashamed to die until you have won some victory for humanity."[136]

Think of the number of people blessed by the landmark inventions of Thomas Edison. How many hundreds of millions have been thrilled and inspired to see the amazing works of Michelangelo? What impact has the Declaration of Independence, coauthored by Thomas Jefferson, had on the world?

How many more Michelangelos would we have if everyone had the same feelings as President Hinckley? He was interviewed for the Church News by Dell Van Orden, who asked this question: "Is there anything you'd like to accomplish personally as you move into the new century?"

He answered, "I'd like to work a little harder. I'd like to do a little more than I'm doing."[137]

Opens Doors to Opportunities

Margaret Thatcher stated, "I do not know anyone who has got to the top without hard work. That is the recipe. It will not always get you to the top, but it should get you pretty close."[138] Hard work opens the doors of opportunity to those willing to pay that price. Some say that successful people, regardless of their field, were born with talent or have just been lucky. But a quote attributed to Tim Notke says, "Hard work beats talent when talent doesn't work hard." There are numerous talented people who never achieve anything of significance in their life. However, when you mix talent with hard work and just a little luck, miracles can occur.

The truth is, successful people almost always work harder than the average person. It is often hard work that opens these doors of opportunity that neither talent nor luck will open. Thomas Jefferson is reported to have said, "I'm a greater believer in luck, and I find the harder I work, the more I have of it." Those who work hard and demonstrate initiative are usually those who get noticed and are considered first when new opportunities appear. Many who achieve great success in life attribute it to the price they were willing to pay to obtain it. Too many depend on their talent or hope for luck on the road leading to success. Most with this philosophy never achieve what they are capable of. It was said of old, "For the drunkard and the glutton shall come to poverty: and drowsiness shall clothe a man with rags" (Proverbs 23:21).

Invitation to Act

1. Start today to follow Thomas Jefferson's philosophy of never being idle.
2. Always have a project underway that will benefit you or others.
3. At the end of each day, account for your time and look for ways to improve.
4. Do a weekly audit of how your time was spent, and make adjustments for the following week.

CHAPTER 8
Early to Bed, Early to Rise

The Lord said, "Retire to bed early," and this is wise advice, but we do not heed it. Now let me say, let us go to bed early, that we may rise early and be refreshed. So far as we can. It is God's plan. He tells us to do it, and we should obey.[139]

President Joseph F. Smith

Monica Tanner

During my freshman year of college, I stumbled into a class that was both uplifting and motivational. Many lessons had direct application to my age and stage of life. One of the many lessons I learned from the teacher was the importance of going to bed early and waking up early. As a first-year college student, this counsel went against everything in me. It took time to implement, but once I did, I instantly recognized the benefits my teacher had promised us. I used this schedule to graduate with honors in only three years. I was grateful for the energy, motivation, and inspiration I received from waking up early.

After graduation, I met the man of my dreams, and we started our family. Somehow, waking up early turned into rolling out of bed at the last possible moment before total chaos ensued. I took a fifteen-year hiatus from the early-to-bed, early-to-rise habit as we raised our four children. Recently, I realized my life mission and wanted to share my excitement with the teacher I had in college, who had become a trusted friend and mentor. He offered his support and then proceeded to give me one piece of advice. Adopt an early-to-bed, early-to-rise schedule. He insisted this one thing would help the inspiration flow more than anything else I could ever do to accomplish my mission. He sent me several research studies and articles listing the benefits of keeping this schedule. Then, he made me promise to try it for a few weeks and write up my experience.

I accepted his challenge and committed to give it my best effort. I made up a plan for the early morning time. It started with an hour of devotional time and journal writing. After my study time, I went to the gym to complete my work out before the rest of my family woke up. Even with my best intentions, I failed miserably the first couple of mornings. When my alarm clock sounded at six o'clock and my body protested, I quickly turned off the awful noise, rolled over, and went back to sleep. I thought, "I am not a morning person, so this is really hard!" I then remembered that my teacher had said, "I never had any trouble as a kid getting up early on Christmas day." I let those words sink in deeply. They have helped me jump out of bed with enthusiasm ever since. Whenever my alarm goes off and I think to myself, "I'm not ready to get up yet," I just picture sitting in my office with a giant bundle of inspirational gifts.

I have seen the benefits of waking up early before the rest of my household springs to life. I love hearing the birds singing just for me outside my office window. I have used the peaceful, early hours for prayer, scripture study, uninterrupted personal reflection, goal setting and evaluating, problem-solving, relationship assessments, journal writing, and research relevant to my life mission. Inspiration comes, thoughts flow freely, and I feel more positive and optimistic early in the morning when the day is still a blank canvas. I have learned exercising early ensures it will get done. Once I've had my own time to fuel up and prepare, I can handle the challenges of the day with more energy and creativity. I have a better attitude and outlook about everything when I've taken the time to gain a better perspective before diving into the day's demands and responsibilities.

Benjamin Franklin's Promise

The early morning hours can be a magical time as life takes on new meaning and excitement. Sadly, many see getting up early as an unpleasant task that should be avoided like the plague. Why? Because it takes self-discipline and consequently eliminates many individuals regardless of the rewards. A drive through a typical neighborhood in the early morning hours will show that most lights are still off, even though some with good intentions may keep hitting the snooze button. There are a rare few who religiously follow an early morning schedule.

We live in a world of bold claims and promises. In our society, we often hear about some miracle program, product, or pill guaranteed to make us happy, rich, or thin in thirty days or less. Almost without fail, we find that anything sounding too good to be true *is* too good to be true. Therefore, a miraculous claim made by Benjamin Franklin over 250 years ago is especially intriguing. He boldly declared if we would do two simple things, which take a few minutes a day to complete, we would receive three things that people around the world desire perhaps more than anything else. These claims seem so bold and far out that the clear majority refuse to even try what he suggests: "Early to bed and early to rise, makes a man healthy, wealthy, and wise."[140]

Can you imagine having health, wealth, and wisdom just by doing something as simple as going to bed early and getting up early? Surely, it can't be so easy. Or can it? The connection between sleep patterns and success in life goes back much earlier than 1758. Aristotle, who died in 322 BC, said, "It is well to be up before daybreak, for such habits contribute to health, wealth, and wisdom."[141] If there is no basis in truth for these claims, why has no one exposed the flawed logic in the past two thousand years?

Three well-known Americans are Benjamin Franklin, Thomas Jefferson, and Thomas Edison. All three are considered polymaths, a term used to describe someone with talents in multiple fields. What they accomplished in their lifetimes is extraordinary. All three seem to attribute their successes in part to something they share. We are all familiar with Franklin's connection between sleep patterns and success, but the other two share his belief as well. Thomas Jefferson declared, "The sun has not caught me in bed in fifty years."[142]

All branches of the military have basic training for new recruits. During this training, there's no such thing as sleeping in. Soldiers usually get up at four thirty in the morning and are in formation by five every day, with lights out at nine o'clock each night. Our missionaries also follow an early-to-bed, early-to-rise routine beginning at the Missionary Training Center and throughout their missions. Why do you think both the Church and the military follow an early schedule? Have both organizations discovered over time these early schedules produce peak performance for those being trained? Weeks spent with these early-to-bed, early-to-rise schedules lead both military recruits and missionaries to enjoy more energy and accomplish more each day.

Wisdom of the Ages

The benefits of following an early schedule have been recognized since ancient time. The three largest religions in in the world—Christianity, Islam, Hinduism with a combined membership of 5.4 billion followers[143]—all teach followers to adopt an early schedule.

- Christianity: "And in the morning, rising up a great while before day, [Jesus Christ] went out, and departed into a solitary place, and there prayed" (Mark 1:35).
- Islam: "Muslims are required to wake up early to pray (Fajr) at dawn (approximately one and one-half hours before sunrise)."[144]
- Hinduism: "A healthy person should get up two hours before sunrise."[145]

Excited about Life

Several years ago, Kevin Rollins, CEO of Dell Inc. at the time, spoke to a group of college students. After his speech, he left time for a question-and-answer session. One of those in attendance asked what time he got up in the morning. Kevin replied, "I get up at five o'clock."

You could hear gasps in the audience. One student joked that he often didn't go to bed until then. Others emphatically stated they were night people. The overall reaction of the students indicated they thought getting up at such an early hour was ludicrous. How interesting that a group of eighteen- to twenty-five-year-old university students, yet to hold a full-time job, basically scoffed at the CEO of a multibillion-dollar company!

The next question was "Why do you get up so early?" I'll never forget the answer. With a sincere smile he exclaimed, "I'm so excited about life, I can't sleep any longer!"

Are we so excited about life we can't sleep past five? If not, it is probably wise to listen to someone who is and to see what's so exciting about it! I asked a group of college students to write down what time they would get up if they had no homework and no place they needed to be. While responses varied, the median time was ten o'clock. By that time, Kevin Rollins (and others like him) would have already been up accomplishing good things for five hours! Prolific Irish writer Jonathan Swift wrote, "I never knew a man come to greatness or eminence who lay abed late in the morning."[146]

With the amazing promised benefits, it is a mystery why more people don't at least try the early-to-bed, early-to-rise principle. Why do so many want to sleep longer than is needful when there is so much good needing to be done in the world?

Let's look at the three benefits mentioned by Aristotle and Benjamin Franklin and other benefits associated with the practice.

Health

Health depends on many factors, one of which is the proper amount of sleep. The connection between mental health and a strong physical body is well documented. We all need to determine the optimal amount of sleep our bodies need to function at the highest level. We've probably all heard that eight hours of sleep a night is optimal. Does this recommendation apply to all ages and all situations? For example, does an infant or a pregnant woman need the same amount of sleep as a healthy adult male? Of course not! The amount of sleep needed varies from one individual to the next and changes over time.

One of the most creative businessmen of our time is Amazon founder Jeff Bezos. When asked about his sleep habits, he said, "I just feel so much better all day long if I've had eight hours."[147] Thomas Edison, on the other hand, needed far less. He said, "For myself I never found need of more than four or five hours' sleep in the twenty-four. I never dream. It's real sleep. When by chance I have taken more I wake dull and indolent."[148] Was this small amount of sleep an unhealthy practice for Edison? Apparently not since he acquired an astounding 2,332 patents worldwide and lived to age 84. Two other polymaths who were early risers, Benjamin Franklin and Thomas Jefferson, died at ages 84 and 83, respectively, when "the average life expectancy during this era was 36."[149]

Although it's a common belief that eight hours of sleep is required for peak health, a six-year study of more than one million adults ages 30 to 102 has shown people who get only six to seven hours a night have a lower death rate than those who get more than this. Researchers from the University of California at San Diego School of Medicine and the American Cancer Society collaborated on the study, which found individuals who sleep eight hours or more, or less than four hours a night, were shown to have a significantly increased death rate compared to those who averaged six to seven hours.[150]

Imagine for a moment that you read a news release announcing that Apple just named a new CEO. Would you be surprised if you found out he was ninety-nine years old? Shocked? What if the next one in line to assume leadership was ninety-one years old? And yet that is exactly the situation we have with President Nelson and President Oaks. Have you ever wondered why our prophets and apostles live so long on average with such remarkable overall quality of life? Living the Word of Wisdom is surely a factor in their longevity, but they must be doing something in addition to just avoiding tobacco and alcohol. How many men do you know even in the Church who could do what they do? Could their early morning schedule be a factor? President Nelson is one of those individuals who knows the blessing associated with this practice. He said, "I get up before anybody else, and that gives me time for personal scripture reading, private prayer, and about a half-hour playing the hymns. . . . By the time I leave home in the morning, my mind is filled with good things—the scriptures and fine music. This gets my day off to a good start better than any other way I've found."[151]

It should come as no surprise that President Oaks also keeps an early schedule. Chris Pendleton reported on a talk given at Southern Virginia University: "Elder Oaks then briefly described his morning routine. Rising around 4:30 a.m.—but never after 5 a.m.—Elder Oaks begins his day by walking a few miles, praying, studying the scriptures, and then praying again, asking that he 'might be guided by the Holy Ghost' that day."[152]

Going to bed early and getting up early not only appear to help physical health but also could have an impact on our mental health. The first few hours often set the mood for our entire day. We live in a world filled with stress, sadness, and depression. Many spend large sums of money searching for joy, not realizing "joy cometh in the morning" (Psalm 30:5). President Nelson shared this counsel: "To those who feel defeated and downtrodden, look to the early hours of the day for your rescue. . . . The dawning of a brighter day heralds a time of forgiveness. Shadows of yesterday's grief melt in the rays of early morn's opportunity."[153] Several studies now show those who arise early are often more optimistic, more focused on the positive, and have more satisfaction in life. Those who stay up late and sleep late lean more toward depression and other psychological challenges. Dr. Joerg Huber of Roehampton University said, "There are morning people and evening people, and morning people tend to be healthier and happier as well as having lower body mass indices."[154]

Wealth

How many times have you heard of an extremely successful and respected business leader with a daily routine of arising at ten o'clock? Early risers have been associated with wealth and success for centuries. For example, King Solomon said, "Love not sleep, lest thou come to poverty; open thine eyes, and thou shalt be satisfied with bread" (Proverbs 20:13). Much later Benjamin Franklin said, "He that riseth late, must trot all day, and shall scarce overtake his business at night; while Laziness travels so slowly that Poverty soon overtakes him. Drive thy business, let not that drive thee."[155]

When one of our sons-in-law was a university student, he rode an exercise bike at five in the morning while watching news on television. Later, he asked me why I thought the first ad he saw at that early hour was for a luxury car. I expressed my thoughts and later asked one of my business-minded sons why he thought they were advertising an expensive car at that time in the morning. He said they were obviously targeting wealthy people, because they are the only ones up that early. Surely large, successful companies have conducted market research before spending valued advertising dollars. They know when their potential customers are watching. Contrast that with late-night infomercials for cheap gadgets that appeal to impulse buyers. Marketers are like Santa Claus—they see you when you're sleeping and know when you're awake.

Multiple surveys have been conducted to determine daily routines of Fortune 500 company CEOs. Not surprisingly, the majority are early risers. Some may believe that the reason successful CEOs get up early is because their demanding schedules force them to. The other possibility, however, is that they are CEOs because they are early risers. This chicken or egg concept was examined by Professor Christoph Randler, who said, "When it comes to business success, morning people hold the important cards. My earlier research showed that they tend to get better grades in school, which get them into better colleges, which then lead to better job opportunities. Morning people also anticipate problems and try to minimize them, my survey showed. They're proactive. Several studies have linked this trait, proactivity, with better job performance, greater career success, and higher wages."[156]

Wisdom

Ralph Waldo Emerson made this observation about the morning hours and wisdom: "In the morning a man walks with his whole body; in the evening, only with his legs."[157] He obviously thought the peak time for learning was in the morning when the mind is fresh and alert, assuming a person has had a good night's sleep.

One scientific study conducted by researchers at Brigham Young University found that "students who habitually go to bed late and sleep late the next day have lower grade point averages (GPAs) than students with early-to-bed and early-to-rise sleeping habits. The later students slept in the morning, the lower their grades tended to be. Out of all the factors studied, weekday and weekend wakeup times had the strongest association with students' GPAs. Each hour over the average that students slept in on weekdays was associated with a 0.13-point drop on the GPA (0.0-4.0 scale)."[158]

Web MD reported, "College students who are 'morning people' may have a higher chance of graduating near the top of their class. In a study at a Texas university, early birds had an average grade point average (GPA) that was a full point higher than night owls: 3.5 vs. 2.5."[159] Unfortunately, many college students, as well as the broader population, tend to do the opposite of these research findings.

President Packer obviously believed that an early schedule is associated with knowledge acquisition. He said, "I counsel our children to do their critical studying in the early hours of the morning when they're fresh and alert, rather than to fight physical weariness and mental exhaustion at night. I've learned the power of the dictum, "Early to bed, early to rise." When I'm under pressure, you won't find me burning the midnight oil. I'd much rather be in bed early and get up in the wee hours of the morning, when I can be close to Him who guides this work."[160]

Productivity

Imagine driving away from your home with no idea where you are going. That is essentially what many do when they sleep until right before they throw on their clothes and rush out the door in a daze with no thought-out plan for the day. Those who rise early and use the early morning hours to plan, set goals, and get organized are obviously more productive than those without a plan. Some believe the Six P Formula is essential to productivity: "Proper Prior Planning Prevents Poor Performance."

Benjamin Franklin was a master of productivity. What was his secret? He had a daily schedule that he left for the world to see, and surprisingly, there were only twenty-four hours in his day just like ours. He went to bed at ten every night and got up at five every morning. He immediately washed up and wrote down this question: "What good shall I do this day?" He must have realized by asking this question in the stillness of the early morning hours, it would generate inspired ideas. He used this time to plan, read, set goals, and prepare for the day. He ate breakfast and began work at eight. Can you imagine having three hours every morning before you needed to be at work? From noon until two, he ate, read, and looked over his accounts. From two until six, he worked. Then from six until ten, he tidied up, dined, enjoyed music and conversation, and recapped how he did in his quest to do good.[161]

Self-improvement guru Paul J. Meyer reminded us, "Productivity is never an accident. It is always the result of a commitment to excellence, intelligent planning, and focused effort."[162] Detailed planning is seldom possible for those who get up late because of the many things that need to happen to start the day. Early risers have time to plan for greater productivity. Usually, it is in the early morning hours when the mind is clear that flashes of inspiration come. It is a time to be proactive and come up with solutions to challenges we face. Former college president Joe J. Christensen pointed out that, "The world is a more beautiful place early in the morning. Life is so much more calm. Much more can be accomplished in a shorter amount of time."[163]

Productivity is a huge benefit to those who do not sleep longer than is needful. Think of what you could accomplish if you had some extra time during the week. Why not do an experiment to see how much sleep you really need to act efficiently? Set your alarm back 10 minutes each night until you figure out the right amount of sleep your body needs. Let's say you have been sleeping 8 hours a night but discover you only need 7. That would give you an extra 365 hours a year or the equivalent of nine 40-hour weeks to accomplish those important goals you have in life. Imagine how many 40-hour weeks you could add to your waking hours if you made this a lifetime practice.

Self-Discipline

Going to bed early and getting up early takes self-discipline. We often make big plans for the next day before going to sleep at night. We may plan to get up at five thirty, read scriptures, meditate, plan our day, write in our journal, run two miles, eat a healthy breakfast, and write a note to a friend. But the next morning something terrible happens. The clock that remained silent for hours suddenly starts making an irritating noise while we are still trying to sleep. At the same time the mattress, which was our dear friend during the night, suddenly gets aggressive and tries to hold us down. It is the first battle of the day and one we must face every day for life. The same mattress that tried to hold us down in the morning seems to shoo us away at night. Isn't it interesting that both the first and last battle of the day involves our mattress?

Stephen R. Covey often encouraged his students to get up early and "sharpen the saw." He explained why getting up early is such a struggle in these words:

> During the first few minutes in lift-off the astronauts were strictly controlled and were powerfully buffeted by the forces of nature struggling to keep them on earth. This is somewhat comparable to the pull of the flesh when our alarm goes off early in the morning. Unless we put "mind over mattress" and carry out the resolves made the night before, we will experience our first defeat that day. Not sufficient to finish. Mission aborted.
>
> But if we overcome the pull and "get up and get at it," we will have won a victory. We kept our own resolve. We can then move to other

> things, for by small means great things are accomplished. Thus, even this "one small step" is also in another sense "a giant leap."[164]

If you get up early after a good night's sleep, your willpower will be at its peak. With most of the world still asleep, you will face few distractions. You can focus on your own improvement and how to help others.

Revelation

There is another benefit of going to bed early and getting up early that is greater than all others. Years ago, Joe J. Christensen and his wife, Barbara, had a chance to chauffeur President Marion G. Romney and his wife, Ida, from Provo to their home in Salt Lake City. Along the way, President Romney told an experience he'd had while serving as a stake president. One general conference, he attended a session in the Salt Lake Tabernacle. During this meeting, he was sustained as a new General Authority, even though no one had talked to him about the calling beforehand. He was shocked and nervous, so he went to his good friend Elder Harold B. Lee, a member of the Quorum of the Twelve Apostles, for advice.

> Elder Lee said, "If you are to be successful as a General Authority, you will need to be inspired. You will need to receive revelation. I will give you one piece of advice: *Go to bed early and get up early.* If you do, your body and mind will become rested and then in the quiet of those early morning hours, you will receive more flashes of inspiration and insight than at any other time of the day."
>
> Years later, reflecting on that experience, President Romney said, "From that day on, I put that counsel into practice, and I know it works. Whenever I have a serious problem, or some assignment of a creative nature with which I hope to receive the influence of the Spirit, I always receive more assistance in the early morning hours than at any other time of the day."[165]

We often hear discussions concerning the best ways to receive personal revelation. Never once have I heard anyone mention going to bed early and getting up early related to inspiration as President Lee did. Often the first piece of advice mentioned is prayer. Joseph Smith and Enos have been used as examples of individuals who prayed and received revelation. Is it possible that both received the inspiration to go and pray in the early morning hours? While we do not know the exact time of day Joseph awoke when he received the First Vision, he did mention "it was on the morning of a beautiful, clear day" (Joseph Smith—History 1:14). And while Enos does not mention a wake-up time on the day he prayed, he does say, "all the day long did I cry unto him" (Enos 1:4). Others get a little more specific, tying early morning hours to revelation. There seems to be a pattern for connecting the early morning hours with revelation. Here are a couple of Old Testament examples:

- "And Abraham gat up early in the morning to the place where he stood before the Lord" (Genesis 19:27).
- "And he hewed two tables of stone like unto the first; and Moses rose up early in the morning, and went up unto mount Sinai, as the Lord had commanded him, and took in his hand the two tables of stone" (Exodus 34:4).

The Heroic Minute

Many arise depending on what time they go to bed. If they go to bed late, they usually get up late. The key is to arise when you say you will. Thomas Jefferson said, "Whether I retire to bed early or late, I rise with the sun."[166] Getting up when you say you will is not easy. I've noticed through the years that my employers didn't change the start time at work depending on what time I went to bed the night before. What is your set time to get up?

Isn't it time you tried an experiment to see if the early-to-bed, early-to-rise routine will be beneficial for you? It takes less than a minute to actually get into bed and less than a minute to get out of bed, but the promised results of doing so are amazing. Catholic priest Josemaría Escrivá advised, "Conquer yourself each day from the very first moment, getting up on the dot, at a fixed time, without yielding a single minute to laziness. If, with God's help, you conquer yourself, you will be well ahead for the rest of the day. . . . The heroic minute. It is the time fixed for getting up."[167]

Over the years, I have challenged thousands of people to determine the amount of sleep they need and try the early schedule. Here are some of the positive benefits mentioned by individuals who go to bed and get up early:

- Become closer to the Lord
- Have extra exercise time
- Have greater desire to eat healthy
- Develop more good ideas
- Feel more alert
- Love winning the first battle of the day
- Have more energy
- Work harder during the day
- Procrastinate less
- Be excited for life
- Find the world more beautiful
- Feel less stressed
- Get more done in less time
- Increase in personal revelation
- Learn more easily
- Be more loving and less judgmental
- Resist temptation better
- Increase in self-discipline

In Doctrine and Covenants 88:124 we read, "Retire to thy bed early, that ye may not be weary; arise early, that your bodies and your minds may be invigorated." I never understood the promise the Lord made here until I looked up the meaning of the words *weary* and *invigorated.* Using the dictionary definitions changed everything for me. The reason we are to go to bed early is so we are not *weary*, which means "exhausted in strength, endurance, vigor, or freshness."[168] We get up early so that our bodies and minds may be *invigorated*, which means "to give life and energy to."[169]

Randal: Recently I had the opportunity to speak at BYU Campus Education Week. One of the class topics was the importance of following an early-to-bed, early-to-rise schedule. I received an email after returning home from popular speaker Merrilee Boyack, who was in attendance. Here is part of what she said:

"Then you quoted the scripture (Doctrine and Covenants 88:124) and said, 'I *promise* you that your mind and your body will be invigorated,' I grabbed hold of that promise and thought, "I'm going to hold you and God to that!" I cannot even begin to tell you what an astounding difference it has made—just absolutely incredible. My energy has been great, my sleep pretty good, but my spirit has been soaring! I feel like the heavens have opened and revelation is just pouring in. It stays with me all day long. I feel like for the first time in ten years, I can start moving forward significantly again. I feel like I'm finally making strides instead of just trying to stay afloat. Incredible. So thank you, my friend, for teaching me a great truth that has profoundly affected my life."

Finally, coauthor Scott O'Neil works in a career that requires many late nights. While working on this book, he accepted a challenge to get up early at five thirty for fourteen days straight and keep a daily journal of his experience. Here are excerpts from his journal:

> *Day 1:* Late night shopping last night in Las Vegas, but getting up at five thirty was easy because I was on West Coast time. . . . Got on an earlier flight and got a ton of work done on the plane and on the long ride back, but was physically and mentally exhausted when I arrived home late.
>
> *Day 2:* Got up with the alarm at five thirty. It is draft day, and we have the number one overall pick! I feel happy and energized. I sent a sarcastic email to Randal telling him that this was the wrong week for this crazy challenge. I curse Ben Franklin for his early-to-bed, early-to-rise statement.
>
> *Day 3:* Draft night was successful and fun since we got the number one pick. But very tired getting home late again. I slept through alarm until six thirty (fail). Yikes! Came up with sarcastic phrase brushing teeth: early to bed, early to rise makes a man, exhausted, poor, and brain dead.
>
> *Day 4:* Home by ten fifteen, stayed up until eleven chatting with Alexa, Kira, her friend Isabell, and Eliza. Much tougher going to sleep early than waking up early. A very fun day. I promise myself no more misses and considered how I am going to write up "sleeping in until six thirty."
>
> *Day 5:* Up at five thirty to alarm. . . . This is Saturday morning. I am a bit sleepy, but happy, content, relaxed, and grateful to be up

and hear nothing but the driving rain. It is peaceful and calm—two words that do not exactly define the O'Neil house. It's allowing me to type this journal, a plus.

Day 6: I saw the most beautiful sunrise. The entire sky was a pinkish-orange, and the clouds looked like cotton candy. It brings me back to college when I worked for a farmer's market from four to noon and fell in love with sunrises. The house is still. I hear the birds chirping. I am at peace.

Day 7: Monday morning and the sunrise was magnificent. I am happy to be up. Having gotten a full night's sleep, I am ready to tackle the day. It is going to be a long day ending with the NBA Awards show in NYC. I had an incredibly spiritual Sunday.

Day 8: Was in NYC last night for the first-ever NBA Awards show. It was a fun night, but I got home late. The five-thirty bell came early, and I did what I didn't think I would do. . . . I rolled over and hit snooze, twice! Yikes! I do feel alive, awake, and happy, but still not quite like Ben Franklin.

Day 9: I feel a good burst of positive energy. I feel clear of mind and at peace. Getting up in the stillness of the morning—when I can hear the birds chirping outside and the sound of the keyboard is the loudest sound of the morning—puts me at peace. I cannot help but notice this morning that I long for more quiet and peaceful moments in my life. Pure serenity. I am committing to this.

Day 10: I got to bed late again but popped out of bed. It seems to be getting easier to get up. I started convincing myself that this shouldn't be just a two-week experiment. I have found myself truly appreciating and enjoying the time of peace and reflection. I feel energized and alive.

Day 11: The weekends! That is when the time is most cherished. That seems to be the easiest for me to get up and get going. I am feeling extra thankful today. I am going to sign off and write in my gratitude journal before digging into some emails before the troops are up and swirling.

Day 12: A fun and busy day. . . . We started with a 5k Bubble Run, moved on to an escape room, and finished with a misnamed family talent show. Another late night, but ton of laughs, quality time, and fun. Kira steals the show with a butterfly dance to a song she had created on the computer.

Day 13: I continue to feel relaxed, energized, and at peace for the five-thirty wake up and what I am calling my "peace time." We are still in a hotel, so when I quietly leave the room and head to the lobby, it isn't the stillness as I find at home, but the rhythmic music becomes white noise.

Day 14: Ironically, this morning is July Fourth, Independence Day, and the two-week challenge is up. I am happier, more productive, more connected when my kids awake, full of energy, and committed to continue the "get up and stay up" program.

Invitation to Act

1. Determine how much sleep you need each night to operate at peak performance the next day.
2. Set a specific time to arise each morning and time to go to bed.
3. Come up with a morning routine for yourself, listing what you will follow each day before heading to work, school, or other tasks.
4. Try the early-to-bed, early-to-rise schedule for fourteen days. Keep a brief daily journal of your experience. See for yourself if the blessings promised with this practice occur, then record what happened during the experiment.

CHAPTER 9
Have a Positive Attitude

So much in life depends on our attitude. The way we choose to see things and respond to others makes all the difference . . . We can't direct the wind, but we can adjust the sails. For maximum happiness, peace, and contentment, may we choose *a positive attitude.*[170]
President Thomas S. Monson

Darol Wagstaff

In May 1988, I was asked to be the keynote speaker for the Arizona Association of Student Councils State Convention in Mesa, Arizona. Mr. Judd, the executive director, told me about a young high school student named Carl Crawford who had recently been paralyzed from the chest down in an accident. He and three friends were on their way to prepare for senior prom when the truck they were riding in overturned. Mr. Judd asked if I could make time to visit Carl to encourage him, because he was suffering from deep depression. I mentioned to Mr. Judd that the National Speakers Association was having its annual convention in Phoenix and that Art Linkletter would be speaking. My twin brother and I had met Art previously when we acted with his daughter Diane in plays and musical productions. I told him I would see if Art could come with me to visit Carl. Art Linkletter agreed to accompany me. However, on the day of our visit with Carl, Art's flight itinerary changed, and he could not go.

I knew that the Crawford family and friends were waiting for us and especially waiting to meet Mr. Linkletter. As I walked through the lobby wondering what to do, I saw a man in a wheelchair. The thought came to my mind to ask him to come with me to meet Carl. As I got closer, it became apparent he had been severely burned. His face was disfigured, and his fingers had been burned from his hands. As I introduced myself, we shook hands, and he told me his name was W. Mitchell. I explained my situation and asked him if he would go with me to encourage Carl. With a big smile he said, "I'd love to go with you."

While I drove across town, Mitchell told me his story. In 1971, he was riding his motorcycle on his way to work and was hit by a laundry truck driver who ran a stop sign. About 60 percent of Mitchell's body was burned. He fractured his pelvis, along with other injuries.

Four years later, after becoming a successful businessman, he and four friends were in Mitchell's small plane taking off from Gunnison, Colorado, when the plane malfunctioned on takeoff. Mitchell had no choice but to crash-land the plane. His friends were not injured, but Mitchell broke his back and became paralyzed from the waist down.

After he told his experiences, I learned one of the greatest lessons of my life. He said, "It's not what happens to you. It's what you do about it that makes the difference." He has now taught thousands this message as an award-winning international keynote speaker for corporations and associations. He is fond of sharing this statement: "Before I was paralyzed there were 10,000 things I could do; now there are 9,000. I can either dwell on the 1,000 I've lost or focus on the 9,000 I have left."[171]

As we pulled up to the Crawfords' home, everyone was waiting for Art Linkletter. Mitchell settled into his wheelchair. When we got to the door, Carl exclaimed, "You are W. Mitchell, aren't you?"

Mitchell replied, "Yes. How did you know?"

Carl answered, "We watched a movie about your life in our rehabilitation unit before I came home." They conversed for an hour or so, and at the end of their conversation, Carl thanked Mitchell for coming and said, "Your caring enough to come here today has literally saved my life!"

Although Art Linkletter couldn't visit with Carl Crawford that day, he probably would have taught him a lesson he taught me years before: "Things turn out best for the people who make the best of the way things turn out."[172]

What Really Counts

The great songwriter Irving Berlin said, "Life is 10 percent what you make it and 90 percent how you take it."[173] W. Mitchell is a product of this statement. He proved we can control our attitudes toward the situations we find ourselves in. Some tend to see themselves as victims rather than agents free to choose their attitudes.

Perhaps many have read "The Moral Bucket List," the thought-provoking article by David Brooks. He reflected on the rare people, like W. Mitchell, who seem to radiate a kind of inner light. He wondered what created this light, how they obtained it, and how he could have what they had. He then shared this insight:

> It occurred to me that there were two sets of virtues, the résumé virtues and the eulogy virtues. The résumé virtues are the skills you bring to the marketplace. The eulogy virtues are the ones that are talked about at your funeral—whether you were kind, brave, honest, or faithful. Were you capable of deep love?
>
> We all know that eulogy virtues are more important than the résumé ones. But our culture and our educational systems spend more time teaching the skills and strategies you need for career success than the qualities you need to radiate that sort of inner light. Many of us are clearer on how to build an external career than on how to build inner character.[174]

Having a positive attitude while facing trials put things in perspective for W. Mitchell. He has helped many with similar situations face their trials bravely. Harvard philosopher and psychologist William James said, "The greatest discovery of my generation is that a human being can alter his life by altering his attitudes."[175]

Life Will Have Bumps

Life is full of ups and downs. It seems there is always something to take the joy out of life, if we choose to look at it that way. No one has smooth sailing every day. It is extremely unlikely anything will change this. A short story illustrates this point.

> A fortune-teller studied the hand of a young man and said, "You will be poor and very unhappy until you are thirty-seven years old."

> The young man responded, "Well, after that, what will happen? Will I be rich and happy?"
>
> The fortune-teller said, "No, you'll still be poor, but you'll be used to it after that."[176]

Popular speaker Bradley R. Wilcox was teaching a large group of active sixth graders and would sometimes get frustrated when things didn't go exactly as planned. He told me that one day he came home and vented to his wife, Debbie, about how difficult things were. He then asked why life had to be such a roller coaster. His wife, a registered nurse, said something that helped him put things into perspective. She essentially said we should be grateful life is a roller coaster with all its ups and downs and twists and turns. He was confused, wondering why anyone would want a life filled with highs and lows. She simply responded with, "The last thing you want is to flatline!"

Failing Is Tough

Scott: Failing is tough. Failing publicly is tougher! Failing publicly and being out of work, out of luck, and out of money makes simple failure feel like some sort of family barbecue. It is hard to put things in perspective when you are going through difficult times. That is where I found myself after leaving the Philadelphia Eagles to chase internet fame and fortune. It was a quick, fun, roller coaster type of ride. And then it was over. The internet bubble burst and with it our hopes, dreams, and the fifty-one people I worked with. We had tried to ramp down spending at the end, cutting all salaries in half a couple times, but it was too little, too late. I stayed on for the last month or so to negotiate out of contracts and wind down the company. That wasn't fun.

Then I faced the harsh reality of being embarrassed, flat broke, and out of work. I was an emotional wreck. I felt like a failure. To add to my worries, my wife, Lisa, had recently become a stay-at-home mom after the birth of our first daughter, Alexa. Adding even more pressure, we had recently purchased a home. It was hard to put things in proper perspective when I felt so low. I spent a lot of time reading, thinking, playing basketball, and going for long walks with Alexa. I also spent time talking to Lisa to get my confidence back and find the inspiration I needed to start looking for a job.

In time, I stopped seeing what I didn't have and saw what I did have. I realized without a doubt I had married the right woman, because she supported me 100 percent. I learned later that in her full protecting mode, she hid our foreclosure notices until I could find my way. During this time, I found what has become my favorite book of all time, *Leadership and Self Deception: Getting Out of the Box* by the Arbinger Institute. This book helped me see things from a new perspective, put the smile back on my face, and gain a new energy for life.

Winston Churchill said, "Success is not final, failure is not fatal: it is the courage to continue that counts."[177] I realized that individuals throughout history have faced despair and depression and have learned wisdom from living through challenging circumstances.

As I look back, I can see many valuable lessons from this experience that have helped me tremendously in my personal life and career. When we fail to put our challenging experiences in the proper perspective, we increase our chances of viewing them out of proportion and then overreacting. We let our emotions take over and throw out sound judgment.

With a new view of my situation, I was ready to get back in the game. I had built relationships and friendships over the years and turned to them for help. In a matter of weeks, I had three job opportunities. I was offered and accepted a job with the NBA after my friend Seth Berger recommended me to current NBA commissioner Adam Silver.

Our Attitudes Affect Those around Us

Having a positive or negative attitude not only affects individuals but also those with whom they associate. A story about a mother driving with her young son shows this. The inquisitive little boy asked, "Mom, why do all the idiots only come out when Dad drives?" At an early age this young man realized his dad had a bad attitude, at least while driving. He, like all of us, could adopt that same negative attitude or choose to take a more positive approach.

Randal: At age nineteen I was drafted into the US Army and sent to Basic Training from the middle of May to the middle of July at Fort Bliss in El Paso, Texas. The heat was oppressive that summer with multiple days over 100°F. During the seventh week, we were taken to the White Sands Missile Range in New Mexico for a multiday encampment in an unsheltered area. We were transported to and from the site in converted cattle trucks. Staying several nights in small tents in the heat and sand was miserable. The intense physical exertion required for training during the day was even worse. Our trip back to Fort Bliss at the end of the week proved dismal. We were all exhausted and packed like cattle in the trailer for the trip back to our post. With no air conditioners or fans, the smell of body odor was intense, and the filthy profanity many of the soldiers used that day was even baser than normal.

When things couldn't have gotten any worse, a brief pause occurred in the complaining and lewd language. Suddenly a soldier did a perfect imitation of a cow. He let out a bellowing moo followed by a higher pitched one. It was the best imitation of a cow I had ever heard. The timing was perfect for our disgruntled group, and almost everyone in the trailer began laughing. Before long almost every soldier in the cattle trailer took his turn mooing like a cow, laughing and joking. This humor changed our collective sullen state of mind to an astonishingly positive attitude. The drill sergeants tried to get everyone to stop mooing, but their commands fell on deaf ears. Harvey Mackay said, "Positive thinking is more than just a tagline. It changes the way we behave. And I firmly believe that when I am positive, it not only makes me better, but it also makes those around me better."[178] That day, the sound of one lone cow imitation instantly changed the negative attitudes of the entire herd of soldiers. Frederick William Faber explained, "There are souls in this world which have the gift of finding joy everywhere and of leaving it behind them when they go."[179]

Think Positively

When things don't seem to be working out exactly as planned, why not at least have a positive attitude and hope for the best? When our oldest son Nathan was seven, he, his younger brother Nolan, and a few cousins decided to try their hand at entrepreneurship with a lemonade stand. It was an extremely hot and humid summer day. They stood out in the heat waiting for their first customer. Time dragged on, and it appeared their hope of turning a profit looked bleak. In fact, the hope of getting a single customer looked unlikely. Sweat poured off their faces as they patiently waited for someone to buy their lemonade.

The boys' grandfather heard about their plight and, being a businessman himself, was sensitive to their situation. Living close by, he pulled into the driveway right beside their lemonade stand. The boys seemed excited since he was their first customer of the day. He ordered two glasses of lemonade. As soon as he placed the order and it was being processed, Nathan said, "Papa, you are going to have to move your truck out of our driveway."

A little surprised, his grandfather asked, "Why do I need to move?"

Nathan explained, "We're expecting a lot of customers here any minute."

No matter how bleak our present situation looks, we can look on the bright side and have hope of better things to come.

In 1 Samuel 17, we read the well-known story of David and Goliath. These two names are now synonymous with a small opponent facing off with a larger, stronger one. The Philistines gathered their armies to battle against the men of Israel. Each army stood on a mountain with a valley in between. The Philistines sent out their champion giant Goliath, who challenged the Israelites to send down a man to fight him with this condition: "If he be able to fight with me, and to kill me, then will we be your servants: but if I prevail against him, and kill him, then shall ye be our servants, and serve us" (1 Samuel 17:9). When the Israelites heard this, they were extremely afraid. Their opponent appeared so big, and they knew no one in their army who could win a one-on-one battle against him. Their doubts led to downtrodden attitudes.

David, the youngest son of Jesse, who experts believe was a young teenager at the time, volunteered to go against Goliath. He was motivated by the thought that he would be fighting for a righteous cause. He walked fearlessly onto the field of battle. Refusing to put on armor, he took only his staff, a sling, and five stones from a brook. His outlook was different from the army's. His attitude seemed to say, "This guy is so big I can't miss!" David hurled a stone from his sling with the skill mastered from much practice and hit Goliath in the center of his forehead. Despite his armor and size, Goliath fell to the ground on his face. Thomas Carlyle said, "The block of granite which was an obstacle in the pathway of the weak, becomes a stepping-stone in the pathway of the strong."[180]

At times, it can seem as if we are up against our own Goliaths. In the 1980 Winter Olympics, I watched as a David versus Goliath battle commenced for the gold medal in the hockey competition. The Soviet Union team consisted of mostly professional players with extensive international experience. They had won the gold medal in five of the six previous Winter Games and were heavily favored to win again. A year earlier the Soviet team overwhelmed the NHL All-Stars 6–0 to win the Challenge Cup. The 1980 US Olympic team was comprised of young amateur players that year. Just three days before the start of the Olympics, the US team played the Soviet team in an exhibition game at Madison Square Garden in New York City and were crushed 10–3. However, in what is now called the "Miracle on Ice," the US team beat the Soviet team 4–3 and won the gold medal, showing the world that with a positive attitude and determination, miracles are possible.[181] Thomas Jefferson is said to have remarked, "Nothing can stop the man with the right mental attitude from achieving his goal; nothing on earth can help the man with the wrong mental attitude."

Some justify having a negative attitude when their circumstances are less than ideal. However, as W. Mitchell and many others have demonstrated, our attitudes often have little to do with the challenges we face. While some people are extremely happy, others working right beside them appear downtrodden. Money doesn't seem to change anything since there are happy as well as miserable millionaires. Many inflicted with severe physical disabilities or even terminal illnesses still enjoy positive attitudes. President Hinckley was as positive as ever in his final years. He joked in general conference by saying, "I am now in my 97th year. The wind is blowing, and I feel like the last leaf on the tree."[182] Our situations, whether good or bad, don't determine our attitudes.

We Are Free to Choose

Viktor Frankl, born into a Jewish family in Vienna, Austria, in 1905, received a doctorate in medicine and later a doctorate in philosophy. During the Second World War, Nazis sent Viktor and his wife, Tilly, along with Viktor's parents, to concentration camps in Germany. His father died from exhaustion after a year and a half. His sixty-five-year-old mother was put to death in the gas chamber at Auschwitz. Tilly died at age twenty-four in the Bergen-Belsen concentration camp. During Viktor's imprisonment, he became aware of the last freedom he knew his enemies could not take away from him. He could decide for himself how his situation would affect him. He realized the ability to choose one's attitude is one of the greatest gifts humans are given. Viktor decided not only to keep a positive attitude amid intense trials but also to comfort those around him. He was one of the fortunate Holocaust survivors and after the war became an internationally famous neurologist and psychiatrist.[183]

Viktor wrote, "We who lived in concentration camps can remember the men who walked through the huts comforting others, giving away their last piece of bread. They may have been few in number, but they offer sufficient proof that everything can be taken from a man but one thing: the last of the human freedoms—to choose one's attitude in any given set of circumstances, to choose one's own way."[184]

Pleasant people are a joy to be around and tend to lift and cheer others. They help put difficult situations into perspective. A good-natured person is like a lighthouse and can radiate good feelings that catch on in a household, office, store, or school. A positive attitude is a valuable treasure that we should seek after, nurture, and practice.

Suggestions for Having a Positive Attitude

We can practice and internalize the steps that cultivate a positive attitude. The following ideas may help.

Look on the Bright Side

It is often easy to be positive and look on the bright side when things are going well and you are winning. However, when things take a downward turn and you are losing, it is far more difficult to stay upbeat. But having a positive attitude does not have to be tied to winning or losing.

My older brother Jack was on a high school football team with a 0–9 record going into the last game of the season. They were predicted to win the last game since they were playing against another 0–9 team that appeared very weak. On the last play of the tied game, a receiver on the opposing team caught a pass and ran for a touchdown, making the final score 6–0. Jack was the defender on the play that night, leaving his team with an 0–10 record. Many years have passed since that embarrassing night and season. Recently I heard Jack being asked if he had played high school sports. After learning Jack had played football, the person then asked how his team had done his senior year. Jack said his team went five and five that year.

"Well, that wasn't so bad," the person replied.

Jack hesitated for a moment and jokingly answered, "Yeah, we had five losses at home and five losses on the road."

Sounds better, right? Besides, maybe the ten teams that beat Jack's team that year just happened to be the ten best teams in the state. If that were the case, maybe his team was the eleventh best. I'm certain that was not the case, but it is a positive way to think about it.

Humor Always Helps

Elder Carlos E. Asay once had a serious illness and was in the intensive care unit of the hospital. At a critical time, his bishop brought him a box full of cards, messages, and drawings from the primary children of his ward. Elder Asay described one of the drawings: "One young lad drew a picture of me stretched out on a coffin. Protruding out of my chest was a single rose. Off to the side of the sketch were these words: 'Please get well, but if not, have fun!' I laughed so loud and hard that the nurses came rushing into the room, wondering what was wrong. Those moments of humor were lifting to my spirits and, I believe, healing to my body."[185]

Isn't it interesting that someone could go from distress to laughter in such a short time? One day while feeling discouraged, I stopped by my brother's business. Noticing my downcast attitude, he played a small clip from radio commentator Paul Harvey that he had just recorded. In his unique voice, Harvey read a classified newspaper notice that went something like this, "Lost dog! Has a missing leg, one eye, a broken tail, and has the mange! He answers to the name of Lucky!" I immediately put my own situation in perspective and started laughing. I realized how lucky I was and forgot about my own challenges that seemed so stressful moments before.

Avoid Negative Media and People

Our world is filled with an endless supply of negative media content. Through television, radio, or internet content, we are almost certain to be bombarded with negativity along the way. Even reading or listening to the news in the morning can put you in a negative mood. For example, the headlines of today's local news included articles about an illegal credit card data skimmer, a shooter killed by police, a murder-for-hire scheme, a carjacking, a rape and murder trial, a local mayor accused of illegally crossing the US-Mexican border, a car crash that killed one, and the CEO of a national company who resigned after using a racial slur.

Unfortunately, it is not just in the media where negativity exists. You may also have acquaintances, coworkers, or even family members who bring you down with their negative attitudes. Albert Einstein is reported to have said we should limit time spent with negative people because they have a "problem for every solution." To keep a positive attitude, it is important to surround yourself as much as possible with people who are optimistic. It is difficult to change the people around you, but you can often change the people you are around. Research shows that people tend to become like the people they are most around.[186] President Monson said, "Choose good friends. Friends help to determine your future. You will tend to be like them and to be found where they choose to go. Remember, the path we follow in this life leads to the path we follow in the next."[187]

Take the David Approach

The scriptures and Church history depict individuals who faced their own Goliaths with a positive attitude. Nephi and his older brothers were confronted with a giant task named Laban, who had the brass plates they were commanded to obtain. Laman and Lemuel murmured about the hard thing required of them. However, Nephi's attitude—whether it was getting the plates, obtaining food for the group, or building a ship—was that if God commanded it, he would be successful despite the size of the challenge. His attitude is summarized in this verse: "If God had commanded me to do all things I could do them. If he should command me that I should say unto this water, be thou earth, it should be earth; and if I should say it, it would be done" (1 Nephi 17:50).

The Lord chose Nephi because of his attitude. "Therefore go, my son, and thou shalt be favored of the Lord, because thou hast not murmured" (1 Nephi 3:6). Joseph Smith looked at life the same way as Nephi did. Consider the following statements:

- "And as for the perils which I am called to pass through, they seem but a small thing to me, as the envy and wrath of man have been my common lot all the days of my life. . . . Deep water is what I am wont to swim in. It all has become a second nature to me; and I feel, like Paul, to glory in tribulation; for to this day has the God of my fathers delivered me out of them all, and will deliver me from henceforth; for behold, and lo, I shall triumph over all my enemies, for the Lord God hath spoken it" (Doctrine and Covenants 127:2).

- "Brethren, shall we not go on in so great a cause? Go forward and not backward. Courage, brethren; and on, on to the victory! Let your hearts rejoice, and be exceedingly glad" (Doctrine and Covenants 128:22).
- "For my part, I think I never could have felt as I now do, if I had not suffered the wrongs that I have suffered. All things shall work together for good to them that love God."[188]
- "If I was sunk in the lowest pit of Nova Scotia and all the Rocky Mountains piled on top of me, I ought not to be discouraged but hang on, exercise faith, and keep up good courage and I should come out on the top of the heap at last."[189]

President Monson, a great example of a perpetual optimist, counseled, "So much in life depends on our attitude. The way we choose to see things and respond to others makes all the difference. To do the best we can and then to choose to be happy about our circumstances, whatever they may be, can bring peace and contentment. . . . We can't direct the wind, but we can adjust the sails. For maximum happiness, peace, and contentment, may we *choose* a positive attitude."[190]

Invitations to Act

1. Go seven days without saying one negative thing about anyone or anything, and write about your experience.
2. Go seven days without any worldly news or social media, and write about your experience.
3. Do your best to change the conversation when talking to negative people or make the encounter as short as possible.
4. If you find yourself being negative, take immediate action by listing the ways you are blessed, listening to uplifting music, reading

a good book, singing or humming a favorite hymn, or finding something beautiful to see.

5. If you are facing ups and downs in life and are frustrated, ask yourself if you would rather have the challenges you face or a "flatline."

CHAPTER 10
The Impact of Our Words

A word of encouragement from a teacher to a child can change a life. A word of encouragement from a spouse can save a marriage. A word of encouragement from a leader can inspire a person to reach her potential.[191]
John C. Maxwell

Tagg Romney

I had two memorable encounters with teachers, both of which stuck with me and shaped me in dramatic ways. Both involved confidence.

First, I really loved and appreciated my fifth-grade teacher. I was picked on regularly by the cool kids, but I always knew that at least I had a believer in my teacher, who liked me for who I was. One day one of the kids punched me in the head and broke his hand. I had not done anything to provoke getting punched. I had been surrounded by a group of bullies, and they insisted that one of the cool kids who had always been fair to me take a swing at me. He resisted at first but then gave in to peer pressure and punched me. I was pretty shaken up and hurt, both physically and emotionally. After recess, Miss B called me out to the hallway and proceeded to yell at me. My world crumbled. To be fair to her, she probably heard a version of the story that was different from my own. And the other kid had departed in an ambulance. I prided myself on being totally nonviolent, kind, and good. I thought she knew that about me and would trust me or at least ask for my version of the story before pouncing on me. Surely, she would know I had not started the fight or intended to cause harm. Her reaction was devastating and had a huge negative impact on my self-confidence.

Six years later, as a junior at Belmont Hill School, I was bumped up to an advanced precalculus class that I probably had no business being in. I was nervous and looked around to see many of the best math students in the school. Unsurprising to me, after the first few tests, my grades fell toward the bottom half of the class. One day my teacher, Mr. Sherman, asked me to stay after class. I thought he was going to get after me for my poor work. Instead he told me that he thought I was one of the brightest kids he had ever taught. He told me that I was quick to understand and get answers, but that it was the simple and silly stuff that was tripping me up. He said that my brain was great at understanding complex concepts and seeing solutions to problems. Finally, he told me that I was bored with the simple stuff and didn't take the time to make sure my work was correct. I believed him. He insisted I use rigor and go back and check all my work all the time. "Rigor, Romney, rigor," he told me over and over. Within a short time, I was performing at the top of the class. And it was not solely because I was double-checking my work, though I am sure that certainly helped. It was mostly because he believed in me. That gave me license to believe in myself. From that time on, my grades in all subjects improved, as did my overall confidence. It is a lesson I have never forgotten. In addition to learning self-confidence, I learned the importance of not belittling others and providing positive feedback even when results may be disappointing.

Words Are Powerful

Through words, confidence can be instilled or shattered. Wars have started and ended. Tender feelings have been hurt or soothed. Courage has been planted, and fear has been stilled. Lives have been destroyed or changed for the better. Think back on your own life when words have hurt you deeply or have comforted you and given you strength, hope, and courage. Our words, like Miss B's or Mr. Sherman's, can have an incredible power for good or bad on those with whom we associate. Tagg experienced what speaker and author Yehuda Berg was referring to when he said, "Words have energy and power with the ability to help, to heal, to hinder, to hurt, to harm, to humiliate, and to humble."192

The authority a few well-chosen words can have over individuals and even nations is amazing. Think of the incredible impact for good that the simple three-word phrase "I love you" has had over time. Those words have led to friendship, romance, marriage, happy families, security, and confidence. The simple three-word phrase "I hate you" has led to broken hearts, divorce, family breakups, destroyed friendships, shattered self-confidence, resentment, and reciprocated hate.

Scott: Just as the wrong words can hurt people for years, encouraging words can motivate a person to accomplish great things in life. My parents' teachings and support have had a huge impact on my life and my siblings' lives. My dad told me I was special every single day. I tear up telling this, but can you imagine someone telling you that you're special each day until you believe them?

I was a pill! I could walk into a room and upset it. I could ruin a dinner in a nanosecond. I could flip over a checkerboard and scream at the top of my lungs. I could slam my door into the wall. I was loving, but I would lose that in a second. My parents tried to take me off sugar. I'm sure I could have been diagnosed with something. My dad would come in and put his arm around me and say things like, "You have skills beyond any boy I have ever met. You could choose anything you want to do, and you would be great. You are special. You could run the country. You could run the world! My only concern for you is that you'll set the bar too low."

Think of the impact on a kid every day. "You're special, you're special, you're special!" And "You can do anything!" And then I started believing him. My parents encouraged their five children, supported us, and taught us what we could become. Currently I'm the CEO of Merlin Entertainments. Sean is the senior vice president of mergers and acquisitions strategy at Fiserv. Michael Jr. is the founder and CEO at GetWellNetwork Inc. Matt is chief content and experience officer at Legends. And my sister, Shannon, is the head national girls lacrosse coach at IMG Academy.

My parents' philosophy was much like the great coach and motivator Pete Carroll, who said, "Each person holds so much power within themselves that needs to be let out. Sometimes they just need a little nudge, a little direction, a little support, a little coaching and the greatest things can happen."[193]

In world history, provocative words have given offense and, in some cases, resulted in the destruction of entire nations. On the other hand, inspired words have motivated millions and led to astonishing results. Here are a few memorable examples:

- Patrick Henry: "Give me liberty, or give me death!"
- Thomas Jefferson: "We hold these truths to be self-evident, that all men are created equal."
- Texan Soldiers at San Jacinto: "Remember the Alamo."
- Abraham Lincoln: "A house divided against itself cannot stand."
- Helen Keller: "The only thing worse than being blind is having sight but no vision."
- Martin Luther King Jr.: "I have a dream."
- Neil Armstrong: "That's one small step for man, one giant leap for mankind."
- Ronald Reagan: "Mr. Gorbachev, tear down this wall!"

Negative Words Spoken to Us

Do you remember the old proverb "Sticks and stones may break my bones, but words will never hurt me"? I'm not sure who came up with this phrase, but it is far from the truth. Words can and do hurt us, and they often destroy our confidence and our perceived value to society. One short derogatory comment can destroy friendships and linger with a person for life. Unfortunately, we live in a society in which we are bombarded with negativity, name-calling, and character assassination. Television, radio, newspapers, magazines, social media, and other media have provided a platform for this type of language to be broadcast to the world in a never-ending barrage. No matter how brilliant the article, how amazing the YouTube performance, or how great the food, there is always someone willing to say that it is trash. Tune in to social media and you will likely hear talk that is belittling, critical, demeaning, disrespectful, malicious, dishonorable, minimizing, sarcastic, mocking, slanderous, spiteful, unflattering, judgmental, disrespectful, rude, and on and on. Can you imagine if media used more positive, encouraging, uplifting, and respectful words like Mr. Sherman did with Tagg?

Perhaps all of us have been on the receiving end of words that hurt. On the other hand, we might hurt others with our words. There are many reasons why people say critical or hurtful things to each other. Jealousy, anger, envy, competition, or spite may play a role. The term *crab mentality* may also play a part. According to the popular analogy, a crab dropped into a bucket alone can easily escape, but if other crabs are released in the same bucket, they will grab and prevent each other from escaping. Applied to the human experience, it means if someone begins to have success beyond what is expected for the group, the group will pull that person down. Potential achievers are sometimes brought back into the bucket of mediocrity through criticism, mockery, insults, and slurs. Because of these techniques, self-esteem and confidence are often shattered.

Randal: Several years ago, I took the Dale Carnegie Public Speaking Course. The first night of the course, the instructor asked all participants to introduce themselves. Those in attendance were mostly business executives, managers, trainers, and top salesmen. Then there was Calvin, who was extremely shy and withdrawn. As he introduced himself, he kept his head down and was barely audible when he uttered his name. I think everyone wondered why Calvin had signed up for an expensive communication course when it appeared he had no desire to be there. We soon learned he was a delivery driver for a local bakery. His CEO was taking the class and decided to include his socially challenged employee. During the twelve-week course, a remarkable change came over Calvin. Our facilitator was incredible at seeing hidden strengths and offering encouraging, confidence-building words. By the end of the course, Calvin was looking people in the eye and giving superb speeches. The change we saw in him was amazing.

During Calvin's last speech, he shared a personal experience from his time in elementary school. He was given the lead role in the school play. He was excited but a little cocky about it. His proud mom had him recite his lines to everyone who visited their home. Calvin was confident on the way to the play with his mother and younger cousin. His repeated his lines one last time before arriving at the school. As he finished, his cousin said something that changed the course of his life for nearly forty years. He said, "Yeah, you think you're so smart, but you're gonna get up there and forget everything." Those few words put doubts in Calvin's mind. On stage he panicked, couldn't remember his lines, and ran off the stage humiliated. He withdrew socially from that point forward.

Calvin's experience isn't really all that unusual. At some point in life, everyone will be the target of words that hurt. A well-known aphorism attributed to Eleanor Roosevelt says, "No one can make you feel inferior without your consent." While the statement is true, it is hard to think positively when negative comments and criticism come our way.

Diane is a friend who owns a successful travel business. Her tours include well-known speakers she calls headliners, who make presentations to those who travel with her. In the early years of the business, she asked travelers to fill out evaluations after their travel experiences. The evaluations were overwhelmingly positive. At the beginning of each tour Diane offered instructions and introductory remarks to her group. After one trip, she read an evaluation from a traveler who said, "I didn't come on this cruise to hear *you* talk. I came to hear the headliner speak!" Because of that one rude comment, Diane quit doing evaluations. It damaged her self-confidence and made her more sensitive to criticism. The sad part is that she missed out on all the positive comments and helpful feedback she would have received from the evaluations.

I asked another friend, named Bill, whether he had anyone ever say things to him that were insensitive or mocking. I didn't think a six-foot-ten former Division 1 basketball player would receive anything but encouragement and praise. He told me he was always tall for his age and got comments about it constantly. Throughout his school years, classmates said things like "How's the weather up there?", "Hey, Daddy Long Legs!", "Are those strings hanging out of your shorts, or are those your legs?", or "Are those your legs, or are you riding a chicken?" He even got emotional several times as he recalled people's insensitive remarks. Toward the end of our conversation, he said the negative comments have never stopped. He was in a supermarket a few weeks earlier when a total stranger came up to him and said, "You are the skinniest person I have ever seen in my life. You need to see a doctor—something is wrong with you!"

Words can have lasting effects. They can color feelings and responses beyond the moment. Bill's comments reminded me of the time when our son Nathan learned he needed glasses. Being on the high school basketball team, he didn't think wearing glasses was the cool thing to do. I assured him that plenty of people wore glasses and that no one would say a word. The day we picked up his glasses, we made a stop at Sam's Club, located about three minutes from the vision center. We had no sooner walked in the store when a little boy pointed at Nathan and said, "Hey, Mom, look at that boy with four eyes." That wasn't really what I was hoping for. As we left the store, the same little boy was behind us. I again heard him say, "Hey, Mom, there's Four Eyes." Those words didn't help my son's confidence. But putting things into perspective, we should not let comments from a four-year-old or an insensitive adult damage our self-esteem!

Put Things into Perspective

Agra, India, is home to the magnificent Taj Mahal, standing at 34,596 square feet and completed in 1653. Named one of the New Seven Wonders of the World by more than one hundred million votes according to the New 7 Wonders Foundation, it attracts seven to eight million visitors a year.[194] On Tripadvisor, 26,944 reviewers rated it five stars (excellent) using phrases such as "the most beautiful place I have ever seen" and "we were astonished to see its beauty." On the other end, 142 reviewers rated it 1 star (terrible) using phrases like, "what a terrible letdown" and "worst wonder of the world ever."[195]

While everyone has the right to his or her own opinion, does the building become less beautiful because of the negative comments made about it? Unfortunately, some people say negative and even cruel things, which often have no basis in truth, about others. In Lehi's dream, people in the large and spacious building "were in the attitude of mocking and pointing their fingers towards those who had come at and were partaking of the fruit" (1 Nephi 8:27). Suzy Kassem perhaps put things in perspective when she said, "A lion does not flinch at laughter coming from a hyena."[196]

There will always be people with positive or negative opinions about travel destinations, movies, restaurants, books, and other people. Do you change your mind if you really enjoy a movie or restaurant just because some critics hate it? What if you love the beach and your friends hate it? Are you okay letting them have a different view than yours? What if you really feel good about yourself, but someone else doesn't seem to care for you? Will you let his or her opinion damage your self-esteem? The great African American social reformer, orator, and writer Frederick Douglass said, "I prefer to be true to myself, even at the hazard of incurring the ridicule of others, rather than to be false, and to incur my own abhorrence."[197]

Douglass chose not to let others determine how he felt about himself. We should do the same. My friend Vaughn once scolded his four-year-old nephew for something he had done. The little boy said, "Uncle Vaughn, me just does the best me can." In other words, the little boy didn't let his uncle's critical words affect him.

There are times when all of us need to be corrected. When that occurs, we don't need to lose our confidence or hold lifelong resentment toward the person who pointed out our indiscretions. It seems strange that when someone shows us how to use PowerPoint more effectively or hold a tennis racket correctly, we are usually grateful. However, if someone tells us we need to clean up our language or lose a few pounds, we often become defensive, and resentment overtakes us. Someone once advised, "If someone criticizes you, their words are either true or false. If they're true, you need to change. If they're false, then don't worry about it."

Use Tact

The need to correct may arise out of duty or love. What is said and how it is said makes all the difference for the recipient. Tact is always necessary when dealing with others. What is tact? Isaac Newton said, "Tact is the art of making a point without making an enemy."[198] Stephanie, a longtime friend, shared how she was corrected tactfully and the impact it had on her:

Several years ago, I was a member of a book group. We happened to all be ladies of varying backgrounds and circumstances and enjoyed each other's company very much. We rarely discussed the book we were assigned but tended to veer the conversation toward more domestic issues of kids, husbands, and hobbies. One night, as I attended a meeting at one of the homes, I was content to listen to the passionate concerns of our host regarding some political issues. The meeting, however, quickly changed into a political party gala, complete with pamphlets, video watching, commitment seeking, and goal setting. I was extremely uncomfortable. I disagreed with the host on some of the issues, and I was disappointed not to have our regular girls' night out. I felt the host abused the fact that we were there for one purpose (book group) and changed it for her own desires.

The following week I was visiting another friend for lunch. While together, I began to share my grievances about the last book group meeting and how disappointed I was that our friend had made that choice. I was upset and wanted company in my misery. My friend stopped me in the middle of my rant, however, and said, "The thing is, Jessica is my friend too." And that was it. I stopped my rant. We continued happily with our lunch. In eight words, my friend showed me that I was allowing my hurt to cloud my better judgment, and I was gossiping. I was embarrassed at my behavior and am grateful for a friend who was courageous enough to stop me.

Stephanie realized she needed to be corrected and was grateful for a true friend willing to help her out. Not only was she not offended by her friend's comments, but she also appreciated the way her friend handled the situation and the tact she used. Elder Marvin J. Ashton said, "A true friend is one who not only is willing to love us the way we are, but is able to leave us better than he found us."[199]

In a graduate level sociology class ,we discussed a small research study involving restaurant servers. According to our professor, the researchers interviewed servers who had made mistakes like dropping food or drink items on the job. Almost all the servers who made the mistakes felt embarrassed or stressed out about what happened. Supposedly the servers were then asked several questions about how their supervisors responded to their mistakes. Not surprisingly, those who had empathetic supervisors who used kind, reassuring words about the servers' mistakes were usually loved. The professor said that the supervisors who showed little or no empathy to the server or used harsh words or irritated looks when dealing with the situation were usually disliked. The lesson is clear not just for supervisors in restaurants but for everyone. When you take away feelings of stress and pressure by using kindness and empathy, you will often draw people closer, and they will likely have positive feelings about you. When people already feel pressure and you add even more with unkind words, judgmental looks, or negative reactions, they will likely resent you.

Elder L. Lionel Kendrick pointed out that it is not just the words we say but how we say them that is important. He said, "Our communications reflect in our countenance. Therefore, we must be careful not only *what* we communicate, but also *how* we do so. Souls can be strengthened or shattered by the message and the manner in which we communicate."[200]

Encourage Others with Your Words

Encouraging words require no more time or effort than disparaging ones, yet they have the potential to change someone's life for good in dramatic ways. Encouragement brings out the best in people while criticism often brings out the worst. It is imperative that we watch our words! Elder Neal A. Maxwell taught, "We can add to each other's storehouse of self-esteem by giving deserved, specific commendation more often, remembering, too, that those who are breathless from going the second mile need deserved praise just as the fallen need to be lifted up."[201]

When we truly care about others, it means we believe in them and encourage them to be the best they can be. When we seek to bring out the best in others, we tend to also bring out the best in ourselves. James Matthew Barrie, the Scottish writer who created Peter Pan, said, "Those who bring sunshine to the lives of others cannot keep it from themselves."202

I love the classic story used in many business schools called "Sweeney's Miracle." In 1965 Dr. James Sweeney was a professor responsible for the Biomedical Computer Center at Tulane University. He believed that anyone, regardless of their educational background, could be taught to be a competent computer operator. To prove his point Sweeney began training George Johnson, who was a janitor at the facility. Johnson would clean during the morning hours and in the afternoon would learn computer skills.

Even though Johnson was making progress, a university administrator decided the experiment needed to stop. It was suggested that a person needed a certain IQ to be able to operate a computer. Sweeney was so certain that Johnson could learn that he threatened to quit if Johnson could not continue. The experiment continued, and Johnson not only learned to operate a computer, but he was also able to train others to use the computers.[203]

Those in any leadership position, whether in the home, school, or workplace can learn valuable lessons from this study. Parents, teachers, or leaders who have high expectations and kind, encouraging words can bring out the best in their children, students, or employees. They are also far more likely to have people who are engaged and unified.

In the business world, "a Gallup study of 7,272 US adults revealed that one in two had left jobs to get away from their manager and thus improve their overall life at some point in their career. Having a bad manager is often a one-two punch. Employees feel miserable while at work, and that misery follows them home, compounding their stress and negatively affecting their overall well-being."[204]

Gallup researchers also found that, "the best managers make a concerted effort to get to know their employees and help them feel comfortable talking about any subject, whether it is work related or not. A productive workplace is one in which people feel safe—safe enough to experiment, to challenge, to share information and to support one another. In this type of workplace, team members are prepared to give the manager and their organization the benefit of the doubt. But none of this can happen if employees do not feel cared about."[205]

An essential aspect of feeling cared for comes from small and large acts and words of kindness. Financial magazine founder B. C. Forbes said, "I've never known any human being, high or humble, whoever regretted, when nearing life's end, having done kindly deeds. But I have known more than one millionaire who became haunted by the realization that they had led selfish lives."[206]

Acclaimed author Og Mandino gave a challenge that can help in our endeavors to treat people with kindness. He said, "Beginning today, treat everyone you meet as if they were going to be dead by midnight. Extend to them all the care, kindness, and understanding you can muster, and do it with no thought of any reward. Your life will never be the same again."[207]

Listen with Love

The power of words comes not only from speaking them but also from listening to them. Philip Stanhope, Fourth Earl of Chesterfield, made an impactful statement when he said, "I would rather be in company with a dead man, than with an absent one; for if the dead man affords me no pleasure at least he shows me no contempt; whereas the absent man very plainly, though silently, tells me that he does not think me worth his attention."[208]

Randal: After reading this statement I made a conscious effort to be a better listener. A few days after making the goal I saw Sarah, who was a university student at the time. She was often in the building where I worked. Even though I had known her for a couple of years, I had never had a real conversation with her. She seemed shy, and I could tell we had different interests. That day as she passed my office, I called out a question to her. She stopped and gave me her typical two-word answer. As she started to walk off, I asked her another question, but this time it was open ended and could not be answered in two words. She stood by my office door. I was determined to give her my full attention. I found out Sarah was a reader and loved fantasy novels. Even though I had never read one myself, I let her talk and just listened. When I asked what she was currently reading, I learned the book was about a man who morphed into a coyote. Even though the books she loved did not interest me in the least, I was interested in listening to Sarah. American psychiatrist Karl A. Menninger once said, "I just tell myself to listen with affection to anyone who talks to me, to be in their shoes when they talk, to try to know them without my mind pressing against theirs, or arguing, or changing the subject. My attitude is: 'Tell me more.' This person is showing me his soul. It is a little dry and meager and full of grinding talk just now, but presently he will begin to think, not just automatically to talk. He will show his true self. Then he will be wonderfully alive."[209]

The more I listened to Sarah that day the more she became wonderfully alive. At one point, she asked me if I had ever read *The Hobbit* or *The Lord of the Rings*. I confessed that I had not and didn't think anything else about it. A few days later I found a brand-new copy of *The Hobbit* on my desk. She bought it for me as a gift. Of course, I had no choice but to read it and, to my surprise, found it fascinating. Later Sarah came by and sat in my office to discuss the book and to give me a crash course on *The Lord of the Rings*. Because I listened to her and spoke encouraging words, we became friends.

Everyone, regardless of age, wants and needs encouragement and a listening ear. When effective communication happens between people, they develop strong bonds and friendships. Those who receive encouragement and listening often excel and have a more positive view of themselves. Elder William R. Bradford stated, "Within each of us there is an intense need to feel that we belong. This feeling of unity and togetherness comes through the warmth of a smile, a handshake, or a hug, through laughter and unspoken demonstrations of love. It comes in the quiet, reverent moments of soft conversation and in listening."[210]

Invitation to Act

1. Use positive, uplifting words to build up those around you every day.
2. If someone points out a weakness they see in you and it is true, don't be offended. Work to change.
3. When put in a position where you need to correct someone, be careful and do it with kindness and tact.
4. Ask people open-ended questions, and listen intently to them when they talk.
5. Treat everyone as if he or she will be dead by midnight.

CHAPTER 11

Building Relationships of Trust

All of us need true friends to love us, to listen to us, to show us the way, and to testify of truth to us so that we may retain the companionship of the Holy Ghost. You must be such a true friend.[211]

President Henry B. Eyring

Paula Jones

When I was twelve years old, I had the opportunity to attend a girls' summer camp for the first time. I was excited to finally meet the age requirement and looked forward to this adventure with great anticipation. However, it only took a short amount of time after my arrival there to realize things were not going to be the way I had imagined.

I was the only girl from my small town, and it seemed that everyone else already had her own group of friends before arriving. I was lonely and homesick, and all I wanted to do was go home.

When I was finally able to call home the first night, I explained my plight to my mother and asked her to please come pick me up. My mom is one of the most understanding people I know, so I knew she would come to my rescue. However, her response was not what I expected or what I wanted to hear. She told me that she wouldn't come get me but that she would share with me how I could have a good experience and be happy at camp. She said she wanted me to look around everywhere I went for the girls who looked lonely or homesick and reach out to them and try to help them have a good time.

My mother's response disappointed me, but I knew I wasn't going home, so I decided to give it a try. For the next five days, whether it was during the craft activity, the hula dance class, or canoeing on the lake, I looked around to see the girls who needed a friend. As the days passed, I made many new friends and had one of the best weeks of my life. At the end of the camp, an award was presented like the Miss Congeniality Award. In the past, it had always gone to one of the older girls who would not be returning to camp the next year, but that year I received it as a first-year camper.

My experience at camp that first year has helped me for the past forty years to be mindful of those around me who might need my kindness. This has brought my life immeasurable joy and happiness. I know it must have hurt my mother's heart to tell me I couldn't come home. But I'm so glad she did the right thing instead of the easy thing. Her advice has made all the difference in my life!

Warm Relationships

Paula's mother gave her a simple challenge that has brought her much joy and happiness through the years. This advice to reach out to those who look lonely, homesick, or sad and help them have a good time is a great way to build relationships. However, it is not just those who are lonely whom we need to befriend. Everyone struggles in some way; we should try to reach out daily to make new friends. President Nelson said, "Each day of your life, strive to enlarge your own circle of friendship."[212]

For some, just the thought of seeking out new friends may seem daunting. However, since the practice brings joy and happiness, it is well worth the effort required. Reaching out to others and building relationships bring multiple benefits. In 1938, Harvard University began a longitudinal study that continues today to discover what leads to health and happiness. The study, directed by Robert J. Waldinger, professor of psychiatry at Harvard Medical School, determined that neither money, fame, social class, IQ, nor heredity led to happiness; rather, close relations with other people bring happiness. The study indicates loneliness can be as damaging to a person's health as smoking or alcoholism. Waldinger said, "Those who kept warm relationships got to live longer and happier."[213]

Another study examining the impact of social relations on health and longevity found across 148 studies (308,849 participants) "a 50% increased likelihood of survival for participants with stronger social relationships.

This finding remained consistent across age, sex, initial health status, cause of death, and follow-up period."[214]

In summary, the effort it takes to build strong personal relationships will likely lead to an increase in happiness, good health, and longevity. Perhaps this is one of the reasons our prophets and apostles are so happy and healthy and live to such advanced ages with unusual quality of life.

Randal: My wife's grandmother Thelma Freeman was an example of someone who developed strong personal relationships with other people. Although she was not in the Harvard study, her life experience certainly confirms what their researchers are finding. A retired schoolteacher, she was always happy and had a positive attitude even though she remained a widow for thirty-seven years. She spent the last few years of her life in an assisted living facility in Billings, Montana. She passed away at age ninety. The last time we visited her, I scanned her visitor's register while my wife and her grandmother reminisced. I was surprised not only by the number of different visitors who had signed in but also by the frequency of the visits. Out of curiosity I went back eight months and counted 1,041 visits from family, friends, and former students, an average of 4.3 visitors a day. She also had stacks of notes and cards in her room from multiple people.

I shared this experience with a group of college students. I asked them to name characteristics Thelma had that would lead to her having close relationships with so many. At first, they seemed confused since no one in the room had any idea who she was. After a short period of silence, hands started to go up, and they began to tell me about Thelma. They said she

- "always acted excited to see visitors,"
- "made people feel special when they were with her,"
- "accepted others the way they were and was nonjudgmental,"
- "listened carefully to what others had to say,"
- "was generous and always willing to help people,"
- "stayed in touch with her friends,"
- "was cheerful and had a good sense of humor," and
- "pointed out people's potential and encouraged them."

At first I was surprised at how accurately they described her even though they'd never met. After thinking about it, I realized they were just describing characteristics of anyone with a lot of close personal relationships. I have wondered how many would visit me in a similar situation. I can't imagine accumulating the list of visitors Thelma had. How many personal visits, cards, emails, and phone calls do you think you would receive in an eight-month period? Are you satisfied that you have enough close friends?

It may help to assume that every person you cross paths with needs a listening ear and encouraging words. While everyone may not respond to your outreach, many will. If you will do your part to reach out, you will certainly deserve a Miss or Mr. Congeniality Award. This is what Paula did at girls' camp and continues to do today. This is what Thelma did.

Reaching out with kindness to others could be a turning point for those you meet. Dorothy Woodhouse, who is our adopted granddaughter, grew up in a single parent home. The summer before her senior year, her mother was killed in a car accident. Later Dorothy served a mission in the England Leeds Mission. When she had been serving for about three months, she was feeling lonely and discouraged. People she attempted to befriend or even communicate with on the street or while knocking doors were uninterested and even rude. She decided she had had enough and was going to leave her mission. Walking back to their apartment, her companion could sense her frustration. Just then a man from the local Methodist church came up to them and said, "I just want to thank you for what you are doing. We need more people like you." He then handed them bottles of water. Dorothy got emotional as he walked away and felt like he had been sent to her at a critical time. In the apartment that day she knelt and asked for forgiveness and made a commitment to stay on her mission. She completed a successful mission, married in the temple, has three young children, and now enjoys befriending and encouraging the young women in her ward.

Seeking to enlarge our friendships may result in a good impression on others. It could be a one-time encounter like the man in Dorothy's experience, but it still can have a lasting influence for good in a person's life. In other cases, reaching out to others could be the beginning of a lifelong friendship. English writer Samuel Johnson said, "If a man does not make new acquaintance as he advances through life, he will soon find himself left alone. A man should . . . keep his friendship in constant repair."[215]

Suggestions to Help Form Meaningful Personal Relationships

Reach Out to New People

President Nelson gave a challenge to members of the Church that could have tremendous benefits if we embrace it. He said, "Reach out to those you do not know and greet them warmly. Each Sunday extend a hand of fellowship to at least one person you did not know before."[216] How do you think we as a people are doing following his inspired counsel? In the past week, how many people have come up to you and introduced themselves, asked your name, and acted like they wanted to get to know you? How about in the last month or year? How many times have you reached out and met someone new?

While there are exceptions, perhaps as a society we are not as friendly as we could be. The Prophet Joseph Smith taught members of the Church that, "Friendship is one of the grand fundamental principles of 'Mormonism'; [it is designed] to revolutionize and civilize the world, and cause wars and contentions to cease and men to become friends and brothers."[217]

Remember People's Names

How does it make you feel when people warmly greet you and call you by name? While it may not seem a big deal to call people by their given names, it is an important component in building relationships that last. Dale Carnegie said, "A person's name is to him or her the sweetest and most important sound in any language."[218] My friend Jim Nielsen put this statement to the test and found evidence to support it. His family moved to a new area at the beginning of his junior year, and he didn't know one person on the first day of his new school.

Jim decided to ask the office receptionist if there were any yearbooks for sale from the previous year. There were. He bought one and began looking at the pictures, memorizing a few names each night. During the next few days as Jim recognized someone in the hallway, he smiled and called them by name. He hoped to eventually learn the names of everyone in his new school. No one ever asked how he knew the students' names or what his name was. However, within a short time, students whose name he called out began to greet him by name. At the end of that school year, the new kid was named the student body president.

Love Them First

Someone has said, "If you don't like someone you can bet the feeling is mutual." While that may not always apply, there is probably some truth to this statement. On the other side of the coin, a New Testament verse explains why Jesus Christ was so dearly loved by His disciples. In 1 John 4:19 we read, "We love him, because he first loved us." That, of course, is what Paula Jones realized at girls' camp.

Tom McMullin, a friend and coworker, shared an experience he had with his daughter Kellie. She had been begging for a kitten for some time, so he finally gave in and took her to pick one out at the local animal shelter. There were several kittens available, and Kellie picked the one she thought was the cutest. However, when she tried to hold the kitten, it pulled away from her. She gave up and picked out another one. This one stiffened its legs, arched its back, and hissed at her when she tried to hold it. At this point, another kitten Kellie had not noticed began rubbing against her leg and purring. Which kitten do you think Kellie took home that day? Are people any different?

When you reach out to people and love them first, they often respond like Kellie did to her new kitten. Friendships begin by offering kindness and love, which are often reciprocated. Writer and political commentator Ben Stein said, "Personal relationships are the fertile soil from which all advancement, all success, all achievement in real life grows."[219]

Randal: Years ago, I was scheduled to speak to a group of about four hundred teenagers at BYU Campus Education Week. As I entered the building where the event was held, Brad Wilcox came out. He came directly to me, introduced himself, then gave me a big hug and wished me luck. Perhaps a casual observer watching the scene from a distance would have thought we had been friends for years. Few would guess it was the first time I had ever met him. I liked Brad immediately because he acted as if he liked me. It is called the reciprocity principle. Caring for someone dramatically increases the chance that person will care about you.

I first met Brad Wilcox the first year I taught at Education Week. He greeted me with a hug and acted as if he was glad to see me even though I had never met him before. I found out that he was a young elementary school teacher at that time. The following year, we were together at an Especially for Youth conference. He not only acted like we were best friends but also treated everyone he met as if they were his best friends. I found that he has a unique gift of making others feel loved. He is now a university professor, professional speaker, and best-selling author who is loved by thousands, with friends around the world. Author Frederick L. Collins explained, "There are two types of people—those who come into a room and say, 'Well, here I am!' and those who come in and say, 'Ah, there you are.'"[220] Brad perfectly fits the description of the second person. Mother Teresa pointed out, "There is more hunger for love and appreciation in this world than for bread."[221]

Act Excited to See Them

Ichi-go ichi-e is a Japanese idiom and cultural concept often translated as "having one chance in a lifetime" or "never again."[222] It refers to cherishing the time you have with others, because there may never be another opportunity to be with that person again. With that thought in mind it is important that we make the most of our time together. One way to do this is to act excited when you see people.

Joseph and Hyrum Smith were great examples of people who lived this principle. According to their close friend William Taylor, who saw them together on many occasions, they always treated each other as if it was a one-time encounter. He said this about their relationship: "Never in all my life have I seen anything more beautiful than the striking example of brotherly love and devotion felt for each other by Joseph and Hyrum. I witnessed this many times. No matter how often, or when or where they met, it was always with the same expression of supreme joy."[223]

Listen to Their Story

One of the secrets to developing lasting friendships is being interested in what others say by intently listening. Wilson Mizner taught, "A good listener is not only popular everywhere, but after a while he gets to know something."[224] A friend named Ed is a successful sales professional with many friends. When he meets someone new he always says, "Tell me your story." He then listens closely to what he or she says. He follows the counsel Dale Carnegie gave when he said, "You can make more friends in two months by becoming interested in other people than you can in two years by trying to get other people interested in you."[225] Can you imagine how different the world would be if we all knew each other's story?

Everyone—whether a child, teen, or adult—wants to be heard. One of the greatest gifts we can give another person is our full attention, with our eyes fixed on them and our body language showing our interest. By paying close attention to others, we will be able to recall details that will let them know we really care about them in future conversations. Henry David Thoreau shared, "The greatest compliment that was ever paid me was when one asked me what I thought, and attended to my answer."[226]

Be Tolerant and Nonjudgmental

Without knowing others' stories, we can easily misjudge them. For the most part, we have no idea what the people we encounter are going through or what trials they've experienced. Once, a teenage girl named Liza stood at the pulpit to give a sacrament meeting talk. Looking up at her, I was shocked to see she had cut her long hair into a buzz cut. I was saddened to see she was following some of the popular female singers of the day and wondered why she would want to do so. I leaned over and asked one of my daughters why Liza had cut her hair. My daughter responded, "She didn't. While she was asleep, her little brother with special needs took scissors and cut her hair down to the scalp in multiple places. She had no choice but to cut it all off." In many cases, we have no idea the real story behind what we are looking at.

If we want to build strong relationships, it is important to leave gossip and judging others out of the mix. People often realize that if someone speaks ill of others to them, that person will probably speak ill of them to others. Benjamin Franklin had many relationships with others and was influential with his associates. He shared this advice that may be related to his secret of success. He wrote, "I will speak ill of no man and speak all the good I know of everybody."[227] When you are tempted to say something negative about another person, stop and find something positive to say.

In life, we interact with people who have views different from our own. The best policy is to be kind to everyone, including those with whom we totally disagree. Abraham Lincoln once said, "I don't like that man. I must get to know him better."[228] Everyone has faults, and everyone has strengths. If we emphasize the positive and overlook the negative, it will go a long way toward building lasting relationships.

Be Supportive and Encouraging

In the movie *My Fair Lady*, Professor Higgins declared he could transform a flower girl named Eliza Doolittle into a refined lady. He worked with her over time and finally succeeded in his goal. At one point Eliza said, "The difference between a lady and a flower girl is not how she behaves, but how she is treated."[229]

During a class I attended, we were discussing the importance of being encouraging and supportive. A sister named Joy shared a personal experience that illustrated this principle. She was about to leave the Missionary Training Center in Provo for the airport to fly to her assigned mission. Although excited about this forward progress, she was anxious about being at the airport among only a few missionaries with no one to support her. Joy understood that her parents, who were in Houston, Texas, couldn't be there because of their responsibilities to their eight other children.

Upon arrival at the airport, Joy noticed multiple families in the terminal offering their goodbyes to their missionaries. She tried to not let it affect her. Then she looked up and began to cry as she saw her parents. When she asked them what they were doing there, her mother said she was reading a talk to the mothers of the Church by President Benson and decided they needed to come. During the talk he counseled mothers to "take time to always be at the crossroads when your children are either coming or going."[230]

George Burton Adams wrote, "Note how good you feel after you have encouraged someone else. No other argument is necessary to suggest that never miss the opportunity to give encouragement."[231] Don't you feel close to those who support you? Showing support and encouragement to others will increase the chance of developing a new friendship and deepening existing ones.

Lyman O. Littlefield was fourteen years old when he participated in the expedition led by Joseph Smith from Kirtland, Ohio, to Clay County, Missouri, called Zion's Camp. Consider the impact the Prophet Joseph Smith's encouraging words had on Lyman. He shared this experience, demonstrating the power of encouragement:

> While there the men were paraded outside of the camp for exercise and instruction. This was an unpleasant feature for me, as I was too young

> and too small of stature to act with the men. This created within me, as I remember, some lonesome reflections. I sat down upon a rock where the men were passing, the better to observe their movements. While thus seated, the Prophet Joseph Smith, who happened to be passing by in quite a hurry, noticed me. He stepped to where I sat alone. It might have been my isolated position that attracted him. I knew not the motive; but that man, who to me appeared so good and so godlike, really halted in his hurry to notice me—only a little boy. Placing one of his hands upon my head, he said: "Well, bub, is there no place for you?"
>
> This recognition from the man whom I then knew was a Prophet of God created within me a tumult of emotions. I could make him no reply. My young heart was filled with joy to me unspeakable.[232]

Love Those You Serve

Many have pointed out that we love those we serve. Speaking after returning from his mission to Puerto Rico, our nephew Jared shared an experience he had with one of the poorer families he worked with. One day he learned that the family's house had burned down, and they had lost everything. Jared and his companion decided to stop by the home where the family was staying. While talking to the father and mother, he said he saw the couple's eight-year-old boy by the mission car. The young man had filled a bucket with water and was washing their car with his shirt. Jared became emotional telling about this experience and how much he loved the family and the little boy. When they went outside to leave, they told the boy what a fine job he had done. Then my nephew pulled out some money to pay the boy. He knew the family desperately needed it.

The boy said in Spanish, "No, no!"

Jared told him he deserved the money and wanted him to take it.

The little boy said, "Please, no. From the heart."

Service makes both the giver and the receiver happy and builds strong relationships between the two. President Monson said, "Often small acts of service are all that is required to lift and bless another: a question concerning a person's family, quick words of encouragement, a sincere compliment, a small note of thanks, a brief telephone call. If we are observant and aware, and if we act on the promptings which come to us, we can accomplish much good."[233]

Sometimes a friend will need much more than just a quick word of encouragement. When you see that a friend needs help, don't ask if there is anything you can do for them. Think of a way to help them out and do it.

I doubt that those nearing the end of their lives wish they would have spent more time at work. Likewise, being the richest person in the cemetery is probably not something many would aspire to as death nears. Deep personal relationships with others bring true happiness.

Anything, Any Time

Scott: A few years ago I had the opportunity to attend Camp Joy with my daughter Kira in Ohio. It was an incredible experience for me as a dad. Kira was eleven at the time and full of joy herself. She is that kind of kid—pleasing, fun, smart, happy, kind, sensitive, and selfless. Her love of family is unmatched.

The camp had several exercises that had me on the edge of my seat, anxious and in tears on several occasions. One was called the Last Walk. The assignment was to spend an hour talking to your daughter as if it were for the last time. What was I going to say? What wisdom could I impart? I was stuck, stunned, and a bit nauseated. Then I thought about my brother-in-law, his two sons, and the fact that he really did have to have this conversation. So I did it. Kira had this beaming smile through the entire walk—it was one of pride, connection, love, understanding and real meaning. She told me she loved me and hugged me when I got choked up—as I am now recounting this time.

It was a moment I will never forget. I am appreciative of her, her light, her listening ears, her special hugs, and the way she sees the world. I couldn't help but wonder as we headed home who this weekend was really for.

Kira: The exercise we did the last night at camp will stick with me for the rest of my life. We were all summoned to the upper cabin. A camp counselor took me and the other girls outside to play a game while the dads were filled in on the activity. When my dad came out of the cabin, his usual smile was gone, and it appeared that he may have been crying. He told me that we were going on a walk, and he was to pretend it was the last time he would ever see me. We were to talk about things that really mattered. He explained that sometimes life is moving so fast, we don't get to have the conversations we should have, and this was a chance to really talk.

"So, Kira," Dad said, "I am going to talk to you about things I want you to always remember."

He started by saying, "There are three things I don't want you to ever forget." I laughed to myself, because it seems like every time my dad gives advice, he gives you a list.

First, family, family, family! Family is something that has always been and will always be a huge part of our lives. We do everything together and have come together through moves, changes, challenges, years, friends, and everything else. Our family will be together forever. We will be there when life is good and when it is bad. We are the roots of the tree, and love is unconditional. We will be the first to celebrate your successes and cheer for you and the first to pick you up when you fall or make a bad decision. This family will be here for you no matter what.

Second, everything will be okay! Things will go wrong, bad, or sideways, and you will think it is the worst thing in the world. But it will always be okay. It will get better. It is just a blip in the moment. Recognize what it is, and know that it will get better or go away. You will always be okay and get through it. Learn to get better, decide what needs to change, and reach out to those of us who can help. There is always hope, no matter the situation.

Third, anything, any time! One of our favorite songs to jam out to in the car is "One Call Away." This song reminds me of my dad, because if I am nervous, sad, or even happy about something, he tells me he is always just one call away. Every day, he sends me a text, voice mail, or email telling me what I can reach for and accomplish during that day.

These three simple phrases have changed the way I see the world and have shaped me to be more like my amazing dad. I know he will be there for me for anything, any time. I find comfort in that. I told him I am here for him too. My dad has always been an incredible enforcer, builder, and lover of family. He shows us with his daily hugs and kisses, his hard work for us, and his nonstop happiness. Yes, everything will be okay with a good family.

Invitations to Act

1. Take the initiative to meet at least one new person every week.

2. Remember the names of the people you meet and warmly greet them, calling them by name each time you see them.
3. Keep friendships alive by reaching out to at least one person every day through a text, email, phone call, or visit.
4. Every week express appreciation or encouragement to those who speak, teach, or share their talents in church.
5. Make "anything, any time" a motto to build relationships with others.

CHAPTER 12

Follow the Voice of the Spirit

The voice of the Spirit comes as a feeling rather than a sound. You will learn, as I have learned, to "listen" for that voice that is felt rather than heard. . . . It is a spiritual voice that comes into the mind as a thought or a feeling put into your heart.[234]

President Boyd K. Packer

Tara Collins

One day I raced through Costco at breakneck speed to finish grocery shopping before my kids returned home from school. I picked the shortest checkout line and frantically unloaded the oversized packages of food onto the conveyor belt. When the belt was reaching capacity, I stopped unloading and noticed the cashier wasn't matching my pace. She stood in aggravated silence as she watched the customer in front of me fumble through her purse.

"Great," I thought. "I never fail to pick the wrong line, especially when I'm late." I folded my arms, let out a slight exasperated sigh, and, if that wasn't enough, rolled my eyes to the customers behind me. We were bonded in our annoyance. As the time ticked by, it was obvious the customer couldn't pay her bill.

"I told you we don't accept that credit card. You will have to pay with cash or with a debit card," the cashier barked as she hardly attempted to hide her irritation. The woman appeared as disheveled as the contents in her purse. She blew strands of unruly bangs repeatedly out of her eyes and tucked other pieces of hair nervously behind her ears. One by one she pulled out old receipts, gum wrappers, coins, crackers, and worn papers—all useless to her as she searched for a way to pay.

"Pay for her groceries," a startling voice said in my head. The positive feeling only lasted a few seconds before I thought, "Oh, sure." Now that I'd made it a point to display my irritation with this woman to everyone around me, how could I step forward to pay for her groceries? I froze. Then I nonchalantly stepped to the side just far enough to see the total bill on the computer screen—thirty-seven dollars. I could handle that, but I just couldn't figure out a way to gracefully execute the transaction. "Pay for her groceries!" When the words came again, my heart started to race. I knew what I needed to do, but I just stood there and stopped myself from doing it. After a thorough self-reprimand and a third prompting to pay for her groceries, I stepped forward and opened my mouth, only to be stopped short by the cashier's exaggerated click of the register and push of the woman's grocery cart to the side. The cashier suspended her transaction and invited her to return for her groceries later if she brought the correct form of payment. I still had a chance to help, but now I was too embarrassed to think of holding up the line for the cashier to input the transaction she had just suspended.

Flushed from embarrassment, the customer turned and slowly walked toward the door. I took my place at the checkout and told the cashier I was in a hurry. I was in no mood for her comments as she tried to engage me in dialogue about ignorant customers. My hurry was no longer to return home. I wanted to get to the parking lot and find that woman. I swiped my credit card and sped out the door as quickly as I could, but I was too late. She was gone. My heart ached with remorse as I loaded my car. I climbed inside and started to sob. I had deliberately ignored the opportunity.

I promised at that moment to never ignore a prompting again, no matter how inconvenient or inconsequential it seemed. I have seen the embarrassed woman at Costco in my mind many times since that day. She is my reminder that when I am urged to do good, I need to act on it.

Listening to Our Inner Voice

There are many words and phrases to describe the voice that came into Tara's mind that day in Costco. Some refer to it as your conscience, defined as "the sense or consciousness of the moral goodness or blameworthiness of one's own conduct, intentions, or character together with a feeling of obligation to do right or be good."[235] Others use words like *intuition, instinct, inner teacher*, or *guide*. In the Book of Mormon, the prophet Mormon described the voice: "For behold, the Spirit of Christ is given to every man, that he may know good from evil" (Moroni 7:16).

A former First Presidency of the Church explained the Light of Christ: "There is a universally diffused essence which is the light and the life of the world, 'which lighteth every man that cometh into the world,' which proceedeth forth from the presence of God throughout the immensity of space, the light and power of which God bestows in different degrees to 'them that ask him,' according to their faith and obedience."[236]

No matter what this inner voice is called, it is available to all mankind regardless of race, religion, or country of origin. It is within everyone. The Light of Christ should not be confused with the Holy Ghost or the gift of the Holy Ghost. In this chapter, we will call the whisperings that help all mankind know good from evil the voice of the Spirit or the inner voice.

American physician and researcher Dean Ornish explained, "We all have an inner teacher, an inner guide, an inner voice that speaks very clearly but usually not very loudly. That information can be drowned out by the chatter of the mind and the pressure of day-to-day events. But if we quiet down the mind, we can begin to hear what we're not paying attention to. We can find out what's right for us."[237]

Two voices influence all mankind. One invites and entices a person to sin (Moroni 7:12), and the other invites and entices a person to do good (Moroni 7:13). Unfortunately, there is no caller ID to identify which voice is speaking. One of the great challenges of life is to learn to quiet the mind and recognize the voice of the Spirit. Some say you can know when the inner voice prompting you to do good is speaking because of how it makes you feel. Some have described the feelings you get as happy, warm, calm, peaceful, emotional, generous, confident, and loving. However, when the inner voice whispered to Tara three times in Costco to pay for a woman's groceries she said, "I froze," "My heart started to race," and "I was too embarrassed!" Based on her experience, it appears that the words *frightening, inconvenient*, and *uncomfortable* should be added to the list of feelings that may come when the voice of the Spirit speaks.

When the inner voice invites a person to do good, it might not always feel warm, peaceful, or comfortable. In fact, it often feels uncomfortable and causes many to either dread acting on the prompting or to outright reject the invitation because it doesn't feel good. When describing the events associated with obtaining the brass plates, Nephi said the Spirit whispered to him four times. He certainly did not appear to be at peace with what he was asked to do. He says, "And it came to pass that I was constrained by the Spirit that I should kill Laban; but I said in my heart: Never at any time have I shed the blood of man. And I shrunk and would that I might not slay him" (1 Nephi 4:10).

Some wonder how Heber C. Kimball and Brigham Young felt the day they left on their two-year mission to England. They were both ill and left their sick wives and children destitute. How did Wilford Woodruff feel the day he left on that same mission? He recorded his feelings with these words:

> Early upon the morning of the 8th of August, I arose from my bed of sickness, laid my hands upon the head of my sick wife, Phoebe, and blessed her. I then departed from the embrace of my companion, and left her almost without food or the necessaries of life. She suffered my departure with the fortitude that becomes a saint, realizing the responsibilities of her companion. . . .
>
> Although feeble, I walked to the banks of the Mississippi River. There President Young took me in a canoe . . . and paddled me across the river. When we landed, I lay down on a side of sole leather, by the postoffice, to rest. Brother Joseph, the Prophet of God, came along and looked at me. "Well, Brother Woodruff,' said he, "you have started upon your mission." "Yes," said I, "but I feel and look more like a subject for the dissecting room than a missionary." Joseph replied: "What did you say that for? Get up, and go along; all will be right with you."[238]

It doesn't appear that the terms *happy*, *warm*, *calm*, and *peaceful* would be used to describe Wilford Woodruff the day he started his mission. Yet he knew for certain that it was the voice of the Spirit that called him, so he responded despite how he felt. The scriptures are filled with great men and women who felt uncomfortable when they were prompted to act on a task they didn't want to do. How did Jonah feel when prompted to go preach in Nineveh? What about Moses, who was prompted to ask Pharaoh to let his people go? His feelings are documented with these words: "And Moses said unto God, Who am I, that I should go unto Pharaoh, and that I should bring forth the children of Israel out of Egypt?" (Exodus 3:11).

When the voice of the Spirit whispers, it is possible that it may make you feel uncomfortable. This point seems obvious if you think about it. Have you ever been asked to accept a Church calling or assignment that made you feel anxious, but you accepted it anyway? Do you feel like you grew from the experience? Was it the right thing to do? In many cases, it is not until a person accepts and acts on a prompting that feelings of joy, peace, and warmth come. Surely the early missionaries to England felt uncomfortable as they left their impoverished families. But imagine the extreme joy, warmth, and satisfaction they felt as they boarded the ship in Liverpool to return home after baptizing thousands.

There are times when we need to act on a prompting immediately or the opportunity will pass. When Tara was invited to pay the woman's bill, she failed to act because she didn't feel comfortable doing it. By the time she decided to heed the prompting, the woman was gone, and Tara missed the chance to help her. When President Monson was a bishop, he had a similar experience that many are familiar with. While sitting in a stake priesthood meeting, he felt prompted to leave the meeting immediately to give a priesthood blessing to a member of his ward who was in the hospital. However, like Tara, he felt uncomfortable leaving while his stake president was speaking and failed to act promptly as directed. Before the closing song and prayer, he rushed out of the meeting. Upon arriving at the hospital, he ran the full length of the corridor to the designated room. A nurse stopped him and asked if he was Bishop Monson. When he answered yes, the nurse told him that she was sorry and that "the patient was calling [his] name just before he passed away."[239]

Determining the Source of Promptings

There is another great danger of always associating the voice of the Spirit with feeling good. Believing that could lead to the "if it feels good, do it" philosophy, one of the biggest weapons in Satan's arsenal. Perhaps one reason people drink, smoke, vape, use drugs, gamble, view pornography, and commit immoral acts is that these vices make them feel good. Unfortunately, the good feelings are usually short lived and come at a terrible cost.

So how do we determine when a prompting is from the Lord and when it is from the adversary? The scriptures give us simple but powerful guides to help. The first answer is found in Moroni 7:13, which says, "Every thing which inviteth and enticeth to do good, and to love God, and to serve him, is inspired of God." The other is from Doctrine and Covenants 9:8, which says, "You must study it out in your mind; then you must ask me if it be right." Imagine how different the world would be if everyone used these guides in their daily life.

Countless examples teach another important principle. Just because something is good and right does not mean it will be easy to do. In fact, acting on what is right may not only be uncomfortable but also extremely difficult at times. This factor can lead many to start down the correct path only to give up when it becomes more challenging than anticipated. For example, how many have felt prompted to take better care of their bodies, so they purchased a gym membership in January, only to quit shortly thereafter? Studies show that within five months of joining a gym, 80 percent have stopped going.[240]

The four sons of Mosiah felt prompted to take the gospel message to the Lamanites. Surely there were some anxious moments as they considered the risks involved in going among their bitter enemies. Imagine the pressure they surely received from worried friends and family members concerned for their safety. But feeling it was the right thing to do, they acted. During their trip in the wilderness, things got difficult, and they became discouraged. In Alma 26:27 we read, "Now when our hearts were depressed, and we were about to turn back, behold, the Lord comforted us, and said: Go amongst thy brethren, the Lamanites, and bear with patience thine afflictions, and I will give unto you success." What a tragedy it would have been had these young men aborted their mission and returned home. Their amazing story demonstrates that sometimes an inspired assignment requires multiple trials and failures before achieving success. Moses, Nephi, Joseph Smith, and countless others have found this out.

While the voice of the Spirit may take you far outside your comfort zone, the blessings of following promptings will be worth the effort. The natural tendency is to run from anything that makes us feel uncomfortable. However, it is often doing those difficult things that helps us grow the most. Perhaps that is why Eleanor said, "You gain strength, courage, and confidence by every experience in which you really stop to look fear in the face."[241]

Understanding the Consequences of Ignoring Promptings

That day in Costco, Tara distinctly heard a voice in her mind telling her exactly what to do. Her fear of looking foolish in front of other irritated customers prevented her from acting. Realizing her mistake, she tried to correct it but was too late. What were the results of her failure? She felt the guilt that often comes when a prompting is ignored. In her words, "My heart ached with remorse as I loaded my car. I climbed inside and started to sob." English writer Mary Wortley Montagu described what Tara experienced: "While conscience is our friend, all is at peace; however, once it is offended, farewell to a tranquil mind."[242]

What would have happened if Tara ignored her racing heart and embarrassment and paid the woman's bill? While we will never know, it may be that instead of sobbing in the parking lot, she would have felt joy associated with acting on a prompting to do good. If the woman had been spared that humiliating experience, perhaps she would have felt tremendous gratitude toward Tara and been more likely to act in similar ways herself. Unfortunately, because Tara ignored that prompting to do good, both women left Costco upset instead of happy.

The good news is we can change and learn to be more in tune with the voice inviting us to do good. Tara learned a valuable lesson from her experience that has shaped who she is today. I asked her what she felt her mission in life was. She replied, "My mission is to never turn down a prompting to do good, while taking as many people with me as I can." President Monson learned the same lesson. After he failed to act immediately on a prompting, "he vowed then and there that he would never again fail to act upon a prompting from the Lord. He would acknowledge the impressions of the Spirit when they came, and he would follow wherever they led him."[243]

Growing into the Principle of Revelation

President Nelson gave wonderful advice to help us receive the revelation we so desperately need in our day. He said: "Pray in the name of Jesus Christ about your concerns, your fears, your weakness—yes, the very longings of your heart. And then listen! Write the thoughts that come to your mind. Record your feelings and follow through with actions that you are prompted to take. As you repeat this process day after day, month after month, year after year, you will 'grow into the principle of revelation.'"[244]

The counsel to pray, listen, record feelings, and act is something we can all do. In our hectic world, it is not easy to set aside a specific time to be alone with our thoughts. However, with proper planning it can be done with amazing results. Stephen R. Covey warned that "we must never become too busy sawing to take time to sharpen the saw"[245] Perhaps the best time to encourage inspiration is in the early morning hours before things get too busy. Someone once said that there has never been a revelation without a question first. During your quiet time, ask questions that are important to you. If you write down a question at the beginning of each day, ideas will begin to pop into your mind almost immediately. Don't believe me? If you have five minutes to spare, try it out. On a piece of paper or your electronic device, write down this question: "How can I be a better person?" Within a short period of time, ideas for self-improvement will come to mind. In other words, the voice of the Spirit will speak to you. Once an idea forms, write it down—even if it seems small. Keep this question in the back of your mind as you go about your day. Write down other thoughts as they come.

It also helps to keep something by your bed that will allow you to capture any promptings or ideas that come during the night. When you have a burning question written down, don't be surprised if you wake with an answer. The bottom line is if you want an answer to a question, ask first, listen closely for answers, write them down, and then act on them.

Acting on Promptings

Randal: A few years ago, I was interviewed by radio talk show host and friend Steven Kapp Perry about a book I had written dealing with learning lessons from life. Turning the tables momentarily, I asked him to share an experience that taught him a valuable lesson. Steven thought for a moment and then shared an experience that applies here.

> When I was sixteen, my friend Brad Wilcox and I enjoyed singing and were part of our high school choirs. It was 1976—the bicentennial of the United States—and Brad heard about a choir being put together made

up of high school students from all fifty states. This choir would represent the US as it toured Europe.

Brad exclaimed, "Let's try out!"

I responded, "Nah, we'd never make it."

He then said something that affected the rest of my life. "Steve, we're already not going to Europe. We've already not made it. What can we lose? We're just taking a chance that we might get to go. The worst that can happen is that our lives will be the same as they are now."

So we auditioned. Of course, I'm telling you this because we made it. We earned the money to go, and at sixteen toured the US and Europe with an incredible choir, having unforgettable experiences. So what do you want to do? Why not try for it? You're already not on the team, in the play, or whatever it is you dream of. Go for it—the worst that can happen is that your life will be just like it is right now—but you're taking a chance on something great happening!

How many times in life have we not acted on a prompting because we'd never make it? Brad pointed out to his friend Steven how illogical this reasoning is. If you don't act, you have already not made it. If you try and are rejected, you find yourself in the exact position as you were before trying with nothing lost. However, when you act, you dramatically increase your chances of getting accepted, being hired, receiving funding, becoming a best-selling author, or being part of a bicentennial choir. Even if you don't make it, you will have learned something valuable from the experience.

Seeing the Spirit as a Personal Assistant for Ideas

We live in a day of instant knowledge. We can ask Google, YouTube, Siri, and Alexa almost anything and get a quick answer. But there are things these technological wonders can't answer. I asked Siri, "What is *my* mission in life?" All I got was "Interesting question!" Can you imagine having a personal assistant willing to whisper to you what is good and right in every situation? How about to offer ideas you had never thought of? Have you wondered where the brilliant ideas of our day come from? Obviously, if no one has thought of them before, they are not available from technological personal assistants.

When Albert Einstein was twenty-six years old, he wrote a paper about the theory of relativity. He once said that he "created it out of whole cloth," meaning it was completely new and not based on any current knowledge. The paper did not have any references or footnotes. So where did it come from? He claimed, "There comes a point where the mind takes a leap—call it intuition or what you will—and comes out upon a higher plane of knowledge, but can never prove how it got there. All great discoveries have involved such a leap."[246] Obviously, an inner voice whispered the ideas behind that stunning theory into his mind.

Five years after thirty-six-year-old Russell M. Nelson accepted a professorship at the University of Utah, he was approached by a Latter-day Saint stake patriarch from southern Utah who asked for his help with what appeared to be a terminal heart condition. The man was very disappointed when he was told by other professionals that he had two faulty heart valves and that one could not be helped surgically. He pleaded with Dr. Nelson to perform the operation anyway, saying, "The Lord will make it known to you what to do."

As the operation commenced, Dr. Nelson successfully relieved the obstruction in the first valve. But when the young doctor exposed the second badly dilated tricuspid value, he had no idea what to do. "While examining this valve, a message was distinctly impressed upon my mind: *Reduce the circumference of the ring*." How? At that critical moment, the answer came. "Then a picture came vividly to my mind, showing how stitches could be placed—to make a pleat here and a tuck there—to accomplish the desired objective. I still remember that mental image—complete with dotted lines where sutures should be placed. The repair was completed as diagrammed in my mind. We tested the valve and found the leak to be reduced remarkably. My assistant said, 'It's a miracle.'"[247]

The patient recovered, and the pioneering surgical procedure has now helped many others with similar heart defects through the years. Where did the idea come from? Not Google! The voice of the Spirit whispered to Dr. Nelson's mind what to do at the very instant he needed it. We all have access to that same source for brilliant ideas if we will ask the questions, listen for the answers, and act on the promptings.

Finding Peace and Happiness

Randal: While attending college, I spent time working with finances at a local landscape architect's office. At the end of a day, I tossed a piece of paper in the trash and noticed an unopened envelope that had obviously been considered junk mail. I heard a little voice in my head say, "Open it!" I felt uncomfortable since it wasn't *my* mail but did it anyway. The envelope contained a mass mailing from an adoption agency in Seattle specializing in children from Korea. As I went to throw it back in the trash can, the thought came, "Take this information to Patty and Jerry Kirk."

Patty was my sister's childhood friend, as well as a distant cousin. I had also been friends with her husband, Jerry, for several years. Patty was unable to have children and was sensitive about the subject. I felt uncomfortable as I approached the door with the letter, not knowing if it would offend them. However, I acted as prompted and handed them the envelope with the comment, "I don't know if you'd be interested in contacting this agency, but I felt like I should drop it by."

They thanked me but didn't have much else to say. I found out later that they immediately contacted the agency and later adopted Spencer, an abandoned little boy from Korea. Spencer thrived in his new home. He is now a returned missionary who married in the temple and has a beautiful family. He obtained a medical degree and is a general surgeon in the Kansas City area. Thinking back on that day I acted on a prompting from the voice of the Spirit makes me feel happy, warm, calm, and peaceful.

All of us at times receive promptings from the Spirit. It is essential to our progress that we learn to recognize and act on these promptings. President Packer gave this counsel to help individuals stay close to the Spirit: "This voice of the Spirit speaks gently, prompting you what to do or what to say, or it may caution or warn you. Ignore or disobey these promptings, and the Spirit will leave you. It is your choice—your agency."[248]

Invitations to Act

1. When you feel a prompting, do not ask if it feels good but rather ask if it is helping you do good, love and serve God, and do the right thing.

2. Pray about your concerns, your fears, your weaknesses, and the longings of your heart. And then listen!
3. Write the thoughts that come to your mind and record your feelings when the Spirit whispers to you.
4. Follow through with any actions you are prompted to take.
5. Repeat this process day after day, month after month, and year after year.

CHAPTER 13
Learning Valuable Life Lessons

Life is a series of lessons. Some are diligent in learning them, and they become pure, wise, and altogether happy. Others are negligent, and do not apply themselves, and they remain impure, foolish, and unhappy.[249]
James Allen

Steve Tedjamulia

I was born in Brazil, but my family moved to Houston, Texas, when I was eleven years old. After graduating from high school, I attended college out of state. While at home for the Christmas holidays, a girl I knew asked if I would be interested in helping with a program that provided holiday meals and wrapped gifts for less fortunate families. That sounded like a lot of fun, as well as being a worthwhile endeavor, so I agreed to help. I had a little wake-up call, however, when I found out that they needed me to play Santa Claus. I realized I had gained a few pounds but hadn't thought it was noticeable.

At that point, I knew I needed to do something to get in better shape, so I decided I would run a marathon. Scrolling through the options, I found one in St. George, Utah, that fit my schedule, so I signed up. I had run a mile once in high school during my tennis-playing days. I figured 26.2 miles shouldn't be that big of a deal since I had several months to train. While filling out the race application, I came upon a question requiring an estimated finish time. I thought about the seven-minute mile I ran the *one* time in high school and figured I could run much faster as a college student with time to train. After some quick math, I entered my estimated time to finish the marathon as two hours and thirty minutes or five minutes and forty-four seconds per mile.

I trained for a few months, and finally race time arrived. After standing in line at the packet pickup, the person at the registration table didn't have my name on the list and asked me to go to another station to sign in. I was surprised at how many promotional items I received compared to those in the regular line but didn't think much about it. At race time, thousands of runners gathered around the starting line. While I was warming up, someone came up to me and said that with my low number I was in the wrong place in the lineup. They escorted me to the front of the massive crowd to a small group of obviously serious runners who acted like they all knew each other. It finally occurred to me that perhaps my estimated time to complete the race may have been a little off. The elite runners looked a little surprised that they didn't recognize me when I joined them at the front of the entire race. Someone asked my name and where I was from. I told them I was from Brazil. That seemed to help explain why I was unknown to them.

It was fun being among the elite runners and in the lead at the start of the race. The thrill only lasted a few minutes, however, as several average runners caught up to and passed me. Out of 4,044 runners at the 2001 St. George marathon, the winning time was two hours twenty minutes, with only five accomplishing the two-hour-and-thirty-minute time I had estimated for myself. On a positive note, I did complete the marathon in three hours and fifty-one minutes—1,480th overall. I missed my estimated ending time by one hour and twenty-one minutes. Maybe I had set my goal a little too high.

It is now Christmas time again—twenty-three years since I last played Santa. Coincidently, I was asked to play Santa again this year. This time I decided to sign up for a triathlon!

Many Kinds of Lessons

With every experience we have or observe in life, there are lessons to be learned. What lesson can you learn from Steve's marathon experience? Maybe the importance of setting realistic goals? A lesson is a useful piece of wisdom, knowledge or insight acquired by experience, study, or observation. Harvey H. Cluff, a business, civic, and educational leader, made this insightful statement: "No intelligent person in youth or old age should merely drift along. Look the world squarely in the face, listen and learn . . . for there are grand lessons before you every minute."[250] Everyone has had experiences that taught him or her lessons.

Years from now, many of you will have hundreds or even thousands of descendants. Will your posterity remember you and the lessons you learned in life from your written records? Or will they only see your name on a tombstone or pedigree chart and know nothing of your life? Recording experiences and the lessons learned can change your life for the better. Natalie Curtis McCullough said this about keeping a personal journal: "I keep a journal to discover what I know, how I know it, and why it matters. I write to unearth treasures and mysteries buried in my heart."[251]

Harvard with No Notes

Imagine for a moment that after working extremely hard for years, you are now among the 4.59 percent of students accepted to Harvard. The cost of tuition, fees, and room and board for an undergraduate was estimated at $79,450 for the 2023–2024 school year or $317,800 for Harvard's four-year degree program.[252] As the first semester begins, you set a goal that perhaps no other Harvard student has ever attempted. You vow to never take any notes during your four years on campus. You plan to attend class and remember everything said. What do you think your chances of success would be?

This implausible goal would be extremely unwise for any university student seeking success. Yet vast numbers do exactly that in the school of life. Bishop T. D. Jakes pointed out, "The world is a university and everyone in it is a teacher. Make sure when you wake up in the morning you go to school."[253] Part of the success in the university of life depends on recording the valuable lessons we learn. A familiar adage says, "If it isn't written down, it didn't happen."

If you or I would take careful notes as a university student to remember what we learned, why would we not keep a journal of the grand lessons learned throughout our lives? The benefit of having a record of these valuable life lessons is inexpressible. Countless lessons can be learned from observing others' experiences. Author Douglas Adams pointed out, "Human beings, who are almost unique in having the ability to learn from the experience of others, are also remarkable for their apparent disinclination to do so."[254]

What a shame so many live their entire lives, learn hundreds or even thousands of lessons from their own experiences and the experiences of others, and then fail to record them. When the tests of life come, our memory is the only resource available. All tests we take in life are open book. Unfortunately for most, there is no book to open because it was never written. Without written records, it is like reinventing the wheel every day.

Reasons People Fail to Journal

Why do so few keep written records of their life lessons when the benefits are so incredible? I have asked hundreds of people over the years if they keep written records of their experiences in life and the lessons learned. Only a small percentage have responded positively. When asked why they failed to do so, these are some of their answers:

- "I just don't have time."
- "I'm not a good writer."
- "The main reason I don't keep a journal is because of laziness."
- "I am distracted by other things and don't get around to it."
- "I feel my daily activities are insignificant and don't need to be written down."
- "It is out of sight out of mind; I just don't think about doing it."
- "It is not a priority for me since I don't see any benefit."
- "The past is something I want to forget."
- "Since I haven't done it in the past, it now feels overwhelming to try to catch up."
- "It takes self-discipline to write, and it's obvious I don't have any."

The main reason given for not keeping a personal record is "I don't have time." Yet many brilliant scientists and inventors through the years have conducted time-consuming experiments, discovered valuable truths, and still found time to record what they learned. Thomas Edison, for example, said, "I enjoy working about 18 hours a day."[255] He could have easily used the "I don't have time" reason not to record what he learned during those long days, but he didn't. Can you imagine if he had not taken time to write the formula for the first practical incandescent light bulb? When he filed for a patent in November 1879, he had written the formula down. By experimenting, discovering great truths, and recording what he learned,

Edison ultimately acquired patents for 2,332 of his inventions worldwide. The Thomas A. Edison Papers Project is a research center at Rutgers University that began in 1978 with a team of editors and scholars who are now turning the five million pages of documents that chronicle Edison's life and achievements into an educational resource.[256] The world has benefited because he wrote down the lessons he learned in life. How many pages of documents will chronicle your life and achievements?

Because great men and women in science followed the same pattern of recording what they discovered, the next generation of researchers can begin where their predecessors left off. This is how we went from the rotary phones of the 1980s to the smart phones of today. This process has led to the most incredible scientific discoveries ever known in human history. Why not follow the same pattern as the scientists to improve our own lives?

Those who fail to keep a record of their experiences and the lessons learned seem likely to live a life not unlike the one portrayed in the 1993 movie *Groundhog Day*. In the movie, Bill Murray plays the part of a self-centered egotist named Phil Connors, a television weatherman in Pittsburg. One of Phil's assignments was to travel to Punxsutawney, Pennsylvania, to cover Groundhog Day, a yearly event that started on February 02, 1887. He was set on getting out of the place as quickly as possible but instead found himself caught in a time loop, repeating the same day. In real life, it appears that few record the lessons they learn and therefore repeat the same day because they can't fully remember what they learned the day before.

Elder Richard G. Scott gave counsel that, if followed, would bring incredible blessings to anyone willing to put forth the effort required. It is a simple yet powerful formula leading to steady improvement throughout life. He said the following:

> I will share a principle that, if understood and consistently applied, will bring enormous blessings throughout your life. It is not difficult for me to explain, nor for you to understand. However, it will require of you significant, determined effort to yield its full potential. With it you can learn vital truths that will bring you greater, enduring happiness and make your life more productive and meaningful. . . .
>
> I will consistently strive to learn by what I hear, see, and feel.
>
> I will write down the important things I learn, and I will do them.[257]

Recalling Past Experiences

Perhaps some realize the importance of keeping a record of life but don't know where to start. Or maybe some think because they haven't recorded their lessons they are forever lost. If you could recall experiences that taught you lessons in the past, would you record them? What if you could record an experience in about eight seconds?

Here is some good news! Many, if not most, of your meaningful experiences are safely stored in your memory and are still accessible. You just need the right words to search the hard drive of your mind. You never know what is stored on the World Wide Web until you enter a search word or phrase. If there is an experience that taught you a valuable lesson, it, too, is most likely still filed away.

Let's try it out. Do you have any physical scars on your body? For some, the answer is no. For most, the answer is yes. Can you remember how you received the scar? If you have a scar, you likely have a memory of how it got there. What if your search words were "frightening experiences" ? Do any come to mind? You can remember because it is stored on your hard drive. Did you learn a lesson from that experience? Isn't it nice to know it is still there? There are likely hundreds or even thousands of experiences stored in your mind waiting for you to recall them. However, if you do not write them down after the recall, they are essentially lost again. Let's assume you are busy person and don't have time to record the experiences you recall.

Three-Word Journal

You only need about eight seconds to record a meaningful experience. It's called a three-word journal. Here is how it works. When you recall an experience you don't want to forget, simply condense it into a three-word summary. At least one of the three words should include a specific person, place, or thing to distinguish it from every other experience.

Let's say I want to recall an experience about gratitude from the past. As soon as I focused on that subject, an experience immediately popped into my mind. The story can be summarized with these three words: Jared Lucky Turtle. While these words mean nothing to the reader, I know exactly what happened and the lesson I learned. Several years ago our neighbors had a seven-year-old son named Jared. His parents bought him a small green turtle from a local pet store. One day Jared and his friend were playing with the turtle. At one point the friend said, "You sure are lucky to have a turtle. All I have is a cat and a dog and a horse." From this simple experience I learned a valuable lesson. Too many of us focus on things we don't have rather than being grateful for the things we do have.

As time permits, write out the details of the experiences summarized in three-word form, adding lessons learned from each. Filing these life lessons by topic will give you instant access for use in giving talks, teaching lessons, helping family members, or recalling for personal improvement. What if you took just one memory prompt a day and focused on coming up with as many three-word summaries as possible on that subject? It is like doing a Google search of your brain and bringing up all your past experiences. In time, you could have hundreds of your important past experiences. You could then file these summaries into topics for instant access.

The thing about leaving your experiences in a three-word format is that your posterity will not know what the summaries mean. However, you can write out the details later and put the stories in sequential order so your posterity can have your life history. If you wrote out just one experience a day, you would have 365 a year. Here are several memory prompts to help you recall past experiences. Just take one memory cue at a time like *father* and think about it as you go about your day. When you think of a specific experience with your father, put it in a three-word summary that includes at least one person, place, or thing. Here are memory prompts to get you started:

- Father, mother, brothers, sisters, grandparents, aunts, uncles, cousins, nieces, nephews
- Friends, neighbors, teachers, coaches, classmates, coworkers, bosses, church leaders
- Christmas, Thanksgiving, Fourth of July, New Year's Day, Halloween, Labor Day
- Best and worst decisions made and the results
- Tragedies, challenges, or frightening events
- Positive and negative family events during vacations, reunions, parties, dinners
- Neighborhoods, houses, cars, pets, bikes, toys, clothes, styles, phones
- Humorous family situations

- Mischief that you, your friends, or your siblings participated in
- Memorable dates, relationships, breakups
- Engagement, marriage, spouse
- Disagreements with friends, family, or others
- Successes and failures
- People who most influenced your life for good or bad and why
- Defining moments that changed the direction of your life
- Sickness or accidents that required a doctor's visit or hospitalization
- Greatest fears or phobias and experiences that may have led to them
- Occasions when you left your comfort zone and the results
- Negative or positive feedback received and how you responded
- Most embarrassing situations
- Times when you quit something and regretted it
- Important events or appointments you were late for or missed
- Pranks, jokes, hoaxes, or tricks you have fallen for, instigated, or participated in
- Results from times you gave in to peer pressure
- Memories of classes, students, teachers, activities, clubs, sports, dances, events
- Experiences with jobs, bosses, and coworkers
- Best and worst news ever received
- Times you felt depressed, unwise, insecure, lonely, or rejected
- Times you felt happy, excited, confident, included, outgoing, or friendly
- Times you were gullible or taken advantage of
- Experiences associated with severe weather
- Special homecomings and difficult departures

You can add a number of additional memory prompts to this list, but perhaps these few will help get you started. We asked several individuals to recall experiences that taught them valuable lessons. You will see a bold search phrase followed by the name of the person, his or her three-word summary, and written details of the experience.

A Time You Stood Up for Your Beliefs

Morgan Jones: "Simeon Sunday Basketball"

When I was in elementary school, playing basketball was one of my absolute favorite things to do. I looked forward to the recreation league season all year, so you can imagine my disappointment when I was eleven years old and found out that the games for my age group would be played on Sunday. My parents taught me from a young age the importance of the Sabbath day, so I didn't play that season. The next season when registration for the season began, my dad went to the recreation center to speak with the director of youth sports, John Simeon, and asked him if he knew when the games would be played. My dad came home excited to report that the games this year were not on Sundays.

A few weeks later, a skills evaluation was held for coaches to eventually select their teams. Each player was expected to shoot a free throw and then dribble in for a layup. The league's coaches privately ranked each player on a scale from one to five. Before the skills evaluation began, John Simeon stood up and welcomed everyone. He then said, "This year's games for this league will be played on Sunday." My heart sank. I was there at the meeting alone. I knew what I needed to do. When they called my name for my turn to shoot, I went to the coach's table and said, "I can still shoot if you would like me to, but I won't be able to play this year if the games are on Sunday." Simeon immediately seemed to understand what the issue was and said, "Go ahead and shoot."

After the meeting, I sat in the hall feeling disappointed as I waited for my dad to pick me up. Suddenly, Simeon came out of the coaches' meeting where they were picking teams and said, "I've talked with all the coaches, and we've agreed to change the games to Saturday mornings so you can play." John Simeon was not, to my knowledge, a religious person, and he probably didn't understand why I didn't feel comfortable playing sports on Sunday. But he respected me and my conviction. In retrospect, this experience set a precedent for the rest of my life. It taught me to believe in the goodness of the people around me and to have the confidence to stand up for my beliefs.

Someone Who Taught You a Valuable Lesson

Trent Kimball: "Pixton Restore Paint"

When I was sixteen years old, I was paired up to do monthly service with an older gentleman named Allan Pixton. He was a retired brigadier general in the Army, although I really didn't know what that meant. I found out later that as a twenty-four-year-old Army lieutenant colonel, he landed on Omaha Beach in Normandy, France, at noon on D-Day, June 6, 1944. He became a military hero and earned thirty-four medals and awards while serving and retired as a two-star general. I don't know how old he was at the time, but he seemed old to me. I was a little intimidated by him, although he was nice to me. At that time, I didn't know anything about the military and couldn't care less that he was a general. I was a junior in high school, very social, and a typical teenage goof-off.

During one of our monthly times together, he commented, "Trent, I have this old car. I want to restore the paint. Can you help me out?" I agreed to help him but told him I was not a painter. He said, "Well, I know how to do it, but I need help with some manual labor. I don't expect you to do it for nothing. I will pay you." I told him again that I would be glad to help. The next month we met up again, and he told me that he was ready to restore the paint on the old car and asked if I could help him that Saturday morning at eight o'clock. I told him I would be there. I didn't think another thing about it. I don't recall what I did that Saturday, but I do know I didn't go help Allan Pixton with his car.

The next month during our scheduled service time, he said, "Trent, let me teach you a lesson. If you say you are going to do something, you do it." That was it. That was the whole lesson, but he said it directly to me.

At the time, I couldn't recall what it was related to, but then I remembered and quickly replied, "Oh, I forgot."

He said, "I was ready to work on the car that day. I set things aside, and then you didn't show up. Do you think you can show up this Saturday?"

This time I remembered and went to his home at the appointed time. The car we were working on was an old Porsche. It was yellow with some rather severe sun damage to the paint job. The color had paled considerably. That morning we took a compound and rubbed it over the entire car to restore the original paint, and then we waxed it. Boy, did it shine! It was rewarding to learn how to do something new.

I never forgot the lesson he taught me. It was just a morning job that took a few hours, and he easily could have done it himself when I didn't show up the first Saturday morning. I don't remember how long we worked in the service assignment together or anything about our visits. But I do remember his kindness and his lesson: "If you say you are going to do something, you do it."

I don't know if it is a pet peeve of mine now, but it is something that I stress in my company because of that one lesson Allan taught me. He made me feel at the time that he was relying on my help for the task at hand, even though he could have easily done it himself. It was simple work. I think he purposefully left the work unfinished so he could teach me a lesson I would never forget.

An Example of When a Dream Came True

Camilla Crawford: "Richards Build Career"

I grew up in Ireland and was at a time of life trying to decide whether to go to college in Ireland or England. During this time, I had a chance encounter in Preston, England, with Randal Wright and his wife, Wendy, from America. It turned out I was good friends with one of their close family members. We became quick friends and stayed in contact by email. Later I came to Salt Lake City to visit friends in America, and the Wrights happened to be there for meetings at the same time. We spent several hours together, and Randal encouraged me to come to school in the United States. At first I totally resisted the idea but then gave in.

A few years later, I was a student at BYU listening to a speech given by Stan Richards, the legendary founder of The Richards Group (TRG), the largest independent advertising agency in America. He was entertaining and among other things spoke about the importance of keeping fit, the fun they had coming up with the famous Chick-fil-A campaign, and the culture at his agency. I remember thinking how fun it would be to work there after realizing there was a far greater opportunity at TRG than a gym and a healthy work-life balance. I could tell that Stan had values that aligned with mine and that he genuinely loved his employees and his work. As I sat there I had an overwhelming feeling that this was *the* agency that I wanted to work for. Soon after the presentation I changed my major to advertising.

The summer I was scheduled to graduate, I applied for several internships. When I got an email telling me I had an offer at The Richards Group, I danced around my room singing "I'm going to Texas" to my poor roommate who didn't have a clue why I was so happy. It was the very scenario I had envisioned.

A short time after beginning my internship, I went to the company gym and happened to see Stan Richards. I went up to him. In my strong Irish accent, I told him I had heard him speak at BYU and he had inspired me to change my major to advertising and to dream of working for TRG one day. He was very gracious to me.

When my internship ended, I decided I would visit my family in Ireland then return to Utah to find a job in advertising. The day before I was to leave, I felt I should say goodbye to Stan and thank him for the opportunity I had been given. He invited me to sit down and talk about my plans. During our conversation, he told me that he hated to see someone like me go. He also said, "Camilla, you can go back to visit your family in Ireland and in Utah, but you can stay here and build a career for yourself." He also asked if I would like an offer from The Richards Group. When I left that afternoon, I sat at my desk shocked at what had just happened. The man who is in the Advertising Hall of Fame and has the advertising program at the University of Texas at Austin named after him offered me the opportunity I first dreamed of when I heard him speak.

Later I wrote him a letter to thank him for what he had done for me. I told him that even though sometimes I felt inadequate and still had a lot to learn, he could rest assured that he would always have at least one employee who is invested in making his agency the greatest in the world. I also promised to always fill out my time sheet honestly and promised to never ask for a 10 percent share of the agency.

An Experience That Changed Your Life

Clark Maxwell: Miss Midnight Curfew

When I was in high school, an experience taught me the importance of keeping your word and being loyal to who you are—no matter what the situation.

One Friday night when I was a senior in high school, I went out with my friends, promising my parents to be home before midnight. My friends and I weren't doing anything bad, but we certainly lost track of time just hanging out, and I got home late. I always checked in with my parents when I got home per our family rule. I prayed they would be fast asleep this time. However, when I walked into my parents' bedroom to report that I was home, my dad was still awake and asked, "What time is it?"

"About one o'clock," I replied.

"What time did you say you'd be home?" he asked.

"By midnight," I replied.

"Why were you late?" he asked.

"Well," I replied, "I just lost track of time hanging out with my friends."

He then paused for what felt like an eternity of silence and then said calmly, but firmly, "Well, you need to decide what's more important, your friends or your word."

His words cut me to the core. I respected my dad and felt sickened to have violated his trust in me. No other words were spoken. I turned around and walked slowly upstairs to my bedroom. Once I got there, I couldn't sleep, I just sat on my bed for over an hour, pondering what had just happened and especially the inquiry "What's more important—your friends or your word?" I resolved that night I would never let it happen again, that I would always be true to my word.

Keep a Journal

A few years back I attended a meeting with twenty-eight successful men in attendance. The instructor talked about the importance of keeping a written record of the lessons learned in life. At one point, the instructor asked the group how many kept a written record. Two men raised their hands that day. If this group were representative of the norm, about 95 percent chose not to take notes in the university of life. An editorial was written in a London publication in the mid-1800s that makes a strong argument for why all should keep a written record of their lives. The writer emphasized,

> "If a man keeps no diary, the path crumbles away behind him as his feet leave it; and days gone by are but little more than a blank, broken by a few distorted shadows. His life is all confined within the limits of to-day. Who does not know how imperfect a thing memory is? . . .

> A man might almost as well not have lived at all as entirely forget that he has lived, and entirely forget what he did on those departed days."[258]

Another thought-provoking editorial appeared in the October 1840 edition of the *Latter-day Saints' Millennial Star* newspaper, believed to be authored by its editor, Parley P. Pratt.

"Do you keep a Journal? If so, well, and you will have your reward; and if not, we would again enjoin it upon you, and upon all who have not before heard the admonition, to commence forthwith to keep a Journal, or write a history; and see to it, that what you write is strictly true and unexaggerated; so that in the end, all may know of all things concerning this last work, and all knowledge may flow together from the four quarters of the earth, when the Lord shall make his appearing, and we all may be ready to give a full account of our mission, our ministry and stewardship, and receive the welcome tidings, 'Thou hast been faithful over a few things, I will make thee ruler over many things: enter thou into the joy of thy Lord.'"[259]

How sad that any of us would live life without recording the experiences and observations we've learned. In the Book of Mormon, Jesus Christ tells Nephi, "Bring forth the record which ye have kept" (3 Nephi 23:7). When Nephi brought forth the records as instructed, Christ reviewed them and asked him if Samuel the Lamanite prophesied concerning many saints rising from the dead after His resurrection. Nephi and the other disciples answered that he did. Christ then asked, "How be it that ye have not written this thing?" (3 Nephi 23:11). According to Parley P. Pratt, a journal will be helpful "when the Lord shall make his appearing, and we all may be ready to give a full account of our mission, our ministry and stewardship, and receive the welcome tidings."[260]

Invitation to Act

1. Use memory prompts to search your brain for experiences or observations from the past that taught you valuable lessons.
2. When an experience comes to mind, summarize it into three well-chosen words, including at least one person, place, or thing.
3. Write out one experience daily in detail and the lesson you learned from it.

4. Constantly be on the lookout for new experiences that teach valuable lessons. Record them in three-word form, and then add details and lessons learned as soon as you get time.

CHAPTER 14

The Amazing Power of Love

A man filled with the love of God, is not content with blessing his family alone, but ranges through the whole world, anxious to bless the whole human race.[261]

Joseph Smith

Dan Packard

During my elementary school years, my teachers had me evaluated by experts who diagnosed me with Attention Deficit Disorder (ADD) and dyslexia. When my performance at school continued to lag, Grandma invited me to her house so she could spend extra time with me. I was happy to have the attention, but I soon learned that we were not going to be watching cartoons and eating cookies. Grandma wanted to teach me the English language. She helped me memorize all the forms of *be* as well as the forty-three most common prepositions. We diagrammed all kinds of sentences and learned how to spell common words, but mostly Grandma had me write short essays, which she called themes. I wrote, and she made corrections and suggestions. I then rewrote the theme, and she made more corrections and suggestions. I wrote and rewrote dozens of themes during those summers, and slowly I started to learn how to organize my thoughts and articulate them in a coherent way. I was never anything special, but English went from being my worst subject to my best, and writing became my strongest academic subject throughout high school, college, and law school. Honestly, I still rely on the things I learned at Grandma's dining room table.

As I reflect on the experience, it seems remarkable that a hyperactive fourth grader who had both dyslexia and ADD would be willing to spend hour after hour in this way. I didn't like diagramming sentences and writing essays any more than the next kid. But I felt truly loved during those sessions with Grandma. Moreover, I was fully cognizant of my academic failures, and I had an unexpressed but profound fear that I did not have the mental horsepower to make it in this world. Grandma was giving me what I really needed. I felt it at the time, so I went cheerfully and received her generous gift of love, knowledge, and time.

Of course, Grandma's teachings involved more than just syntax. Through her actions and demeanor, she showed me how to love—how to love a spouse, how to love children, how to love all the little things in life, and how to love God. She showed me that you can inspire people without judging them. She showed me how joyful people can be when they make life's important relationships their life's work. For me, Grandma Vivian Hayes truly was a teacher come from God.

The Impact of Love

Dan's touching tribute to his grandmother was read at her funeral services. The love she showed was a major factor in helping him overcome the challenges he faced with ADD and dyslexia. He went on to become a champion debater and eventually received a scholarship for college. After graduating with his bachelor's degree, Dan attended law school at Brigham Young University, where he graduated with academic honors. He married Allison, one of his law school classmates, and they have a beautiful family. Dan is now a successful attorney, having argued several high-profile cases with national significance. Through the years, Dan has had the opportunity to serve faithfully in many important Church callings, including president of the Massachusetts Boston Mission.

Vivian Hayes was an amazing example of what it means to love another person. Because of her tireless work with a struggling grandson, countless lives have been blessed. Elder David B. Haight shared this insight: "Someone has written, 'Love is a verb.' It requires doing—not just saying and thinking. The test is in what one does, how one acts, for love is conveyed in word and deed."[262]

Basic Needs

William Glasser, an internationally known psychiatrist and researcher, developed Choice Theory. His theory focuses on individual choice, personal responsibility, and the belief that people can change. He theorized that behavior is driven by five basic human needs:

- Survival: physical needs, food, clothing, shelter, safety, sexual intimacy
- Love and Belonging: relationships, friendship, affection, to feel part of a group
- Power: achievement, skills, competency, recognition, to be listened to
- Freedom: independence, autonomy, to have choices, to control one's life
- Fun: to find pleasure and enjoyment, to play, to laugh, to learn life skills[263]

If Glasser is right, his research has deep implications for individuals, families, and organizations. Imagine working for a company where everyone from top management down fully understood these basic needs and worked hard to see they were being met, where appropriate, in the workplace. Imagine the difference in families if everyone understood the needs of others and helped meet those needs.

Randal: While speaking to a group of parents and teenagers in a southern state, I mentioned the need all humans have for love and affection and the consequences that often occur when these needs are not met. To illustrate, I quoted following experience: "'When my father stopped hugging me, I decided I could either tear up the beautiful book he had given me for Christmas, I could kill myself, or I could try to get hugs from someone else,' says Janie, thirteen, who recently had her first sexual encounter. 'I finally decided to get a boyfriend.'"[264]

When Janie's father stopped giving her hugs, she mistakenly assumed he no longer loved her. This led to her seeking love from a boy who took advantage of her needs for his own selfish purposes. Unfortunately for Janie, her boyfriend likely met all five of her basic needs.

After the speech, a fifteen-year-old girl named Loni came up to talk. She said that for as long as she could remember her dad came into her room every night to share experiences, encourage her, and tell her how special she was. Before leaving he gave her a hug, kissed her on the cheek, and expressed how much he loved her. However, when she turned thirteen, he never came into her room again. As she related her story, she became emotional and said, "Sometimes I just want to shake him and tell him I still need that."

British scholar C. S. Lewis said, "Affection is responsible for nine-tenths of whatever solid and durable happiness there is in our natural lives."[265] On the other hand, the lack of love and affection leads to unhappiness. Those who don't receive it often go looking for love in all the wrong places, as thirteen-year-old Janie did.

As part of a parenting class, I asked Tami, a female college student, what mistakes she thought her parents made growing up. She responded, "Never once did I see my mom or dad show any physical affection toward each other. There was no hand holding or kissing in front of the family. Neither did my father ever once hug or kiss me or tell me he loved me. I think it was the same for my siblings. The only time I remember my mother giving me a brief hug was when I was leaving for college. I think we were all starved for affection and went seeking it outside the home."

Feeling loved at home matters most, but feeling genuine love in other circumstances also matters. Those who do not feel appreciated in the workplace are likely to be less effective, less satisfied, and will often seek employment elsewhere.[266] Maya Angelou observed, "I've learned that people will forget what you said, people will forget what you did, but people will never forget how you made them feel."[267]

Why People Struggle to Show Love

In a marriage class I taught, participants gave multiple reasons why some people struggle to show love and affection to others:

- Parents failed: Those who grew up in homes where they felt deprived of love by their parents or caregivers also tend to struggle displaying affection to others.
- It is considered a weakness: Some have been raised to believe that showing love is a weakness. Because of this, they hide their emotions from others.

- Shyness: Many are shy and have a difficult time expressing love and giving affection to others.
- Fear of rejection: For those who have low self-esteem, showing love may be too risky because of the fear of rejection.
- Desire to be sincere: Some fear that showing or expressing love may be perceived as being insincere, so they refuse to display it.
- Assumption that recipients already know: Many assume that family members, friends, or coworkers know they are cared for, so there is no need to express it.

Regret Not Showing Love

A college friend named Sandy shared an excerpt from her grandfather's journal. Cornelius Kleven was born October 8, 1899, in Norway. His story emphasizes the challenge many face over showing appropriate love and affection.

> In the fall of 1922, four other boys in the neighborhood and I decided to go to America. It took several months to get our papers ready.
>
> In January 1923, we were ready to leave home. On the morning of my departure, my mother came upstairs at 4 a.m. to wake me up. As I lay there, she knelt by my bed and put her arm around me with her cheek against my cheek, and told me how she loved me and how she would miss me. She told me to be a good boy. She felt that she would not see me again in this life.
>
> I had been taught never to cry or show emotion, but at that moment I wanted to put my arms around her. Unfortunately, I let them lie still by my side under the covers. I didn't say or do anything, because I was a man. How could I be so soft to put my arms around my mother, or maybe cry, and tell her how I loved her? I couldn't do that. It wasn't manly. How I have regretted that moment all these years!
>
> I got up, and she walked me two miles in the knee-deep snow to the bus stop. She helped me carry my suitcase. When I got on the bus, I shook hands with my mother and said goodbye. Now for fifty-two years, I have regretted all this.
>
> Thirty-eight years after I came over to this country, I had a chance to go back to Norway for a visit. My mother had died eighteen years before. The first thing I did on the first day I was there was to go to the graveyard. I didn't know where the graves were located. I searched up and down the

> rows till I finally came to the graves of my mother and father. I stood there and looked at them for a minute. All my past days went through my mind, especially the last day I saw my mother.
>
> I knelt down and put my arms around the marker. I put my cheek against her name, and those tears that I should have shed thirty-eight years earlier were shed there. I was not such a big man after all.[268]

Unfortunately, neither Cornelius nor any of us can go back to make up for lost opportunities. What we can do is commit to do better in the future.

Demonstrate Love

Randal: Several years ago, I attended a high school basketball game between two powerhouses vying for the tournament championship. The game was between Port Arthur Lincoln, five-time Texas state champions during the previous decade and the number one team in the state at the time of the game, and Beaumont Westbrook, was led by their six-foot-five star Lucious "Lukie" Jackson, son of Lucious "Luke" Jackson—two-time All-American at Pan American College, a gold medal winner at the 1964 Olympic games, NBA Rookie of the Year in 1965, All-NBA pick, and member of the 1967 NBA champion Philadelphia 76ers.

I was cheering for the Lincoln team but soon switched because Lukie was so fun to watch. Westbrook held the lead for most of the game, but with seconds left in regulation play, Lincoln tied the score. Again, in overtime, Westbrook had a one-point lead with just seconds left. On the final drive, a Lincoln player went up to shoot but was fouled by Westbrook's star player, Lukie. Lincoln's player made the first free throw. That tied the score, and then he made the second, giving Lincoln the victory. Lukie walked off the court totally dejected even though he'd played brilliantly. To lose the game to the number one team in the state because of his foul was obviously devastating.

I wondered what his former NBA All-Star dad was thinking. Would he yell at his son for making a mistake that cost them the game? At that point, I looked to my left and saw Lukie's huge six-foot-nine father descend the steps toward his upset son. My first thought was "Run, Lukie!" I've seen many insensitive fathers negatively react when their children make mistakes in sports. However, when Lukie saw his father walking toward him, he immediately started up the steps to meet him. This loving father put his arms around his son and held him tight. His son laid his head on his father's shoulder, and with Luke patting him on the back, he cried out his frustrations. As a father, I wondered how I would have handled the situation that night.

After the long embrace ended, they talked briefly, and Lukie smiled and ran back down onto the court, hugging players on the Lincoln team and congratulating them on their win. It was a touching scene and one I'll never forget. I learned that night how to be a better father. Lukie went on to play basketball for four years at Syracuse University.

One day I thought about this experience and wondered, as I often had, what the father said to his son that night. I decided to look online and found the phone number for Lucious Jackson. After hesitating several minutes, I placed the call, and he answered. I talked to him briefly and told him I'd be in his area soon and wondered if it would be possible to stop by and visit with him.

On January 16, 2017, I went to the home of Luke and Marva Jackson, his wife of fifty-two years. We talked about what happened at the game. I expressed how much Luke's actions impressed me and offered them a written copy of my version of what happened that night. They were as kind and loving as anyone I have ever met.

I found out that Luke's father abandoned his family when he was young, and his mother raised their five children alone. The first time Luke heard from his father was when he was a senior in college. During his eighth-grade year, the high school was integrated; however, Black students were not allowed to play sports. During his ninth-grade year, he could only take physical education classes. The next year the six-foot-eight sophomore was given an opportunity to move to Bastrop, Louisiana. He lived with the family of Morehouse High School principal Henry Adams so he could play sports. Mr. Adams became a father figure to Luke and taught him how to win and lose like a champion.

I asked the Jacksons if that night was unusual or if love and physical affection was part of their family. Marva said that when she and Luke married, they committed to express love and show it. They have two daughters, Nicole and Andrea, and their son, Lukie. All are college graduates and enjoy successful careers. Marva said when their daughters visit, they immediately give their parents a hug. Then she said when Lukie visits, he immediately goes to his dad and gives him a big hug and a kiss.

Before leaving I got to ask Luke the question I had wondered about for years. I asked if he remembered what he said to his dejected son as they hugged after the demoralizing 1991 tournament championship loss. He assured me that he remembered it well. He said, "I told him to be a champion." That is exactly what both Luke and his son were that night to me.

Be Nonjudgmental

No home or workplace is full of perfect people. Since we all have weaknesses, we should be understanding of each other. Many have grown up in difficult circumstances, while others are perhaps dealing with a bad marriage, insecurities, health concerns, rebellious children, financial issues, and more. Author Sam Keen said, "We come to love not by finding a perfect person, but by learning to see an imperfect person perfectly."[269] If people seem different to you, it probably means that you seem different to them also.

Randal: Years ago while driving home one evening, I glanced down at the dashboard and noticed the gas gauge was past empty. Luckily a self-serve gas station was just ahead, so I pulled in and began to fill the gas tank. After a few moments, an old, dilapidated car pulled up at another set of pumps. The driver had long hair, a straggly beard, and a cigarette in his mouth. As he got out of his car, I noticed that his clothes were tattered. "Poor guy," I thought.

I finished pumping the gas and walked up to pay the cashier. Reaching into my pocket, I found that I had a slight problem—no money! After checking all my pockets, I told the cashier I'd be right back, that I needed to run to the car to get some money. I searched everywhere in the car but found nothing. I had no choice but to go back and explain my dilemma, tell her I would leave my ID, and go home to get the money. Running back to the cashier, I passed the young man I had been judging.

As we passed, he said, "Don't worry about it."

I thought, "Same to you, buddy," although I had no idea what he was talking about.

When I got to the cashier to explain my predicament, she informed me that the young man saw what was happening and paid my bill. "He said to tell you to not worry about it," she said. I quickly ran over to his car to tell him that I really appreciated what he'd done for me, but that I lived close by and would be right back with the money. He said, "Don't worry about it. I know what it's like to be broke." Then he drove off, leaving me standing there feeling foolish.

Later that night I conjured up a mental picture of what it might be like at the judgment bar. I could just see this young man being called up and asked a few questions.

"Did you smoke while you lived on Earth?"

"Yes," came his reply.

"Did you realize that tobacco was not good for the body?"

He said he didn't realize it when he started but then got hooked.

"I'm sorry but that is a minus five on your test of life." He was then asked, "Did you love your neighbor and try to help those in need?"

He answered that he did try to do that.

I spoke up and said that he had helped me at the gas station.

I imagined the words, "Well done, thou good and faithful servant. You took care of the most important things in life."

Then I imagined myself being called up for a few questions. I was still in my nice dark suit. The first imagined question to me was "Did you smoke while you lived on Earth?"

Proudly, I quoted Doctrine and Covenants 89:8, "Tobacco is not for the body."

"Good, that's a plus five in the test of life." Then I was asked, "Did you love your neighbor, or did you judge them?"

What could I say?

Then I could hear the words, "Minus fifty! You forgot to take care of the most important things in life."

I could just imagine the young man saying to me, "Don't worry about it, man. Maybe it won't be that bad!"

Of course, I was just going through these scenarios in my mind. I don't pretend to know the specifics of how the Judgment will work. We do know that Jesus Christ taught that to love God is the first and great commandment and to love our neighbors as ourselves is the second great commandment. He also taught that we should not judge others because we are going to be judged the way we judged them. I have a feeling that the

Lord is saying that not loving others and judging them is more serious than the things we are judged harshly for.

President Uchtdorf taught this about not loving others as we should: "I don't know exactly how to articulate this point of *not judging others* with sufficient eloquence, passion, and persuasion to make it stick. I can quote scripture, I can try to expound doctrine, and I will even quote a bumper sticker I recently saw. It was attached to the back of a car whose driver appeared to be a little rough around the edges, but the words on the sticker taught an insightful lesson. It read, "Don't judge me because I sin differently than you."[270]

Love Them First

If you want someone to love you, show love and kindness to them first. Call people by name. Act excited to see them. Say goodbye. Listen intently. Make eye contact. Give sincere compliments. Make time for others. Ask for advice. Use appropriate touch. Laugh easily. Be easy to get along with. William Arthur Ward said, "Flatter me, and I may not believe you. Criticize me, and I may not like you. Ignore me, and I may not forgive you. Encourage me, and I will not forget you. Love me, and I may be forced to love you."[271]

I became a believer in this principle a few years ago when I was asked to teach a seminar in a nearby city. As I walked into the classroom the first night, I was surprised to see Kylie, the daughter of some good friends. I hadn't seen her since she was in high school but knew she was married with two kids. Kylie and I gave each other a brief hug. Several months later, I attended a meeting, and as I walked into a hallway, I was surprised and happy to see Kylie again. Of course, I greeted her, smiled, said, "Hey, how are you doing?" and gave her a big hug. As I looked closer, I realized she wasn't Kylie and I didn't know for sure who she was. I'm sure my face was red as I quickly said, "Have a good night." I turned and hurried off. At the end of the hall, I asked a friend if he knew who the woman was down the hall behind me. He said her name was Melissa, and she was married to one of his friends.

Several months after that embarrassing situation, I found myself in the same building and came face-to-face with Melissa. I felt like running but she acted excited to see me and quickly hugged me and asked how I was doing. We had a good conversation and got to know each other.

Isn't it interesting that months before I had mistakenly acted as if I was excited to see Melissa and gave her a hug? When I saw her a second time, she did the exact same thing I had done. From that point on, my wife and I really did become friends with Melissa and her husband, Scott. We have gone out to dinner with them and sat by them at several football games. Now, every time I see Melissa, I really am excited to see her. I learned a valuable lesson from my mistake. If you act as if you like someone, it will increase the chance they will act like they care about you. Before long it will no longer be acting as if, because it will be real.

Serve Others

There are many who feel a lack of love and support and many who are under extreme stress. When we show love to others, we help relieve the load they carry. People tend to bond with those who help take pressure away and elude those who add pressure or who are not empathetic to their needs. Researchers at Yale University School of Medicine have also discovered an added benefit of showing love. "Providing help to friends, acquaintances, and even strangers can mitigate the impact of daily stressors on our emotions and our mental health."[272]

When we help others relieve their loads, we also help relieve our own. Going out of our way to help others is not comfortable for many. It is a natural man tendency to be selfish and withhold love from others. However, if we muster the motivation to act despite feelings of reluctance, we can feel the joy that comes when we love and serve others. President Nelson said, "When we love somebody, we show it by doing something nice. So learn to serve: find a need and fulfill a need. Surprise people with a good deed they hadn't planned on."[273]

Express Love

Several years ago I visited a small country cemetery where several ancestors were buried. At one point I sat on a bench and thought about some of those whom I had known and loved. As I sat there I noticed what looked to be a laminated sheet of paper hanging from a tree branch near a tombstone. Curious, I got up and saw that it was a poem titled "If Only I

Had Known," written by a mother whose son was buried beside the tree. The name on the tombstone was Billy Wayne Ezell, born on December 7, 1972, and passed away on February 26, 1994. I felt sad as I read the words:

> If I'd only known it would be the last time,
> That I'd see you walk out the door,
> I'd gave you a bigger hug and kiss
> And called you back for one more.
> If I'd only known it would be the last time,
> I'd hear your laughter and playful way,
> I'd taped each action and word,
> So I could play them back every day.
> If I'd only known it would be the last time
> We would have and extra minute or two,
> I'd been sure to have said once again,
> "Son please know how much I love you.
> If I'd only known it would be the last time,
> I'd be there to share your day.
> Believing there would always be more,
> I wouldn't have let it just slip away.
> If I'd only known it would be the last time
> That I'd see you fall asleep.
> I'd prayed, "Take me Lord, but please,
> Give my son his life to keep."
> If only I had known.
> Love you forever!

This mother reminds all of us that we never know when we will see those we love for the last time. It is important to express that love so that we never have to regret having not done so. President Monson reminded us of this when he said: "What is most important almost always involves the people around us. Often we assume that they *must* know how much we love them. But we should never assume; we should let them know. . . . We will never regret the kind words spoken or the affection shown. Rather, our regrets will come if such things are omitted from our relationships with those who mean the most to us."[274]

Invitation to Act

1. Memorize the five basic human needs suggested by William Glasser and try to help others fill those needs.
2. Tell family members and friends how you feel about them and show appropriate affection.
3. Do something nice for someone every day to show them you care.
4. Call people by name, act excited to see them, say goodbye, listen intently, make eye contact, give sincere compliments, make time for others, ask for advice, use appropriate touch, laugh easily, and be easy to get along with.
5. Express love to those you are close to.

CHAPTER 15
Leaving a Legacy

As we read the stories of great men, we discover that they did not become famous overnight nor were they born professionals or skilled craftsmen. The story of how they became what they are may be helpful to us all.[275]
President Spencer W. Kimball

Shon Hopkin

As a boy growing up in Fort Worth, Texas, I don't think I ever used a swear word. I felt it was completely unnecessary, except for the time I recount here. On a hot summer day, my brother and I were working for my dad painting a rental home that was in bad shape. The beating sun had prompted us to both go inside to get a quick nap before returning to work. I slept a little bit too long, then got up and returned to work. After working for about forty-five minutes by myself, I became annoyed at my brother and went inside to kick him and tell him to stop sleeping and come help. Then I went back outside. He came out about five minutes later, ready for battle. He let loose a string of insults that included a lot of choice words that I wasn't used to being called. I was painting the house while my brother insulted me at the top of his lungs. As he continued, I got more and more worked up, until finally I decided to open the floodgates and respond in kind. I may not have used swear words before, but I chose to use them at that point as loud as I could, trying to outshout my brother as we both swore at each other for about five more minutes. It just kept getting louder and louder. As our yelling match began to wind down, I heard a noise behind my back and glanced over into the neighbor's back yard.

This was an economically depressed part of town, and the next-door neighbors didn't have a fence. Their back yard was full of old tires, magazines, beer bottles, and other garbage. The back door was open, and a little girl's dirty face was pressed against the screen door. She was wide eyed and looked scared as she stared straight at me after she had listened to me use language that shouldn't have ever come out of my mouth. Although it's just a guess based on the state of disrepair of that back yard, I'm guessing that this little girl came from a pretty difficult situation and that this may not have been the first time she had heard people screaming at each other.

At any rate, her big, wide eyes stared straight into my soul. My stomach turned. I felt immediate shame. My mouth snapped shut in shock as I saw myself through her eyes. Two brothers had terrified the little girl and filled her head with garbage. My brother didn't see what I saw and kept yelling for a little bit longer, but I felt totally ashamed. I turned quietly back to the house and continued working. My brother joined me a little bit later. I was quiet the rest of the afternoon and have never sworn in anger from that day to this. I never want to be the cause of anyone feeling terror that way again.

I have learned that our actions are always seen and always have an impact on others for good or ill. When we allow ourselves to act inappropriately, we allow ourselves the luxury of injuring others who may have a deep need for goodness. We have a responsibility to leave a legacy of lifting others and to be a light to the world.

Choosing Our Legacy

While the word legacy has various definitions in many circles, it has generally come to mean something that is passed on. The word is unusual because it can be associated with things both good and evil. For example, if you do a Google search of the phrase "a legacy of", some of the words that come up are abuse, kindness, hate, love, giving, greed, excellence, failure, fear, and hope. So, the legacy one leaves behind can be a positive one, a negative one, or somewhere in between. One thing to remember is that everyone will leave a legacy behind whether it is good, bad, or indifferent, with the potential of having a powerful influence.

In the Book of Mormon, we clearly see the legacy of hate passed on by Laman. Through the generations, that legacy resulted in the death and misery of hundreds of thousands of individuals. "And it was because of the wickedness and abomination of their fathers, even as it was in the beginning. And they were taught to hate the children of God, even as the Lamanites were taught to hate the children of Nephi from the beginning" (4 Nephi 1:39).

On the other hand, we can also see the legacy of love that Nephi passed on. The result was countless attempts made by his descendants to show love and concern for their estranged Lamanite relatives. That legacy continues today as the gospel is being taken with great success around the world. Moroni, the last Book of Mormon writer, declared, "Now I, Moroni, write somewhat as seemeth me good; and I write unto my brethren, the Lamanites; and I would that they should know that more than four hundred and twenty years have passed away since the sign was given of the coming of Christ" (Moroni 10:1).

For Shon, a little girl with a dirty face pressed against a screen door was a wake-up call for what he would leave behind. Through a quick self-examination, while feeling those wide eyes assessing him, he decided at that moment he would not pass on a legacy of anger or inappropriate language. He chose to follow the counsel found in Ephesians 4:29: "Let no corrupt communication proceed out of your mouth, but that which is good to the use of edifying, that it may minister grace unto the hearers." Shon also demonstrated that past mistakes need not determine our future. We can change. Shon passed on to me a desire to achieve more and to have a more positive attitude.

Randal: I worked in the same office with Shon five days a week for six years. We often crossed paths multiple times during a typical day. He put in long hours while also pursuing a PhD in Hebrew studies with a focus on Medieval Hebrew, Arabic, and Spanish literature. The degree was demanding and required him to be proficient in those languages as well. Married with four children at home, Shon lived on four or five hours of sleep a night for most of the time we worked together.

When he shared the experience of arguing with his brother, I couldn't have been more surprised. Imagining Shon angry or using inappropriate language was nearly impossible. During all the years I have known him, he has never once lost his temper, raised his voice, or used profanity. To be truthful, I have never once seen him in a bad mood. He has always been willing to drop whatever he is doing to help anyone at any time.

Shon is now a popular speaker, researcher, and university professor in the Religious Education Department at Brigham Young University. He is a major impact for good and will pass on a legacy of achievement and kindness.

What Will You Leave Behind?

While attending college, I took a sociology class from a popular professor named Reed Bradford. One of our assignments in that class was to write our own obituary. An obituary reports the death of an individual and usually includes a little of the legacy the person left behind. At first I thought this assignment was strange, but it was one that caused me to examine myself closely. Before this task, I don't think I had ever considered how I would be remembered. That assignment turned out to be a pivotal time for me and helped me change in many ways. I felt as if I were being given a chance to be the person I really needed to be instead of just drifting along.

Over the years several premature obituaries have been mistakenly published. This means, of course, that the subjects were not actually deceased at the time their obituary hit the newspapers. Wikipedia has an article on this subject listing the names of over three hundred well-known individuals who have been able to read about their own deaths. Names like Hillary Clinton, Miley Cyrus, Sally Field, Celine Dion, Paul McCartney, Joe Montana, Willie Nelson, and Barack Obama are among those whose deaths were reported erroneously.[276]

In 1888, several newspapers across Europe published the obituary of a Swedish engineer, inventor, chemist, author, businessman, and pacifist named Alfred Nobel. However, it was his brother Ludvig who had really died. Multiple sources state that Alfred had the chance to read his own obituary while still living, and what he read shocked him. One newspaper report called him, "The merchant of death is dead."[277] He knew many people resented him and what he did to amass his large fortune. Yet Alfred had over 350 patents for his inventions. Why would he be considered a merchant of death when he was a pacifist? Perhaps is was because his most recognized invention was dynamite. Many begrudged the fact that he made a fortune manufacturing explosives in more than ninety armament factories.

Perhaps the shock of reading his own obituary and how some remembered him influenced Nobel to reconsider the legacy he was leaving. He set aside nearly his entire fortune to establish a foundation. Its purpose was to bestow prizes in recognition of individuals who contributed in a positive way to cultural and scientific advances. Today, Alfred Bernhard Nobel is remembered as a great humanitarian who created the Nobel Foundation. The Nobel Prizes are recognized as the world's most prestigious awards given in the fields of chemistry, physics, literature, medicine, economics, and peace.[278]

When Alfred Nobel decided to leave his fortune to the Nobel Foundation, he forever blessed the world for good. Think of the impact past Nobel Prize winners like Marie Curie, Albert Einstein, Mother Teresa, Ivan Pavlov, and Martin Luther King Jr. have had on the world. Hundreds of millions have been blessed because of the efforts of those awarded a Nobel Prize. What is it that you would leave behind if you were to die today? If someone close to you assumed you were dead and wrote your obituary, what would be included?[279]

What Will You Leave?

A few years ago, I became acquainted with Sandy, who was unhappy with her life. She had tried various medications and therapies over the years, but nothing seemed to increase her happiness. When asked about the advice she received from her therapist, she explained he told her to focus on herself. As a wife and mother of two boys needing her attention, Sandy unfailingly followed the therapist's advice to focus on herself. After returning home from work, the rest of the evening was spent watching television, browsing social media, playing online games, shopping, and reading. Her husband, who also had a full-time job, was left to do the cooking, help with homework, read bedtime stories, and complete other household chores. Sandy had little interaction with her boys or her husband and became more like an aloof roommate than a wife and mother.

I don't know what her therapist had in mind when he told her to focus on herself. Maybe the self-focus was good advice for a short time if she was feeling overwhelmed; however, it is hard to believe that a total focus on oneself for an extended period could bring anyone long-term happiness. Booker T. Washington, the famous educator, author, orator, and advisor to presidents of the United States, had a different philosophy about life and what brings happiness. He said, "Those who are happiest are those who do the most for others."[280] I had a chance to talk to Sandy and asked how she would be remembered by her husband and boys. She ticked off the list, which included lazy, selfish, and self-centered. Can you imagine? Thankfully she decided a change was in order.

What Are You Currently Leaving?

Have you ever considered the legacy you are leaving behind? What will people say about you? Ray Bradbury insightfully offered, "Everyone must leave something behind when he dies. . . . Something your hand touched some way so your soul has somewhere to go when you die. . . . It doesn't matter what you do, . . . so long as you change something from the way it was before you touched it into something that's like you after you take your hands away."[281]

University professor Jenet Erickson wrote the following tribute to her dad about what his hands have touched. It could easily be his obituary—however, he is still alive.

> I watched Dad's large hand gently lift the tiny spoon to Grandma's mouth. She opened it ever so slightly, and Dad carefully placed the spoon between her lips, where she could draw on the much-needed nourishment. With his other hand he patted her back, assuring her that he would help her and that she was loved. Everything felt hushed as I watched. It was all so tender. No mother could have had a more caring son-in-law.
>
> But it was watching Dad's hands that also quieted me. They are large hands, with bulging vessels and calloused, thick surfaces. Growing up, I watched them do hard work—build fences; plant large gardens; repair cars; dig ditches; cut down trees; carry large, heavy loads; and even knead bread. But I also saw those same strong hands reach out and take Mom's slender fingers while they were walking side by side or when we were sitting close as a family discussing tender things together.
>
> Those hands brought me healing juices and medicine when I was sick, held the cup to my mouth while I drank, fixed my pillow, and pulled up the covers close around my chin as I lay back down. They helped me make my bed almost every morning of my growing-up years. They guided and rescued me during hours of swim lessons where Dad

> was the instructor. And in an innumerable number of other moments, those hands served and blessed me.
>
> In truth, nothing has ever felt warmer or more assuring than when Dad reached out, put his hand on my knee, and patted me, letting me know that he was proud of me and loved me. And I know that his hands have been used to bless all of us in those same meaningful ways. They built a home for all of us, but they also built our hearts. In those hands, service and love were made flesh. And how I love them for it!
>
> I hope one day I can do for Dad what he did for Grandma that night. I hope my hands, too, can be used to assure him that he is safe in my care, that I am proud of him and love him. Could he know how much his kind touch through all those years still brings tender feelings of love and assurance, filling me with gratitude for all he has done for me? How precious are the memories of the kind touch and service of Dad's remarkable hands!

Jenet's father is leaving a legacy of love, kindness, and hard work to his posterity that will not be forgotten by those who know him. Notice how he is passing those same characteristics to his daughter. Benjamin Franklin shared this advice for those who want to make a difference in the world. He said, "If you wou'd not be forgotten as soon as you are dead and rotten, either write things worth reading, or do things worth writing."[282] Surely one goal we should all share is to live a life that will be emulated when we are gone.

In contrast to the legacy Jenet's father is leaving her is Tom, a divorcé living with his teenage son, Luke. For years, by his own account, he was stern, had a short temper, and often saw the world through a narrow and judgmental lens. Tom shared with me a wake-up call he had that began to change how he viewed life. He said he came home from work one day and noticed dirty dishes in the sink and became irritated with his son. He scolded Luke about not keeping the house clean. He felt his son should be more grateful for all the hard work he was doing for him. He was surprised when his son Luke asked, "What do you do around here, Dad?"

Tom was irritated at first but then asked himself if his son's question was valid. As it turned out he had to admit it was. He realized Luke had no idea how hard his dad worked at his construction job and why he felt he needed a break when he came home. All his son could see most days was an irritated man sitting in a chair watching television and barking orders. Luke probably felt like he worked hard every day at school, dealing with tests, homework, and projects, and needed a break too. Tom had never considered why his son would think he had just as much responsibility to keep the house clean. Tom recognized that day the legacy he was passing down to his son was not the one he wanted. He began the difficult process of changing.

Children tend to be natural mimics and often follow the actions of their parents rather than their words. A friend named Sandra was concerned about her three-year-old son's ever-present attitude. When she asked him to do something, he often flippantly replied, "I don't think so!" She had no idea where he picked up the phrase but knew it needed to stop.

One day, while discussing their son's problem with her husband, he observed, "You know where he got that line, don't you?"

Sandra assured him she had no idea.

"From you," he remarked.

Shocked, her spontaneous response was "I don't think so!" Realization hit as her face turned red.

Focus On Things That Matter Most

Scott: A few years ago, my professional position required that I learn more about the music and entertainment business. A friend who works in that field suggested I go with him to Los Angeles to get a glimpse of what I would be dealing with. During the trip, he took me to the to the world-famous Beverly Hills Hotel to meet Martin "Marty" Erlichman, an award-winning producer and veteran manager in the entertainment industry. He is best known for discovering Barbra Streisand and managing her career for the past fifty years. Marty and I hit it off and had a great time exchanging stories.

At one point, Marty became serious. He asked, "Scott, do you want to know the meaning of life?" As soon as he said that, I used my phone to record what he was about to tell me. He looked at me and said, "What are you doing?"

I said, "If you're about to tell me the meaning of life, I'm going to capture it on film so I can go home and tell my girls!"

"Are you serious?" he quipped.

I asked him if he was serious.

He said, "Yeah."

So I said, "Well, let's go then."

He quickly started, "Number one, you wake up in the morning, put your feet on the ground, and are so passionate about what you do that you sprint to work every day. Number two—this one is slightly more important than number one—in the evening, after a hard, challenging day at work, you sprint home with equal passion."

Think about how simple that is. Run to work with passion and run home with equal passion. It was a valuable gift I received from Marty that day and one I will never forget! It is scary to realize how quickly time flies by and that time is the one thing you cannot save. The only thing you can do is spend it in ways that you will not regret later. Today is the only day we have to give our attention to the things that matter most.

Creating a Legacy

During his mortal ministry, Jesus Christ gave a masterful discourse that is referred to as the Sermon on the Mount. As part of His message, He admonished His followers to "let your light so shine before men, that they may see your good works, and glorify your Father which is in heaven" (Matthew 5:16). His message seems to be that we live in a dark world and should be a light that others can follow. Professor Felix Adler observed, "The hero is one who kindles a great light in the world, who sets up blazing torches in the dark streets of life for men to see by. The saint is the man who walks through the dark paths of the world, himself a light."[283]

The way others perceive us generally comes by what they see and hear from us or about us. If we are to be a light to others and leave an inspiring legacy behind, we must constantly examine ourselves and ask if we are being that light to others. People are not usually impressed with lazy, grouchy television watchers who bark out orders. In Acts 10:38 we read, "God anointed Jesus of Nazareth with the Holy Ghost and with power: who went about doing good." Our goal in life should be to go about doing good. Those who follow the example of the Savior are those who seek to do good in life.

One who tried to be a light to the world was President Monson. At his funeral services, daughter Ann M. Dibb paid her father this tribute:

"Today I am profoundly grateful for my father and the legacy he created—a legacy of love and service."[284]

President Monson left a legacy of love and service like few others. His name is associated with those characteristics in his family, among friends, in the membership of the Church, and with any whom he crossed paths. At age twenty-two, he was made a bishop of a Salt Lake ward with 1,080 members that had a heavy welfare load. His large ward also included eighty-five widows. During his tenure, he regularly visited these widows to ensure both their spiritual and temporal needs were met. They became not only "his widows" but also his lifelong friends. He was well known at the rest homes where many of these sisters ended up in their twilight years. He was often by their hospital beds during their last hours. President Monson said this of his eighty-five widows: "While they might feel they benefit by my visit, I know I come away a better man for having spent perhaps a half hour or hour reminiscing with each of these sweet sisters who are in the late years of their lives."[285]

One of President Monson's favorite stories was when he visited Melissa, his former primary president. She was in her nineties and living in a nursing home in Salt Lake. He described the experience in these words:

> I found Melissa in the lunchroom. She was staring at her plate of food, teasing it with the fork she held in her aged hand. Not a bite did she eat. As I spoke to her, my words were met by a benign but a blank stare. I took the fork in hand and began to feed Melissa, talking all the time I did so about her service to boys and girls as a Primary worker. There wasn't so much as a glimmer of recognition, far less a spoken word. Two other residents of the nursing home gazed at me with puzzled expressions. At last they spoke, saying, "Don't talk to her. She doesn't know anyone—even her own family. She hasn't said a word in all the years she's been here."
>
> Luncheon ended. My one-sided conversation wound down. I stood to leave. I held her frail hand in mine, gazed into her wrinkled but beautiful countenance, and said, "God bless you, Melissa. Merry Christmas."
>
> Without warning, she spoke the words, "I know you. You're Tommy Monson, my Primary boy. How I love you." She pressed my hand to her lips and bestowed on it the kiss of love. Tears coursed down her cheeks

and bathed our clasped hands. Those hands, that day, were hallowed by heaven and graced by God."[286]

President Monson's Church commitments frequently required him to travel throughout the world for days and even weeks at a time. Yet he found the time in his busy schedule to speak at the funeral services of all eighty-five of his widows. Elder Jeffrey R. Holland said this about the service President Monson constantly gave others: "Those who know him well understand that he has not done these things simply because his parents expected him to do so or because the widows were the responsibility of a bishop or because it was his role as an Apostle. He has given this kind of selfless service because that is who he *is*. Thomas S. Monson does those things because they are what his Savior would have done."[287]

You don't have to be a prophet to be a saint. Former UCLA basketball coach John Wooden left a coaching legacy that will likely never again be duplicated. At one point, his teams won eighty-eight consecutive games and ten national championships in twelve years. But he left far more than basketball championships. Sportswriter Doug Robinson wrote what could have easily been a paragraph fitting for Wooden's obituary. Notice the words he used to describe this coaching legend. "A great coach, he is a better man, and that has always been his broad appeal. Grace, wit, wisdom, perspective, humility, love, competence, devotion, and spirituality have rarely been packaged so well in one tiny man. One of his players was recently asked to choose one word to describe Wooden. He chose 'Saint.'"[288] Surely the legacy of an exemplary life far exceeds the legacy of being a champion, winning prizes, or finding financial success.

Do you feel like you will be remembered the way you would like to be remembered? If not, you can change just as Alfred Nobel did and truly become the person you want people to remember. It is important to think often about how your name will be remembered. To make sure it is positive, consider the words of Shannon Alder, who said, "Carve your name on hearts, not tombstones. A legacy is etched into the minds of others and the stories they share about you."[289]

Invitation to Act

1. Write your own obituary as you would want it to read. Then live it.
2. Make a detailed list of the good things you need to do that you have been procrastinating doing.
3. Use Matthew 5:16 as a guide for your daily living: "Let your light so shine before men, that they may see your good works, and glorify your Father which is in heaven."

Notes

1. *Merriam-Webster*, s.v. "crossroad (*n.*)," https://www.merriam-webster.com/dictionary/crossroad.

2. Henry B. Eyring, "Raise the Bar," (Brigham Young University–Idaho devotional, January 25, 2006).

3. Thomas S. Monson, "Choices," *Ensign* or *Liahona*, May 2016, 86.

4. Donald L. Hallstrom, "What Manner of Men?" *Ensign* or *Liahona*, May 2014, 53.

5. Norman Vincent Peale, *Enthusiasm Makes the Difference* (Upper Saddle River: Prentice-Hall, Inc.), 13.

6. Naryana Murthy, "Think Big and Act Boldly," *Infosys Annual Report 2013–14*, April 2014, https://www.infosys.com/investors/reports-filings/annual-report/annual/documents/infosys-ar-14.pdf.

7. Dieter F. Uchtdorf, "Forget Me Not," *Ensign* or *Liahona*, November 2011, 120.

8. Benjamin Franklin, *The Autobiography of Benjamin Franklin* (London: J. Parsons, 1793), 38.

9. Franklin, *The Autobiography of Benjamin Franklin*, 38–39.

10. Phyllis G. McDaniel, *By the Grace of God: Principles for Daily Living* (self-pub., Lulu, 2015), 102.

11. Kathryn Petras and Ross Petras, *Change Happens: A Compendium of Wisdom* (New York: Workman, 2018), 167.

12. Thomas S. Monson, "Pathways to Perfection," *Ensign*, May 2002, 100.

13. Thomas S. Monson, "The Will Within," *Ensign*, May 1987, 68.

14. Nadia Chadhury, "Aaron Franklin's Favorite Barbecue, When One Direction Visited Whataburger, and More A.M. Intel," *Eater Austin*, Aug 7, 2015. https://austin.eater.com/2015/8/7/9115903/franklin-barbecue-favorite-whataburger-one-direction-news.

15. Emily Brandon, "10 Ways Retirees Spend Their Newfound Free Time," *US News and World Report*, June 26, 2015, https://money.usnews.com/money/blogs/planning-to-retire/2015/06/26/10-ways-retirees-spend-their-newfound-free-time.

16. "What We Can Learn from Church Leaders about Growing Older, 'Living Life in Crescendo,'" *LDS Living*, August 24, 2018, https://www.ldsliving.com/what-we-can-learn-from-church-leaders-about-growing-older-living-life-in-crescendo/s/89152.

17. Thomas S. Monson, "The Will Within," 68.

18. Richard G. Scott, "To Live Well," (Brigham Young University commencement address, April 21, 2011), speeches.byu.edu.

19. Gordon B. Hinckley, *Skyline High School (Utah) Seminary Fireside*, Salt Lake City, April 30, 1995.

20. Kahlil Gibran, The Prophet (New York, NY: Alfred A. Knopf, 1923), 35.

21. Neal A. Maxwell, "Overcome . . . Even As I Also Overcame," *Ensign*, May 1987, 71.

22. Victor Niederhoffer, *The Education of a Speculator* (Hoboken: Wiley & Sons, 1996), 113.

23. Joan Garrett, *The Journey Continues: Life's Travel Guide for Teens and Young Adults* (Bloomington: iUniverse, 2010), 22.

24. Karl Kraus, *Half Truths & One and a Half Truths* (Chicago: University of Chicago Press, 1990).

25. Ezra Taft Benson, *God, Family, Country: Our Three Great Loyalties* (Salt Lake City: Deseret Book, 1974), 145.

26. "How Many Products Does Amazon Carry?," Retail TouchPoints, https://www.retailtouchpoints.com/resources/how-many-products-does-amazon-carry.

27. Ann Jordan and Lynne Whaley, *Investigating Your Career* (Mason: Thomson South-Western, 2007), 113.

28. "Tobacco-Related Mortality," Centers for Disease Control and Prevention, https://www.cdc.gov/tobacco/data_statistics/fact_sheets/health_effects/tobacco_related_mortality/index.htm/.

29. Randal A. Wright, *Achieving Your Life Mission* (Springville: Cedar Fort, 2009), 155.

30. Thomas S. Monson, "Decisions Determine Destiny," (Brigham Young University devotional, November 6, 2005), 4, speeches.byu.edu.

31. Stephen R. Covey, *The Wisdom and Teachings of Stephen R. Covey* (New York: Free Press, 2012).

32. Merlin R. Lybbert, "A Latter-day Samaritan," *Ensign*, May 1990, 82.

33. William Walker Atkinson, *The Secret of Mental Magic* (London: L. N. Fowler, 1907), 174.

34. Roy T. Bennett, The Light in the Heart: Inspirational Thoughts for Living Your Best Life (Cleveland, OH: Roy T. Bennett, 2020), 56.

35. *Oxford English Dictionary*, s.v. "constitution (n.)," https://www.oed.com/dictionary/constitution_n?tab=meaning_and_use#8393654https://www.oed.com/dictionary/constitution_n?tab=factsheet#8393654.

36. Dallin H. Oaks, "The Divinely Inspired Constitution," *Ensign*, February 1992, 68.

37. Tony Augarde, *Oxford Dictionary of Modern Quotations* (Oxford: Oxford University Press, 1991), 291.

38. Wilford Woodruff, *Conference Report*, April 1898, 57.

39. Joseph Smith, *The Wentworth Letter*, March 1, 1842.

40. Reinhard Maeser, *Karl G. Maeser: A Biography* (Provo: Brigham Young University, 1928), 130.

41. Ernest L. Wilkinson and Cleon W. Skousen, ed., *Brigham Young University: A School of Destiny* (Provo: Brigham Young University Press, 1976), 84.

42. Wilkinson and Skousen, *Brigham Young University: A School of Destiny*, 85.

43. Dorothy Herrmann, *Helen Keller: A Life* (Chicago: University of Chicago Press, 1999).

44. Helen Keller, in *Dunn County News*, January 22, 1916.

45. "Time 100 Persons of the Century," *Time*, June 14, 1999.

46. Michael Barrier, *The Animated Man: A Life of Walt Disney* (Oakland: University of California Press, 2008).

47. "Walt Disney Parks and Resorts Growth Fact Sheet," Disney Parks Blog, accessed November 30, 2023, https://disneyparks.disney.go.com/blog/.

48. Charles Clay Doyle, Wolfgang Mieder, Fred R. Shapiro, The Dictionary of Modern Proverbs (New Haven, CT: Yale University Press, 2012), 62.

49. Dave Kraft, *Leaders Who Last* (Wheaton: Crossway, 2010), 121.

50. Spencer W. Kimball, "Education for Eternity," (Brigham Young University devotional, September 12, 1967), 12, speeches.byu.edu.

51. Neal A. Maxwell, *Religious Studies Center Symposium* (Provo: BYU Press, 1982), 115.

52. Spencer W. Kimball, "The Years that the Locust Hath Eaten," *The Improvement Era* 73, no. 12, (December 1970): 75.

53. "John Goddard's Life List," John Goddard (website), accessed November 30, 2023, https://www.johngoddard.info/life_list.htm.

54. Tiffany Kelly, "Adventurer Known as 'Real-life Indiana Jones' Dies at 88," *Los Angeles Times*, May 22, 2013.

55. Randal A. Wright, "Plan Your Life," Achieving Your Life Mission, http://www.achieveyourlifemission.com/stories/plan_your_life2.

56. Jack Canfield, David Bebee, The 30-Day Sobriety Solution (New York, NY: Simon and Schuster, 2016), 128.

57. "BYU Trackster Honors Her Fallen Teammate," *Deseret News*, June 15, 2008.

58. Michele Gorman, "Yogi Berra's Most Memorable Sayings," *Newsweek*, November 4, 2018.

59. Russell M. Nelson, "Becoming True Millennials," (worldwide devotional for young adults, January 10, 2016), Gospel Library.

60. Robert Collier, *The Secret of the Ages* (Tarrytown: Robert Collier Publications, 1951), 48.

61. Tom Rath, Barry Conchie, Strengths-Based Leadership: The 4 Things Followers Need (New York, NY: Gallup Press, 2008), 7.

62. Elaine S. Dalton, "Dare Great Things" (Brigham Young university–Idaho devotional, October 12, 2011), byui.edu.

63. Nicole Kekeh, "Liberian President Ellen Sirleaf Johnson: 'Bullish' on the Future," *Forbes*, June 27, 2011.

64. Bryant S. Hinckley "The Sublimity of Mankind," *The Latter-day Saints' Millennial Star* 98, no. 40, (October 1, 1936): 626.

65. Randal A. Wright, *Achieving Your Life Mission* (Springville: Cedar Fort, 2008), 104.

66. Neil Farber, "New Year's Resolutions Become Dissolutions," Psychology Today, January 9, 2017, https://www.psychologytoday.com/us/blog/the-blame-game/201701/new-years-resolutions-become-dissolutions.

67. Thomas S. Monson, in *Conference Report*, October 1970, 107.

68. Gail Matthews, "3 Ways to Help Your Employees with Goal-Setting," *Entrepreneur*, March 29, 2016.

Max Anders, 30 Days to Growing in Your Faith (Nashville, TN: HarperCollins Christian Publishing, 2021), 313.

70. Ryan M. Frischmann, *A Skills-Based Approach to Developing a Career* (self-pub., Trafford, 2013) 5.

71. Wright, *Achieving Your Life Mission*, 164.

72. Brigham Young, in *Journal of Discourses*, 6:315.

73. Gordon B. Hinckley, "Our Solemn Responsibility," *Ensign*, November 1991, 49.

74. Franklin, *The Autobiography of Benjamin Franklin*, 82.

75. Gordon B. Hinckley, "And Peter Went Out and Wept Bitterly," *Ensign*, May 1979, 65.

76. Monson, "Choices," 86.

Paul Selby, The Life, Stories and Speeches of Abraham Lincoln (Chicago, IL: George M. Hill Company, 1900), 224

78. *Merriam-Webster*, s.v. "good (*n.*)," https://www.merriam-webster.com/dictionary/good.

79. *Merriam-Webster*, s.v. "evil (*n.*)," https://www.merriam-webster.com/dictionary/evil.

80. *Messages of the First Presidency*, comp. James R. Clark, 6 vols. (Salt Lake City: Bookcraft, 1965–75), 6:179.

81. "Excessive Drinking Is Draining the U.S. Economy," last reviewed April 14, 2022, Centers for Disease Control and Prevention, https://www.cdc.gov/alcohol/features/excessive-drinking.html/.

82. K. Alex, *Managerial Skills* (Ramnagar: S. Chand, 2013), 163, Google Play Books.

83. Jet Parker, *ABC's for CEOs: 26 Vital Skills for Business Chiefs* (Success DNA, 2003), 68.

84. Marvin Gardner, "Elder Russell M. Nelson: Applying Divine Laws," *Ensign*, June 1984, 13.

85. Richard A. Singer Jr., *Now: Embracing the Present Moment* (Winchester: O-Books, 2011), 25.

86. H. Norman Wright, *Success Over Stress* (Eugene: Harvest House Publishers, 2013).

87. *Merriam-Webster*, s.v. "comfort zone (*n.*)," https://www.merriam-webster.com/dictionary/comfort%20zone.

88. M. Russell Ballard, "Do Things That Make a Difference," *Ensign*, June 1983, 70.

89. "Ideas for Being a Successful Insurance Agent," Insurance Guide Local, accessed November 30, 2023, https://www.insuranceguidelocal.com/information-for-insurance-agents/ideas-for-being-a-successful-insurance-agent/.

90. Joseph B. Wirthlin, "Sticking to It," *New Era*, October 2000, 14.

91. David E. Drew, STEM the Tide: Reforming Science, Technology, Engineering, and Math Education in America (Baltimore, MD: Johns Hopkins University Press, 2011), 38.

92. "Cement Flows for Permanent Plug of BP's Gulf Well," MPRNews, September 18. 2010, https://www.mprnews.org/story/2010/09/18/gulf-oil-spill.

93. Mark Rosen, Best Seat in the House (Minneapolis, MN: MVP Books, 2012), 275.

94. *Oxford Dictionary of Modern Quotations*, ed. Elizabeth Knowles (Oxford: Oxford University Press, 2008) 76.

95. R. Cort Kirkwood, *Real Men: Ten Courageous Americans to Know and Admire* (Nashville: Cumberland House Publishing, 2006), 65.

96. *Merriam-Webster*, s.v. "perseverance (*n.*)," https://www.merriam-webster.com/dictionary/perseverance.

97. Alan Cohen, Dare To Be Yourself (New York, NY: Ballantine Books, 1994), 279.

98. Jim Gentil, *Positive People Power* (Sevierville: Insight Publishing Company, 2001), 121.

99. *Teachings of Heber J. Grant* (Salt Lake City: The Church of Jesus Christ of Latter-day Saints, 2011), 35.

100. *Teachings of Heber J. Gran*t, 35.

101. *Teachings of Heber J. Grant*, 36.

102. Ekaterina Walter, "30 Powerful Quotes on Failure," *Forbes*, December 30, 2013.

103. Malcolm Moore, "Grandmother Passes Driving Test at 960th Attempt," *The Telegraph*, September 5, 2010.

104. *Teachings of Heber J. Grant*, 36.

105. *Merriam-Webster*, s.v. "endure (*v.*)," https://www.merriam-webster.com/dictionary/endure.

106. *Poems That Touch the Heart*, comp. A. L. Alexander (New York: Doubleday, 1941), 35.

107. Thomas S. Monson, "Believe, Obey, and Endure," *Ensign* or *Liahona*, May 2012, 129.

108. Gordon B. Hinckley, "Farewell to a Prophet," *Ensign*, July 1994, 37.

109. J. Reuben Clark Jr., in "What of the Future in this Plan?," *Improvement Era* 40, no. 4 (April 1937): 208.'

110. Hank Flick, *The Unweddables Among Us* (Bloomington: WestBow Press, 2014), 71.

111. Leonardo DaVinci, in *T. P.'s Weekly* 11 (April 3, 1908), 428.

112. *Merriam-Webster*, s.v. "busy (*adj.*)," https://www.merriam-webster.com/dictionary/busy.

113. *Merriam-Webster*, s.v. "work (*n.*)," https://www.merriam-webster.com/dictionary/work.

114. Thomas S. Monson, "What Have I Done for Someone Today?" *Ensign* or *Liahona*, November 2009, 85.

115. Anne Frank, *The Diary of Anne Frank: The Revised Critical Edition*, comp. H. J. J. Hardy, ed. David Barnouw, Gerrold van der Stroom (New York: Doubleday, 2003), 706.

116. Jacqueline Howard, "Americans Devote More than 10 Hours a Day to Screen Time, and Growing," CNN, July 29, 2016, https://www.cnn.com/2016/06/30/health/americans-screen-time-nielsen/index.html.

117. Christopher Muther, "Instant Gratification Is Making Us Perpetually Impatient," *Boston Globe*, February 2, 2013.

118. Barbara Kramer, *The Founders of Famous Food Companies* (Berkeley Heights: Enslow Publishers, 2002), 37.

119. Viktor Frankl, *Man's Search for Meaning* (New York: Pocket Books, 1985), 131.

120. Mark A. Escobar, *Thorns and Thistles: Pathways to Discipleship—Cycle C* (Bloomington: Author Solutions), 118.

121. George Bull, *Michelangelo: A Biography* (New York: St. Martin's Publishing Group, 1998).

122. Tom Kington, "Sistine Chapel Tourists to be Vacuumed and Cooled to Protect Frescoes," Guardian, December 21, 2012, https://www.theguardian.com/world/2012/dec/21/sistine-chapel-tourists-vacuumed-cooled.

123. Frederick A. Owen, *Normal Instructor*, vol. 39, (Dansville: F. A. Owen, 1929), 19.

124. "Famous Quotes by Thomas Edison," Edison Innovation Foundation, https://www.thomasedison.org/edison-quotes/.

125. Matthew Josephson, *Edison: A Biography* (Lexington: Plunkett Lake Press, 2019).

126. "Famous Quotes by Thomas Edison," Edison Innovation Foundation.

127. The American Presidency Project, "Remarks at a Dinner Honoring Nobel Prize Winners of the Western Hemisphere," April 28, 1962. https://www.presidency.ucsb.edu/documents/remarks-dinner-honoring-nobel-prize-winners-the-western-hemisphere.

128. Willard Sterne Randall, *Thomas Jefferson: A Life* (New York: HarperCollins, 2014).

129. Sarah N. Randolph, *The Domestic Life of Thomas Jefferson* (New York: Harper & Brothers, 1871), 121.

130. Gordon B. Hinckley, "Watch the Switches in Your Life," *Conference Report*, October 1972, 107.

131. Sterling W. Sill, in *Conference Report*, April 1960, 70.

132. Og Mandino, *A Better Way to Live: Og Mandino's Own Personal Story of Success* (New York: Random House, 2010), 58.

133. H. David Burton, "The Blessing of Work," *Ensign*, December 2009, 43.

134. Gordon B. Hinckley, "Testimony," *Ensign*, May 1998, 69.

135. Dieter F. Uchtdorf, "Are You Sleeping through the Restoration?" *Ensign* or *Liahona*, May 2014, 59.

136. Ernest Stabler, *Founders: Innovators in Education 1830–1980* (Edmonton: University of Alberta Press, 1986), 86.

137. "Church's Past Is 'Prologue to the Future," Deseret News, December 11, 1999.

138. Howard Breen, *A Page from a CEO's Diary* (Bloomington: AuthorHouse, 2009), 83.

139. Wright, *Achieving Your Life Mission*, 176.

140. Benjamin Franklin, *Poor Richard: The Almanacks for the Years 1733–1758* (Paddington Press, 1976), 32.

141. Tryon Edwards, *A Dictionary of Thoughts* (Detroit: F.B. Dickerson, 1908), 132.

142. John Whitcomb and Claire Whitcomb, *Real Life at the White House: 200 Years of Daily Life at America's Most Famous Residence* (New York: Routledge, 2002), 20.

143. Pew Research Center, *The Global Religious Landscape*, December 2012, https://assets.pewresearch.org/wp-content/uploads/sites/11/2014/01/global-religion-full.pdf.

144. Ahmed S. BaHammam, Munir M. Sharif, D. Warren Spence, and Seithikurippu R. Pandi-Peruma, "Sleep Architecture of Consolidated and Split Sleep Due to the Dawn (Fajr) Prayer among Muslims and Its Impact on Daytime Sleepiness," *Annals of Thoracic Medicine* 6, no. 4 (October-December 2011): 187–192, https://www.ncbi.nlm.nih.gov/pmc/articles/PMC3277040/.

145. Sangeetha Rajah, "Dinacharya," accessed November 30, 2023, http://www.hindupedia.com/en/Dinacharya.

146. Edwards, *A Dictionary of Thoughts*, 132.

147. Nancy Jeffrey, "Sleep Is the New Status Symbol for Successful Entrepreneurs," *The Wall Street Journal*, April 2, 1999.

148. Maria Popova, "Thomas Edison, Power-Napper: The Great Inventor on Sleep and Succsess," Marginalian, accessed November 30, 2023, https://www.themarginalian.org/2013/02/11/thomas-edison-on-sleep-and-success/.

149. "Life and Death in the Liberty Era, 1750–1800," Legacy, accessed November 30, 2023, https://www.legacy.com/life-and-death/the-liberty-era.html.

150. Daniel F. Kripke, Lawrence Garfinkel, Deborah L. Wingard, Melville R. Klauber, and Matthew R. Marler, "Mortalitiy Associated with Sleep Duration and Insomnia," *Archives of General Psychiatry* 59, no. 2 (February 2002): 131–136.

151. Gardner, "Elder Russell M. Nelson: Applying Divine Laws," 13.

152. Chris Pendleton, "Elder Oaks Makes Surprise Visit During Sister Oaks' Keynote Address at SVU," *Deseret News*, June 5, 2016.

153. Russell M. Nelson, "'Joy Cometh in the Morning,'" *Ensign*, November 1986, 70.

154. Nick Collins, "Early Risers Get Ahead of the Game," *The Telegraph*, September 15, 2011.

155. Benjamin Franklin, *Poor Richard*, 98.

156. Christoph Randler, "Defend Your Research: The Early Bird Really Does Get the Worm," *Harvard Business Review* (July–August 2010), https://hbr.org/2010/07/defend-your-research-the-early-bird-really-does-get-the-worm.

157. Joel Porte, ed., *Emerson in His Journals* (Cambridge: Belknap Press of Harvard University Press, 1982), 215.

158. Mickey T. Trockel, Michael D. Barnes, and Dennis L. Egget, "Health-Related Variables and Academic Performance Among First-Year College Students: Implications for Sleep and Other Behaviors," *Journal of American College Health* 49, no. 3, (November 2000): 125–131.

159. "Early Birds Get Better Grades," WebMD, June 9, 2008. https://www.cbsnews.com/news/early-birds-get-better-grades-09-06-2008/.

160. Boyd K. Packer, *Teach Ye Diligently* (Salt Lake City: Deseret Book, 1991), 245.

161. Franklin, *The Autobiography of Benjamin Franklin*, 146.

162. Shu Hattori, *The McKinsey Edge: Success Principles from the World's Most Powerful Consulting Firm* (New York: McGraw Hill, 2015), 105.

163. Joe J. Christensen and Barbara K. Christensen, *Making Your Home a Missionary Training Center* (Salt Lake City: Deseret Book, 1985), 33.

164. Stephen R. Covey, *Spiritual Roots of Human Relations* (Salt Lake City: Deseret Book, 1978), 94.

165. Randal A. Wright, "Filled with Life and Energy," *Liahona*, July 2015, 43.

166. Robert Walsh, ed. *American Quarterly Review*, Volume 6, (Philadelphia: Carey, Lea & Carey, 1829), 521.

167. Jenny Uebbing, "Responding to the 'Heroic Minute,'" Catholic Exchange, November 9, 2016, https://catholicexchange.com/responding-heroic-minute/.

168. *Merriam-Webster*, s.v. "weary (*adj.*)," https://www.merriam-webster.com/dictionary/weary.

169. *Merriam-Webster*, s.v. "invigorated (*v.*)," https://www.merriam-webster.com/dictionary/invigorated.

170. Thomas S. Monson, "Living the Abundant Life," *Ensign*, January 2012, 4.

171. Sheryl Towers, Seeds of Success: 17 Ways to Nurture the Greatness Within You (New Orleans, LA: Pelican Publishing, 2009), 107.

172. Art Linkletter, *Yes, You Can: How to Succeed in Business and Life* (New York: Simon & Schuster, 1979), 31.

173. Roy B. Zuck, *The Speaker's Quote Book* (Grand Rapids: Kregel Publications, 1997), 27.

174. David Brooks, "The Moral Bucket List," *New York Times*, April 11, 2015.

175. Tom Morris, *True Success: A New Philosophy of Excellence* (New York: G. P. Putnam's Sons, 1994), 210.

176. James S. Hewett, *Illustrations Unlimited: A Topical Collection of Hundreds of Stories, Quotations & Humor* (Carol Stream: Tyndale House Publishers, 1988), 16.

177. Jane Bluestein, The Perfection Deception (Deerfield Beach, Florida: Health Communications, 2015), 194.

178. Harvey MacKay, in United Feature Syndicate, January 20, 2013, https://tulsaworld.com/news/local/business/harveymackay/harvey-mackay-positive-thinking-helps-achieve-goals/article_1120c061-331d-5fea-a24b-b6096b776595.html.

179. Frederick Faber, in T*he Business Woman's Magazine* 1, 1903, 28.

180. Geri O'Neil and Herbert S. Robinson, *Make the Best of the Rest of Your Life* (Bloomington: AuthorHouse, 2005), 71.

181. Michael Burgan, *Miracle on Ice: How a Stunning Upset United a Country* (Mankato: Capstone, 2016).

182. Gordon B. Hinckley, "The Things of Which I Know," *Ensign* or *Liahona*, May 2007, 83.

183. Anna Redsand, *Viktor Frankl: A Life Worth Living* (New York: Clarion Books, 2006).

184. Frankl, *Man's Search for Meaning*, 86.

185. Carlos E. Asay, *Family Pecan Trees* (Salt Lake City: Deseret Book, 1992), 100.

186. "Surround Yourself with the Right People, *Forbes*, August 20, 2010.

187. Thomas S. Monson, "In Harm's Way," *Ensign*, May 1998, 47.

188. Joseph Smith, *History of the Church*, vol. 3 (Salt Lake City: Deseret Book Company, 1948), 286.

189. George A. Smith, "History of George Albert Smith by Himself," *George Albert Smith Papers 1834–75* (Salt Lake City: The Church of Jesus Christ of Latter-day Saints), 49.

190. Thomas S. Monson, "Living the Abundant Life," *Ensign*, January 2012, 4.

191. Jeffrey I. Moore, "50 John Maxwell Quotes About Becoming an Amazing Leader," *Everyday Power*, everydaypower.com.

192. Yehuda Berg, "The Power of Words," *Huffpost*, September 14, 2010.

193. Jayson Jenks, "Seahawks Coach Pete Carroll Leads Players with Positive Approach," *The Seattle Times*, August 29, 2014.

194. "Taj Mahal," New 7 Wonders of the World, accessed November 30, 2023, https://world.new7wonders.com/wonders/taj-mahal-1630-a-d-agra-india/.

195. "Taj Mahal," Tripadvisor, accessed November 30, 2023, https://www.tripadvisor.com/Attraction_Review-g297683-d317329-Reviews-Taj_Mahal-Agra_Agra_District_Uttar_Pradesh.html.

196. Suzy Kassem, Rise Up and Salute the Sun: The Writings of Suzy Kassem (Phoenix, Arizona: The Awakened Press, 2010), 20.

197. Scott Martineau, The Power of You!: How YOU Can Create Happiness, Balance, and Wealth (Hoboken, New Jersey: John Wiley and Sons, 2006), 45.

198. Wolfgang Mieder, ed., *A Dictionary of American Proverbs* (Oxford: Oxford University Press, 1991), 796.

199. Marvin J. Ashton, "It's No Fun Being Poor," *Ensign*, September 1982, 73.

200. L. Lionel Kendrick, "Christlike Communications," *Ensign*, November 1988, 23.

201. Neal A. Maxwell, *Notwithstanding My Weakness* (Salt Lake City: Deseret Book, 1981), 10.

202. James Matthew Barrie, *The Outlook: A Family Paper* 52, no. 15, October 12, 1895, 599.

203. Robert Rosenthal and Lenore Jacobsen, *Pygmalion in the Classroom* (New York: Holt, Rinehart & Winston, 1968), 3.

204. Gallup, "What Employees Want from Managers," *State of the American Manager: Analytics and Advice for Leaders*, 18, https://m100group.files.wordpress.com/2015/07/stateofamericanmanager_0515_mh_lr.pdf.

205. Gallup "What Employees Want from Managers," 19.

206. Barry C. Forbes, *Forbes* 158, Issues 1–7, 243.

207. Og Mandino, A Better Way To Live (New York, NY: Bantam Books, 1990), 90.

208. Philip Dormer Stanhope Chesterfield, *Letters Written by the Earl of Chesterfield to His Son* (Miami: Hardpress, 2017), 253.

209. Karl Menninger, *Love Against Hate* (New York: Harcourt, Brace, 1942), 276.

210. William R. Bradford, "Selfless Service," *Ensign*, November 1987, 75.

211. Henry B. Eyring, "True Friends," *Ensign*, May 2002, 29.

212. Russell M. Nelson, "Be Thou an Example of the Believers," *Ensign* or *Liahona*, November 2010, 48.

213. Liz Mineo, "Good Genes Are Nice, but Joy Is Better," *Harvard Gazette*, April 11, 2017.

214. Julianne Holt-Lunstad, Timothy B. Smith, and J. Bradley Layton, "Social Relationships and Mortality Risk: A Meta-analytic Review," *PLOS Medicine*, July 27, 2010, https://journals.plos.org/plosmedicine/article?id=10.1371/journal.pmed.1000316.

215. James Boswell, *The Life of Samuel Johnson* (Oxford: Talboys & Wheeler, 1826), 230–31.

216. Nelson, "Be Thou an Example of the Believers," 48.

217. *Teachings of the Prophet Joseph Smith*, comp. Joseph Fielding Smith (Salt Lake City: Deseret News Press, 1965), 316.

218. Jacquelyn Smith, "6 Easy Ways to Remember Someone's Name," *Forbes*, April 5, 2013.

219. "5 Types of People to Never Let Go," Power of Positivity, www.powerofpositivity.com.

220. Frederick Collins, in *The Reader's Digest* 144, issues 861–866, 19.

221. Bob Hughes and Judy Hughes, *Love Focused: Living Life to the Fullest* (Laguna Hills: Crossroads Publishing, 2008), 31.

222. Wikipedia, s.v. "Ichi-go ichi-e," last modified November 21, 2023, 00:44, https://en.wikipedia.org/wiki/Ichi-go_ichi-e.

223. William Taylor, in *Young Woman's Journal*, vol 17, no. 12 December 1906, 547–48.

224. Michael J. Gelb and Kelly Howell, *Brain Power: Improve Your Mind as You Age* (Novato: New World Library, 2011), 141.

225. Dale Carnegie, *How to Win Friends and Influence People* (New York: Pocket Books, 1936), 52.

226. Henry David Thoreau, "Life Without Principle," *The Atlantic Monthly* 12, no. 71 (October 1863): 484.

227. Benjamin Franklin, in *The School Executive* 64 (1944): 43.

228. V. Neil Wyrick, The Spiritual Abraham Lincoln (Carlsbad, California: Magnus Press, 2004), 5.

229. *My Fair Lady*, directed by George Cukor (1964; Burbank, CA: Warner Bros), 02:34:06–10.

230. Ezra Taft Benson, "To the Mothers in Zion," *Eternal Marriage: Student Manual* (Salt Lake City: The Church of Jesus Christ of Latter-day Saints, 2003), 355.

231. Laura Barrette Shannon, *Be Happy Now: Simple Steps for Enjoying Life* (Bloomington: Balboa Press, 2012), 102.

232. Nels Benjamin Ludwall, *The Fate of the Persecutors of the Prophet Joseph Smith* (Salt Lake City: Bookcraft, 1952), 283.

233. Thomas S. Monson, "Three Goals to Guide You," *Ensign* or *Liahona*, November 2007, 121.

234. Boyd K. Packer, "Counsel to Youth," *Ensign* or *Liahona*, November 2011, 17–18.

235. *Merriam-Webster*, s.v. "conscience (*n.*)," https://www.merriam-webster.com/dictionary/conscience.

236. Joseph F. Smith, Anthon H. Lund, and Charles W. Penrose, "'Receiving' the Holy Ghost," *Improvement Era* 19 no. 5, (March 1916): 460.

237. Dean Ornish, *Dr. Dean Ornish's Program for Reversing Heart Disease* (New York: Ivy Books, 1990), 110.

238. Matthias F. Cowley, ed., *Wilford Woodruff* (Salt Lake City: Bookcraft, 1964), 109.

239. Jeffrey R. Holland, "President Thomas S. Monson: Man of Action, Man of Faith, Always 'on the Lord's Errand,'" *Ensign*, February 1986, 11.

240. Rebecca Lake, "23 Gym Membership Statistics That Will Astound You," CreditDonkey, February 26, 2020, https://www.creditdonkey.com/gym-membership-statistics.html.

241. Eleanor Roosevelt, *You Learn by Living* (Louisville: Westminster Press, 1983), 29.

242. Freeman-Smith, Five Minutes in the Morning: Daily Devotions for Women (Brentwood, TN: Howard Books, 2006), 270.

243. Holland, "President Thomas S. Monson," 11.

244. Russell M. Nelson, "Revelation for the Church, Revelation for Our Lives," *Ensign* or *Liahona*, May 2018, 95.

245. "Habit 7: Sharpen the Saw," FranklinCovey Benelux, accessed November 30, 2023, https://www.franklincovey-benelux.com/en/resources/habit-7-sharpen-the-saw/.

246. "Death of a Genius," *Life*, May 2, 1955, 64.

247. Russell M. Nelson, "Sweet Power of Prayer," *Ensign* or *Liahona*, May 2003, 8.

248. Boyd K. Packer, "Personal Revelation: The Gift, the Test, and the Promise," *Ensign*, November 1994, 60.

249. James Allen, *Out from the Heart* (Chicago: Science Press, 1906), 53.

250. Harvey H. Cluff, *Autobiography of Harvey Harris Cluff Autobiography*, prelude, 1908 http://boap.org/LDS/Early-Saints/HCluff.html.

251. Dawn Hall Anderson, Susette Fletcher Green, and Dlora Hall Dalton, ed., *Clothed with Charity: Talks from the 1996 Women's Conference* (Salt Lake City: Deseret Book, 2010), 66.

252. "How Aid Works," Harvard College, accessed November 30, 2023, https://college.harvard.edu/financial-aid/how-aid-works.

253. Patrick McDermott and Ferol Arce, *Mind Body Spirit: The Triangle of Life* (New York: iUniverse, 2007), 76.

254. G. Keith Sill, *Introduction to Crowd Science* (Boca Raton, FL: CRC Press, 2014), 27.

255. "Thomas Edison's Secret Trick to Maximize His Creativity by Falling Asleep," Huffpost, October 28, 2017, https://www.huffpost.com/entry/thomas-edisons-secret-trick-to-maximize-his-creativity_b_59f4d276e4b06ae9067ab91c.

256. "Thomas A. Edison Papers," Rutgers, accessed November 30, 2023, edison.rutgers.edu.

257. Richard G. Scott, "To Acquire Knowledge and the Strength to Use It Wisely," (Brigham Young University devotional, January 23, 2001), 1, speeches.byu.edu.

258. "Keeping a Diary," *Deseret News*, July 16, 1862.

259. Parley P. Pratt, ed., "Do You Keep a Journal?," *The Latter-day Saints' Millennial Star* 1, no. 6 (October 1, 1840): 160–61.

260. Pratt, "Do You Keep a Journal?," 161.

261. Joseph Smith, "Charity, The Pure Love of Christ," *Teachings of the Presidents of the Church: Joseph Smith* (Salt Lake City: The Church of Jesus Christ of Latter-day Saints, 2011), 426.

262. David B. Haight, "Love All," *Ensign*, November 1982, 12.

263. William Glasser, *Choice Theory: A New Psychology of Personal Freedom* (New York: HarperCollins, 2010).

264. Kathleen McCoy, "Is Your Child Flirting with Sex?" *Reader's Digest*, September 1989, 114.

265. C. S. Lewis, *The Four Loves* (New York: Harcourt, Brace 1960), 53.

266. Gary Chapman and Paul E. White, *The 5 Languages of Appreciation in the Workplace* (Chicago: Moody Publishers, 2012).

267. Michael Strahan, Wake Up Happy: The Dream Big, Win Big Guide to Transforming Your Life (New York, NY: 37 INK, 2015), 116.

268. Randal A. Wright, *Power Parenting in the LDS Home* (Springville: Cedar Fort, 2014), 132.

269. Sam Keen, *To Love and Be Loved* (New York: Random House, 1997), 43.

270. Dieter F. Uchtdorf, "The Merciful Obtain Mercy," *Ensign* or *Liahona*, May 2012, 75.

271. Catherine Frank, *Quotations for All Occasions* (New York: Columbia University Press, 2000), 23.

272. Emily Ansell, Elizabeth B. Raposa, and Holly B. Laws, "Helping Others Dampens the Effects of Everyday Stress," *Clinical Psychological Science* 3, no. 7 (December 10, 2015), https://medicine.yale.edu/news-article/ansell-helping-others-dampens-the-effects-of-everyday-stress/.

273. Russell M. Nelson, "Focus on Values," *New Era*, February 2013, 4.

274. Thomas S. Monson, "Finding Joy in the Journey," *Ensign* or *Liahona*, November 2008, 86.

275. Spencer W. Kimball, "The Angels May Quote from It," *New Era*, October 1975, 5.

276. Wikipedia, s.v. "List of Premature Obituaries," last modified November 28, 2023, 00:19, https://en.wikipedia.org/wiki/List_of_premature_obituaries.

277. Aditya Agrawal, "Merchant of Death: The Story Behind the Nobel Prize!," The Times of India, April 5, 2020, https://timesofindia.indiatimes.com/blogs/unheardshepherd/merchant-of-death-the-story-behind-the-nobel-prize/.

278. Kenne Fant, *Alfred Nobel: A Biography* (New York: Arcade Publishing, 2007).

279. Michael Worek, *Nobel: A Century of Prize Winners* (Richmond Hill: Firefly Books, 2010).

280. Booker T. Washington, *Up from Slavery: An Autobiography* (New York: Doubleday, 1901), 66.

281. Ray Bradbury, *Fahrenheit 451* (New York: Simon & Schuster, 1951), 150.

282. Benjamin Franklin, *Poor Richard, An Almanack for the Year of Christ 1738, Being the Second after Leap Year* (Philadelphia: B. Franklin, 1738), https://founders.archives.gov/documents/Franklin/01-02-02-0035.

283. Felix Adler, The New Outlet, Vol. 9, 1956, 61.

284. Ann M. Dibb, "A Legacy of Love and Service," *In Memoriam: President Thomas S. Monson*, supplement to *Ensign*, February 12, 2018, 22.

285. Heidi S. Swinton, T*o the Rescue: The Biography of Thomas S. Monson* (Salt Lake City: Deseret Book, 2010), 142.

286. Thomas S. Monson, "A Doorway Called Love," *Ensign*, November 1987, 69.

287. Jeffrey R. Holland, "President Thomas S. Monson: In the Footsteps of the Master," supplement to Ensign, June 2008, 3.

288. Doug Robinson, "Wooden's Medium is Basketball, but Life Is His Art," *Deseret News*, April 13, 1997.

289. Shannon L. Alder, *Three Hundred Questions to Ask Your Parents Before It's Too Late* (Springville: Horizon Publishers, 2011).

About the Author

Randal A. Wright obtained an M.S. in Family Studies from Lamar University and a Ph.D. in Family Studies from Brigham Young University. His research focused on the impact of electronic media on the attitudes and behaviors of adolescents. He worked as an Institute Director for Seminaries and Institutes as a career. He has spoken in over 250 cities, 34 states, and several foreign countries at various events, including BYU Campus Education Week, Especially for Youth, and on cruises and land tours with Bountiful Travel.

Randal is the author of several books, including *The Book of Mormon Miracle, Achieving Your Life Mission, Make Every Day Meaningful,* and *Power Parenting.* He has also written chapters in several books and articles in the *Ensign*, *LDS Living*, and other magazines.

He and his wife, Wendy, are the parents of five married children and live in San Antonio, Texas.